Ronald Watkins

Ronald Watkins is the author of four previous works of non-fiction. He holds a BA in history and an MS in justice studies. He is a member of The Hakluyt Society and The Society for the History of Discoveries. In the course of his writing he has travelled throughout South-East Asia, India, Mexico and Central America. He previously lived in Portugal where he was inspired to write this book. He now lives in Phoenix, Arizona. For more information please visit www.RonaldJWatkins.com.

Other books by the author

Birthright
High Crimes and Misdemeanours
Evil Intentions
Against Her Will

UNKNOWN
SEAS

How Vasco da Gama
Opened the East

RONALD WATKINS

JOHN MURRAY

First published in Great Britain in 2003 by John Murray (Publishers)
A division of Hodder Headline

Paper edition 2004

A CIP catalogue record for this title is available from the British Library

ISBN 0 7195 6417 4

Typeset in Monotype Bembo by Servis Filmsetting Ltd

Printed and bound by
Clays Ltd, St Ives plc

Hodder Headline policy is to use papers that are natural, renewable and recyclable
products and made from wood grown in sustainable forests. The logging and
manufacturing processes are expected to conform to the environmental regulations
of the country of origin.

John Murray (Publishers)
338 Euston Road
London NW1 3BH

Dedicated, with all my love, to
Stephen, Theresa and Elizabeth,

and to

Brianna and Elena

Contents

Illustrations

The author and publishers would like to thank the following for permission to reproduce illustrations: Plates 1 and 3, National Library, Lisbon; 2, 15 and 18, Library of Congress, Washington, DC; 4, 5, 6, 8, 9, 14 and 19, Institute of Portuguese Museums; 7, 13, 16, and 21, City Museum of Lisbon; 11, The Pierpont Morgan Library, New York © 2001, Photo Pierpont Morgan Library/Art Resource/Scala, Florence. Plates 10, 12, 17, 20, 22 and 23 are from the author's collection.

Map

Vasco da Gama's First Voyage to India, 1497–1499

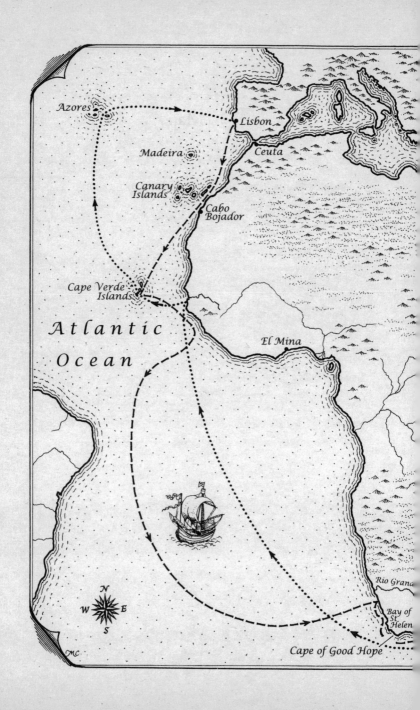

Azores

Lisbon

Madeira

Ceuta

Canary
Islands

Cabo
Bojador

Cape Verde
Islands

Atlantic

Ocean

El Mina

Rio Grande

Bay of
St
Helen

Cape of Good Hope

N
W E
S

MC

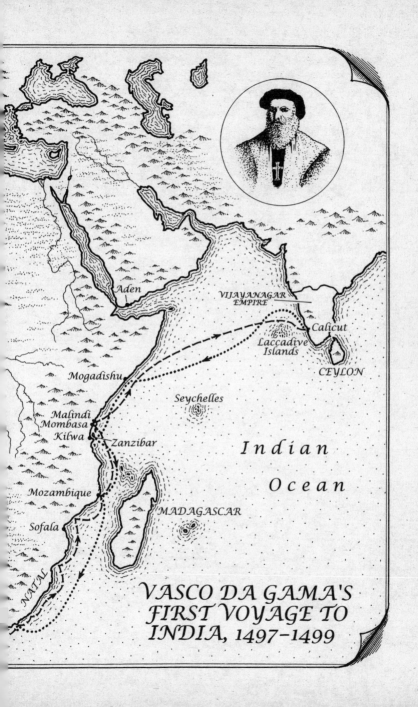

Aden

VIJAYANAGAR
EMPIRE

Calicut

Laccadive
Islands

CEYLON

Mogadishu

Seychelles

Malindi
Mombasa
Kilwa · Zanzibar

Indian

Ocean

Mozambique

MADAGASCAR

Sofala

NATAL

VASCO DA GAMA'S FIRST VOYAGE TO INDIA, 1497–1499

From Iberia
Would any sovereign with sense endured,
Hither send Missions, and confide his fleets
To seas unknown, remote and unexplor'd?

Luis Vaz de Camoens
The Lusiads

Introduction

Although unaware of the winter seas and prevailing winds confronting him, in January 1493 Admiral Christopher Columbus⋆ ordered his two surviving caravels, the *Pinta* and the *Niña*, to set sail so that he might carry the news of his discoveries to Spain.

What awaited him and his men those winter months were north Atlantic storms among the worst in recorded history. One gale after another drove ships near the Atlantic coast from the sea to seek safe harbour where they could. Hundreds of vessels were trapped in harbours from November on, unable or unwilling to face the continual violent winds and seas. By March, twenty-four ships had sunk off Flanders alone. The triumphant returning Columbus sailed into the teeth of this storm, recording in his log that he was uncertain his ships could survive.

Throughout this most difficult passage Columbus found it all but impossible to fix his position and was never confident where he was, only that the coast of Europe lay somewhere to the east. Fearful he would perish and that word of his momentous discoveries die with him, he made a record of his voyage, sealed it in cloth and wax, then placed it into a wooden barrel he had cast into the raging waters, telling his fearful crew he was performing an act of devotion.

⋆ Under the terms of his title from the Spanish sovereigns Columbus had been made admiral, viceroy and governor upon discovering lands to the west. The ceremony had been performed on his first landfall. The *Santa María*, a sluggish deep-drafted vessel that had served as flagship, had been run aground off Hispaniola and lost.

During one especially violent night his two ships were separated and were forced to sail on alone, to be eventually reunited in Spain. Yet the most dangerous weather awaited Columbus and the *Niña* as he approached the coast of the Iberian peninsula, where all sails save one were rent to shreds by the gale-force winds. With that single sheet of canvas the ship scarcely held her bearing and Columbus was compelled to rely on dead reckoning to approximate his location. Winds are estimated to have reached force 10 on the Beaufort scale.

The direction of merging storms forced the small ship ever northward, on a course away from any Spanish port. On 3 March, the most dangerous night of the return passage, 'they went under bare poles because of the great storm of wind and sea, which from two directions was swallowing them up.' That terrible night, again and again, the crew gave themselves up as lost and prayed for deliverance. The seas 'seemed to lift the caravel in the air. And [they had] rain from the sky and lightning all around.'[1] Winds off the coast of Portugal were observed in excess of 100 miles an hour, hurricane strength.

Then, at first light, as if by a miracle, Columbus spotted land. It was the Rock of Sintra, which he knew all too well and which told him he was at the mouth of the Tagus river and the port of Lisbon, Portugal – the last place on Earth he wished to be. With no alternative, he gave the order to attempt to enter the river, God willing. The ship slowly clawed its way against the seas and winds towards salvation, or death at the Cabo da Roca, the resting place of countless lost ships and seamen.

That morning the residents of the small port of Cascais, some 25 miles west of Lisbon and the first town at the approach to the Tagus river, spied the lone, heavily weathered *Niña* beating its way against the winds and current to seek safety in its harbour. Villagers gathered just up from the enormous waves crashing on the shore to watch the imminent disaster while others rushed to the nearby church to pray for the safety of the unknown mariners. The *Niña* was so battered that witnesses reported she resembled a ship that had miraculously survived a fierce naval battle.

Amid lightning, thunderclaps and violent whirlwinds the small caravel with just the single sail was driven back repeatedly, but again and again Columbus ordered its bow to be turned into a perilous tack, only to be forced aside, putting the ship in danger of capsizing. Finally Columbus relented and ordered the helmsman and crew to give up the struggle. The ship turned away from the safe harbour of Cascais to a more easterly course and then, almost imperceptibly at first, slowly made its way uncertainly amid the gale entering the mouth of the Tagus, finally passing the threatening bar into safety. With the dangerous seas now behind, the *Niña* soon arrived at Belém, Lisbon's outermost port, where it dropped anchor as the crew knelt and gave thanks to God for their salvation.

To safeguard the approach to the port of Lisbon a warship lay at anchor near by. In a short time a longboat was launched, and as it was rowed towards the Spanish ship Columbus wondered if he would leave this place alive. For a number of years the new admiral had made his home among the Portuguese and was considered by many of them to be a native son. Portugal was the focal point of European discoveries and the most advanced nation in the world in navigation, shipbuilding and mapmaking. Columbus's first wife had been the daughter of the hereditary Portuguese governor of Porto Santo, and it was there on Madeira that he had learned from the Portuguese the secrets they had mastered in their decades of exploration.

But when the Portuguese king John II had denied Columbus support for his venture to discover a sea route to India by sailing west, he had gone to the hated Spanish monarchs, Ferdinand and Isabella. There were many in the Portuguese court and nation who considered Christopher Columbus a traitor. Now that he was returning from having 'discovered' the Indies, as he believed, he could not but help fear for his fate as King John's violent deeds were legendary.

Some time after he arrived, and before the port official reached his ship, Columbus learned the Portuguese king was not far off. He hurriedly wrote and dispatched a personal note to the sovereign, hoping to stave off disaster at the moment of his life's triumph. In his note he requested immediate permission to sail upriver and anchor at Lisbon because he feared that, as he wrote in his journal, 'evil-doers, thinking that he brought much gold, while he was in a deserted harbour might' board and loot his ship. In his communication he cited his credentials from Ferdinand and Isabella and assured King John that in no circumstance had he been to the region of Africa known as Guinea, which was under Portuguese control and closed to Spain. Apprehensive, he watched his letter on its way, for if the king refused to believe him Columbus might very well be executed.

From the longboat stepped the Grand Captain of the port, none other than Bartholomeu Dias, who was surprised to find that the captain of the battered caravel was Christopher Columbus. The two men knew each other. They had served at the Portuguese fort of El Mina on the west African coast, and just four years earlier Columbus had been present when Dias had returned from his discovery of the Cape of Good Hope and made his presentation to the king and his court.

But on this day, when Dias made the customary request for papers and instructed Columbus to go ashore to explain his anchorage and receive formal permission, Columbus refused, saying that he was now an admiral of the 'sovereigns of Castile and that he would not give such an account to such persons nor would he leave' his ship except by force, which he would resist unto death as 'was the custom' of Spanish admirals. He then briefly related a startling tale, claiming he was returned from having discovered India – by sailing directly west, across the Atlantic Ocean.

Dias asked to see these papers from the Spanish king and queen, and Columbus was only too glad to hand them over. Satisfied, Dias returned to his ship and reported what he had learned. The captain of the warship then went 'with great ceremony, and with kettledrums, trumpet, and horns sounding gaily to the *Niña*', where he greeted Columbus and treated him with honour. They would await directions from the Portuguese king.

Word quickly spread throughout the local region that

Columbus had returned from the Indies. A large crowd journeyed from nearby Lisbon and elsewhere to view this ship, which had come from so far, and to see for themselves the 'Indians' the new Spanish admiral had brought back with him. With typical Portuguese generosity they gave thanks to God that 'such an increase of Christianity' should come to the king and queen of Spain as they had laboured so hard to this end. We can assume that among these were friends of the admiral who had known him during his Lisbon years and that it was for Columbus an extremely satisfying moment, even as he quietly pondered his fate.

On 8 March word arrived from King John inviting Columbus to join him and issuing orders for the *Niña* to be reprovisioned and made ready to sail once the inclement weather sufficiently abated. Though fearing treachery, Columbus went none the less as he had no choice. He had written another summary of his discoveries during the most violent portion of the storm off the coast of Portugal and dispatched it by messenger to the Spanish sovereigns. Should anything happen to him, at least his titles and honours would be secure for his oldest son.

Mules were provided for Columbus and for the members of his crew he chose to take, and to carry some of the bits of gold and other articles he possessed in order to prove he had discovered a new land. He also took a selection of the healthiest 'Indians' he had with him. The weather was scarcely better ashore so it was not until the night of 9 March, a Saturday, that he reached the king.

A pestilence had struck Lisbon, earlier than customary since they typically arrived with summer, so King John and his entourage were staying at a monastery located in a pine forest some 30 miles from Lisbon. To spare the resources of the surrounding area, the queen, with whom Columbus had always had good relations, was housed elsewhere with her court.

This was not the first occasion on which the Portuguese king had met Columbus. At this time Columbus is believed to have been forty-two years old; the king was thirty-seven. Despite his relative youth, the king was not in good health. He had lost his heir just two years earlier, a loss from which he was never to

recover. But the discovery of the sea route to India had been perhaps the greatest passion of his reign, having been given responsibility for it by his father, Alfonso V, at an early age, and he
would hear the story of its discovery from the lips of this new
Castilian admiral.

Nine years earlier, shortly after John II had assumed the
throne, he granted a meeting with Columbus. For years the
Genoan had lobbied the previous king and his advisers to support his venture of reaching to India by sailing west. The
Portuguese were methodically seeking to reach India by working their way down the coast of Africa, hoping with each expedition to find the tip of the continent. The endeavour had taken
so long that King John was at least willing to hear the persistent
man out. João de Barros records in *Décades da Asia* that, though
Columbus was respected in some areas of his knowledge and
experience, John considered the Genoan 'to be a big talker and
boastful in setting forth his accomplishments, and full of fancy
and imagination'.

Despite this, after their meeting the king referred the matter
to his Junta dos Mathemáticos for a final decision and they soon
informed him that Columbus was simply wrong. His idea to
reach the Indies by sailing west was not original and had been
studied in the past. The distance from the Canary Islands to
Japan, where Columbus said he would first arrive, was known to
be just over 10,000 miles (10,600 in fact), not 2,400. The true
distance was beyond the reach of any contemporary ship without making repeated stops for provisions and maintenance.
Rebuffed nine years earlier, Columbus had taken his efforts to
Spain and in time been granted his wish.

Columbus had been viewed as something of an eccentric by
the Portuguese court during the years he had lobbied the crown,
and his conduct in 1493 on the occasion of this second meeting
with the king bordered on the irreverent. Losing his apprehension at the occasion, he was taken with his own self-importance
and demanded that he be addressed by the august titles to which
his discoveries entitled him. He was more than eager to remind
the king that the passage to India by sailing west could have been

his, if only he had placed his faith in Columbus. The new admiral related his story arrogantly, displaying 'discourtesy and insolence' and behaving as a 'braggart'.[2]

As proof of his achievement Columbus produced not the spices, silks and exotic treasures that were to be expected from a voyage to Asia, but a few natives he called 'Indians', some minor bits of gold jewellery and a number of interesting, though primitive, artefacts. When his lack of spices, known to be common in Asia, was pointed out, Columbus argued he had only reached the outer islands of Japan. Still, what he described and the paltry items he displayed appeared nothing like the objects Europeans had received overland from Asia for centuries.

Columbus wrote that he was well received by both the king and his principal officers, that they showed him much honour and favour, and that John II in particular said he was very pleased that his voyage had ended so favourably. And that probably is what the Portuguese king said and the face he presented. But there was another observer who wrote of the same scene and his account is quite different. According to the king's chronicler, Rui da Pina, King John's expression of pleasure was insincere. In fact, he was furious at this turn of events but kept his anger to himself. He was enraged that time and again Columbus elevated his position and so obviously exaggerated the truth about his discovery, 'and made the tale of gold, silver and riches much greater than it was'.

The king politely suggested to Columbus that this new discovery was of lands within 'the seas and boundaries of his Lordship of Guinea, which was prohibited' to the Spanish.[3] The Treaty of Alcáçovas of 1479 stipulated that all land south of the Canary Islands, discovered or yet discovered, belonged to Portugal. Of course, the treaty actually meant just Africa itself and those lands discovered near it, but it could be interpreted as meaning a line drawn across the Atlantic. To this 'the Admiral answered that he had not seen the treaty nor did he know anything else except that the sovereigns had ordered him not to go to La Mina or anywhere in all of Guinea.'[4] The king smiled becomingly and allowed that he was certain there would be no need for arbiters to settle the matter.

When Columbus retired for the evening there were those of the royal advisers who, though they doubted the validity of the navigator's claim, advised that he be killed rather than risk his return to Spain. They argued the Portuguese monarchy had invested too much in the quest for the passage to India to run the slightest risk of its falling to their enemy. Further, the Genoan deserved death if for no other reason than his discourteous manner towards their sovereign. But the king would not hear of it. Columbus would be permitted to sail to Spain.

Following Mass the next day the two men met for an extended briefing. King John examined the 'Indians' at some length, joined by a large contingent of locals who marvelled at them. When Columbus bragged about the intelligence of the men, the king summoned a quantity of dry beans and asked one of the natives to use them to draw a map of their lands. The man squatted down and with great presence of mind used the beans to depict his island and those surrounding it in detail, explaining himself in his own incomprehensible language. The king mixed the beans up and directed one of the others to reconstruct the picture, which he promptly did, adding still more lands.

Whatever doubts King John had had until now, he could no longer conceal his chagrin at the extent of this new discovery, whether it was truly the gateway to India or not. Had he but listened to Columbus, they were lands that should have been his. In private, it is reported, the king struck his breast repeatedly in anger and cried out, as recounted in the stilted language of his chronicler, 'O man of little comprehension! . . . Why did I let slip an enterprise of so great importance?'

The next morning, as Columbus prepared to return to his ship, the king gave him a message for Ferdinand and Isabella, then bade him farewell. Columbus detoured to pay a brief courtesy call on the queen, Leonor, as she had asked to see him before he left. Her entourage was present for their meeting and the admiral's description of his voyage and the discoveries. Among them was the queen's younger brother Dom Manuel, the Duke of Beja, unaware he was destined to become king of Portugal within two years.

The next day Columbus received word that King John was prepared to give his party all they needed to make the journey to Spain by land if he wished. Fearing this to be a ruse during which he and his men would be murdered and the affair dismissed as banditry, Columbus noted that word of his success had already been sent to Spain. He refused the offer and instead promptly returned to his ship, now restored and provisioned.[5] At eight o'clock on the morning of 13 March the *Niña* set sail with the ebb tide and, graced by a fair wind, entered the still rolling open sea. Two days later Admiral Christopher Columbus sailed into the harbour at Saltes, from which he had departed eight months earlier, and took his place in history.

Despite the absence of substantive proof, this unexpected development was disturbing to King John. He was especially concerned over the complexion of the 'Indians' with Columbus, which was not dark; nor was their hair curly like that of the African slaves in which the Portuguese dealt. They might very well be Asians. If what Columbus claimed was true, and despite what he had told the admiral, Spain might now hold exclusive rights to trade with Asia by sailing west. Even should the Portuguese succeed in reaching India by rounding the cape of Africa, it would, by treaty and papal bull, be a Spanish monopoly from which the Portuguese would be excluded.

After due consideration, however, the king's junta reached the conclusion that Columbus was simply wrong. He had discovered new lands in the Atlantic, just as the Portuese had, but he had not reached India. That prize still lay unclaimed.

Columbus's voyage was, however, a cautionary event. Since Dias's return from the tip of Africa the Portuguese had yet to launch a fleet for the final push to India. It was apparent now that if the Portuguese delayed, the prize of the ages could well slip from their grasp. With this in mind and against the steady clock of his own looming death, John II made preparations for the final effort.

Bordered by its historic enemy Spain, Portugal faces the Atlantic. Off the beaten path, it has lain since its founding in the early twelfth century in quiet, beautiful isolation. However, for a brief time in history it was the centre of the greatest explorations the world has ever seen. From those discoveries came to the Portuguese unimaginable wealth and a worldwide empire that stretched from the Chinese coast to Java, from there to Sri Lanka and Gôa, to Angola and Brazil. To this day Portuguese names dot the world map.

The vast sweep of the Portuguese discoveries during the fifteenth century is generally unappreciated for its consequences on the world at large. It is not too much to say that the world as we know it, for better and for worse, came into being because of the Portuguese.

It was the Portuguese who opened the way into the Atlantic. They were the first to sail south down the west coast of Africa, the first Europeans to pass the equator, to double the African continent, the first to reach India by sea from Europe. They were the first Europeans to reach Ceylon, Sumatra, Malacca and Timor, the first to find the mythical Spice Islands, the Moluccas. They were the first Europeans to reach and trade with both China and Japan by sea, the first to view Australia. And in the Americas they 'discovered' Brazil. There is credible evidence they were the first to land on North America in 1500. The methodical Portuguese expeditions were all a part of a decades-long, systematic exploration and discovery of the unknown world.

Before this monumental undertaking Europe was an island of civilization in a vast world of obscurity. The rest of the Earth existed as tradition, legend, rumour or myth. Although many of the maps of that era were fundamentally accurate as far as they went, they were contradicted by others of apparently equal merit. There was no single repository of reliable knowledge. Information came by word of mouth, or from faded documents of dubious worth, few of which agreed on much of anything.

Ships of all the European nations sailed within sight of land, venturing into blue water only briefly or inadvertently to flee pirates or as the result of a storm. There was no certain profit in sailing into new seas – and much peril. Ships and crews were routinely lost on well-established routes, so why risk the unknown? The purpose of sailing was not discovery or pleasure but to move goods and passengers for value.

Although the enormous fortune to be made by wresting control of trade with the East from the Muslim infidels was one motive, and a very powerful one, the Portuguese explorations were always about more than empire and spices, although that has become the standard textbook telling. The Portuguese equally sought to establish contact with long-lost pockets of Christians known to be in the East, convert pagans and colonize new lands; and, as much as anything else, they were driven by the desire to know.

At Sagres in the extreme south-west of Portugal, Prince Henry – Henry the Navigator as he came to be known – welcomed his crews home with lavish dinners and spent long nights being regaled by his captains with stories of what they had seen and experienced. The world was a mystery and every reliable word of what lay beyond the known was eagerly embraced and carefully documented. Henry's captains were noted for their courage, their seamanship and their steadfast, reliable temperament. Henry wanted reports in which he could have faith and selected men who would give them to him.

The story of the Portuguese explorations is not one of quaint men in picturesque wooden ships. It is a tale of passion, of blood and treachery, of incomparable bravery, of majestic sweeps of vision, of nation- and empire-building. It is a drama played across a world stage, in a time that will never be repeated, for it was the last era when the physical world and its peoples were largely unknown, when each ship returned with new knowledge, when myth was finally separated from reality. It is no wonder 'The Discoveries', as the Portuguese came to call them, filled so many with such hunger and compelled so much sacrifice.

The cost was enormous and in many ways is immeasurable. 'God gave the Portuguese a small country as cradle but all the world as their grave', observed the seventeenth-century Portuguese Jesuit António Vieira.[6] Indeed, the oceans of the world can be described as one vast watery grave for Portuguese seamen.

If the decisions and motives of the players appear alien to us it is because, while technically these were men of the Renaissance, their hearts and thinking were still medieval. It was a time when Muslims and Christians alike converted great populations to the 'true faith' by sword and cannon, or by the expedient of seducing, or buying, the ruler. Where we have doubts, they had none. There was much they did not know about the world at large, but in matters of religion and conquest they were unhesitating. The people they discovered *en route* to India and those they encountered once there – the Moors, blacks, Hindus and others – were in their eyes heathens and, as one Portuguese recorded, possessed 'the badness of all bad men'.[7] A captain wrote on observing the people of Brazil, although he could just as easily have said the same of all those the Portuguese encountered, that 'Since our Lord . . . brought us here, I believe it was not without purpose.'[8]

Only on the most superficial level is this the story about a trade monopoly in spices. For Prince Henry, John I, John II and Manuel, those who had the most to do with directing the effort, it was nothing less than the Crusades, reborn in a different manifestation but with the same objective. It was believed, correctly, that flanking the Muslims who controlled the gateway to Asian spices would weaken the infidel. It was hoped, futilely, this would lead to the reconquest of Jerusalem.

The Portuguese achievement, however, had far greater implications by imposing European superiority in technology and weapons across the world. It spread Christianity and Western culture to the most distant lands, the effects of which are profound to this day and the ramifications of which continue to be felt. The conflict between Christians and Muslims has scarcely played itself out.

This is in large part the story of a number of Portuguese sea captains. They appear to act out their role, stepping into history from poorly recorded pasts, disappearing into obscure futures, but for a period of time the role of each was essential. Gil Eanes, Antão Gonçalves, Nuno Tristão, Diogo Cão, Bartholomeu Dias, all played key roles in the Portuguese feat, each building on the success of those, known and unknown, who went before them.

The pivotal act of the Portuguese accomplishment, however, was Vasco da Gama's discovery of the all-sea passage to India. The story of his first epic voyage forms the single greatest part of this account. Because of his accomplishment Gama became the greatest Portuguese of all time.* No king, no general or admiral, no cardinal or bishop, no writer, poet or artist, even comes close. His name is still spoken throughout the country with respect and awe. It is a significant measure of the character of the Portuguese people that this should be so. But if it had not been Gama, then it would have been another. When he returned to Lisbon two years after his departure preparations for another India fleet were already under way.

The most disturbing aspect of the Discoveries was the intro-duction of black African slaves into the European economy. The Portuguese did not invent slavery, nor did they create African slavery, but they gave it a scale unknown previously and brought untold misery and suffering to countless millions through its merciless application.

They did not see it like that. The Christian nations of Europe, or for that matter the Hindu and Muslim nations who likewise practised widespread slavery, considered it to be the natural state of the world. In Europe it was accepted that it was better for a pagan black African to spend his or her life in Christian bond-age than to remain in Africa and burn in hell for eternity.

Recounting these historic events presents unique obstacles in the telling as historians of this time attached little importance to dates and often failed to include them. This requires a painstaking, occasionally imprecise, reconstruction of events to determine a probable date. Highly regarded historians have made crucial errors in calculations, so every fact must be checked and rechecked.

Certain key documents are also lacking. Many sources that do exist are at best second-hand, relying on original documents that have not survived. Some have simply vanished, while others

---

* The earliest Portuguese writings use 'Gama' as the family name of Vasco da Gama. Despite that, English-language writers usually use the incorrect 'da Gama'.

were destroyed in the devastating Lisbon earthquake of 1755. We know, to name just one conspicuous example, that Gama maintained a log during his first voyage to India, for it existed some time after his death; but it has disappeared.

Sources very close to events, however, have survived. Two are *The Chronicle of the Discovery and Conquest of Guinea*, by the royal chronicler Gomes Eannes da Azurara, and *The Three Voyages of Vasco da Gama and his Viceroyalty*, from the *Lendas da India* by Gaspar Correa. Azurara's work was completed in 1453 and recounts nearly at first hand the early years of the Portuguese discoveries. It is especially fortunate that Azurara interviewed participants in the voyages, and knew and worked with Prince Henry. Correa wrote at the other end of the Discoveries, sailing to India when very young, in 1514. He too drew on interviews with participants in the events about which he wrote. Both works have deficiencies, Correa being the more unreliable, but each possesses remarkable insights and details that would otherwise be unknown.

A third source, and the best, comes from a member of the crew of the first voyage to India by Vasco da Gama who maintained a contemporaneous record that has survived. Known simply as the *Roteiro* (or 'Journal'), its authorship is an unresolvable dispute. A name can be affixed only by an imprecise process of elimination. What matters is that it is accepted as authentic and offers a first-hand account of the voyage and of many of the historic events that took place during it. Also available are English-language selections from *Décades de Asia*, by João de Barros, the most respected of the royal chroniclers but writing at greater distance from events.

Although it was Vasco da Gama who actually reached India by sea, it is Christopher Columbus who is best remembered beyond Portugal. Both men changed the course of the world, but it is arguable which of them changed it more. Adam Smith wrote that, 'The discovery of America and that of the passage to the East Indies by the Cape of Good Hope are the two greatest and most important events recorded in the history of mankind.'

Contemporaries had no doubt which of the two accomplishments was the greater. New lands were being discovered routinely at the time, and their full potential took several centuries to grasp. The Portuguese, and Gama, had opened the way east, and all of Europe appreciated the immediate and lasting implications of this achievement.

In their quest to reach India by sea, the Portuguese invented, or adapted, the latest advances in navigation and modified their ships repeatedly to the needs of the explorations. The reputation of the Portuguese spread throughout Europe with each passing year and each fresh, amazing discovery. When the explorations began, sailors from the Mediterranean nations and northern Europe gazed at the Portuguese caravels (*caravelas*) in Lisbon harbour with the exotic lines of their hulls and triangular-shaped lateen sails (from the word *latin**) and observed that only a Portuguese vessel was capable of rounding Africa. Fifty years, and many accomplishments, later they allowed with awe that only a Portuguese vessel *and* a Portuguese crew were capable of reaching the East.

Yet before the fifteenth century Portugal had been a nation of farmers and of coastal fishermen, with no indication of what was to come. As each captain's success led to the next, by the time of Gama's expedition, less than a century after the first ship set forth, no nation on earth commanded the seas as did the Portuguese. Gama's three-month sweep through the central and south Atlantic to make landfall within 100 miles of his destination, lacking so much as a sextant, was the greatest feat of sailing the world had ever seen and is still ranked as one of the most extraordinary sailing accomplishments of all time.

The strain of the Portuguese achievement was written on the faces of the widows and on those of the mothers who never again saw their husbands and sons. In a nation of scarcely more than 1 million, the drain on manpower to sustain the effort of discovery

---

* The sail would more accurately be described as Arab. The Arabs exploited its use to the point of perfection and introduced it into the Mediterranean, but they too did not invent it. It is all but certain the so-called lateen sail came to them from western India.

was enormous. Men routinely fled the boredom and poverty of the farm to seek the excitement and opportunity of Lisbon, and from there joined the annual expeditions into the unknown. Once the empire was created, fresh soldiers, sailors and administrators were required each year to serve its needs. Official indifference, storms, violence and tropical disease exacted a relentless toll on them. Only a small portion of those who left the shores of Portugal ever returned, and those who did, such as Luis Vaz de Camoens, soldier, royal official, poet and writer, author of *The Lusiads*, the Portuguese national epic, were often prematurely broken in body.

Portugal's greatest modern poet, Fernando Pessoa, centuries later wrote of the sacrifice in the *Mensagem*:

> *O sea. How much of your salt*
> *Consists of Portugal's tears.*
> *How many mothers have wept,*
> *How many children in vain have prayed,*
> *How many brides remained single*
> *For you to become ours, O sea.*

Fado, the native Portuguese music, was born on these long voyages of discovery. Its haunting melodies and melancholy laments tell of the sorrow and heartache the men experienced on distant seas so far from home. Bartholomeu Dias returned from the tip of Africa with a depleted crew, and even these survivors were seriously ill. Many ships never returned at all. Because of the secrecy imposed on much of the explorations the full cost of the Portuguese achievement will never be known.

The historian E. G. Ravenstein, in his foreword to the *Roteiro*, questions 'whether Portugal would not be happier now, and richer, too, had . . . her strength not been wasted in a struggle to which she was materially unequal, and which ended in exhaustion and ruin'.[9] Such a thought is sacrilege to the contemporary Portuguese, who hold no such view.

The first passage to India by sea was the equivalent in its time not of a moon shot but of a mission to Mars. Gama sailed with

16

the best vessels available, using the latest technology, manned almost entirely by volunteers, many of them veterans of the earlier Dias expedition which had discovered the tip of Africa and opened the way east. To complete this voyage Gama sailed further than the distance around the world following the equator, an estimated 23,000 nautical miles.

The obstacles to the Portuguese were enormous. Ships slowly disintegrated in the warm waters of the south Atlantic, Indian Ocean and Arabian Sea. Scurvy was a new disease brought on by the amazing distances the Portuguese innovations had made possible, one that took a terrible toll on the sailors.

The conduct of the Portuguese captains is often criticized for being both unreasonably and disproportionately violent. The use of force was not limited to the Portuguese, who were in its application no more vicious than captains from Italy, Flanders, Spain or England. In the case of Vasco da Gama, he was intruding into a part of the world dominated by Muslims who profited enormously from their trade monopoly and who despised all Christians as 'dogs'. The history of the Muslims and Hindus, among themselves and against each other, was also particularly violent and destructive. Success meant nearly unimaginable honours and riches, while failure meant death for him and his crew.

The consequences of the Portuguese voyages of discovery for Europe, Asia and the world are all but incalculable, certainly the most significant in world history. That Portugal, the poorest and one of the smallest nations of Europe, should have led the way is nothing less than astounding.

*There will come an age in the far-off years, when Ocean shall unloose
the bond of things, when the whole broad earth shall be revealed . . .*
— Seneca, *Medea*
Translated by Frank Justus Miller

I

'I sing the greatness of the race'[10]

Had John II only listened to Columbus, Portugal would have added the rest of the Americas to its collection of nations, depriving Spain of its place in history's sun. Still, by 1650, not yet 200 years after his finally meeting with the Genoan, Portugal commanded more of the world and of world trade than any nation in history. The Portuguese were the first to have a world seaborne empire, the last to give it up, and of all the European nations to hold such empires the legacy of the Portuguese has lasted longest.

During the period of exploration and the establishment of empire Portugal's population was never much more than 1 million; the nation had just 1,000 doctors, lawyers, judges, municipal and crown officials of every kind. The population at large was uneducated and generally ill treated by the nobility. Yet the Portuguese were fiercely patriotic, a patriotism fed in part by the all but constant wars against the Moors and Castile.

Other nations, however, had a people just as hardy and explorers as brave and resourceful as the Portuguese. Control of the spice trade was the greatest single prize of the age. The Italian city-states were profiting from the existing Muslim control of the market since they had insinuated themselves into the lucrative position of middleman. They were formidable sailors and explorers themselves, and had at different times shown an interest in rounding Africa.

The English and Flemish both coveted the sea route to India, but once the Portuguese seized the initiative neither of them was ever in the running. Castile might have made the push, and certainly wanted to, benefiting as it did from its possession of the strategically placed Canary Islands off the coast of West Africa, but instead for most of the crucial century it was preoccupied with creating Spain from Aragon and Castile and with the effort to push the last of the Moors from Iberia.

Although Portugal sits in a largely forgotten corner of Europe, it was a united country throughout the fifteenth century, with little internal strife. Both its isolation and its relative tranquillity proved great advantages. During the time of the Discoveries western Europe was gripped by the Hundred Years War, England by the Wars of the Roses, while other nations were occupied by civil war or foreign invasion.

Yet there was nothing to suggest the Portuguese would be the people to lead the European expansion into the world. At the beginning of the fifteenth century there was little reason to believe the Portuguese would carve for themselves the all-sea route to Asia and the spice monopoly that went with it. In fact, the Portuguese achievement seems incomprehensible as they were not a nation of seafarers. In the early fifteenth century they sailed from Oporto and Lisbon to the Mediterranean and northward towards Flanders and England, but hugged the coast, as did all sailors of the time. Yet within the span of less than a century Portugal explored and recorded nearly half of the world. Primarily through their efforts oceans that had been insurmountable barriers became highways of commerce, conquest and colonization. Regular systems of transport and communication were established and the face of the modern world took shape.

In the end it fell to the Portuguese, not by chance, location or default, but because it was they who saw the way and relentlessly pursued it over more than eighty years of sacrifice and fearful loss of life. It was an achievement without precedent for a such a small nation. Possessed of few natural resources and no great wealth, the monarchy struggled every year to remain solvent and nearly every generation fought to hold its power against the powerful counts. It was difficult for the population merely to survive on the land, large portions of which lay fallow, ravaged by plague and the wars with Castile. In retrospect, however, reasons can be found.

For all of its history Portugal has compared itself to and defended itself against the much larger and more populous Castile, and later Spain itself. Yet during its first three centuries Portuguese kings strove by conquest and marriage to unite the two nations of Castile and Portugal, under Portuguese rule. As it was, the eventual union of Castile with Aragon was less likely than union with Portugal since it involved Castile in Aragon's persistent disputes with France. Union with Portugal would have allowed Castile a better avenue for overseas exploration and expansion.

If Castile saw the advantages, it was the Portuguese who finally rejected the realization. When an opportunity for uniting the two countries did arise, the Portuguese rejected the rightful heir to their throne by a Spanish-born queen, uniting instead behind the bastard son of the king's Portuguese mistress. The Portuguese saying goes, 'No good wind and no good marriage comes from Spain'.

Confronted to the north and east by its historic enemy and unable to conquer it, the Portuguese instinctively looked west-ward, across the unknown and unexplored sea for expansion, wealth and glory. From earliest times the Iberian peninsula was occupied by many people, speaking different languages, with diverse cultural practices. Both the land and existing culture in the peninsula worked their effect so that every new people came to see themselves in time as Hispanic. The Romans occupied large portions of the region and profited from its silver mines, but they had never managed to subdue it entirely, although they left a lasting legacy of administrative regions, a common lan-guage and a well-established network of roads. The Spanish and Portuguese languages, although quite similar, are not derived one from the other; rather, they stem from a common root. Of the two, Portuguese was the first committed to writing and, because it lends itself more easily to romance, was for centuries the language preferred by the poets of both nations.

The closest land mass to Portugal is Africa and it is natural that the Portuguese, by reason of proximity and history, should be drawn there. The distance from Faro, on the southern coast of

Portugal, to Tangier is less than 150 miles. At certain times of the year it was possible to stand on the Portuguese shore and smell the scent of Africa blown by storms across the short expanse of sea. Strange and exotic plants were tossed on to the coastline of Portugal by massive north Atlantic storms. Ancient maps and legends also identified islands and lands in the vast ocean, the locations of which had been lost over time.

In addition, the 350-mile Portuguese coastline possessed many safe, deep harbours. The country's significant rivers flowed into the Atlantic, and at or near their mouths the major cities of Portugal developed and prospered. Oporto and Lisbon were excellent harbours for ships plying their trade from the Mediterranean to northern Europe and England. In Lisbon at any given time during the Middle Ages ships of every country and description could be seen. No other nation was more ideally situated to develop the sea route to India.

There was also the force of nature. Each summer the coast of Portugal receives a steady flow of wind along its western coast from the north to the south. This wind continues down the coast of north-west Africa in an even, predictable flow and was the natural course any sailing ship would take. It tugged at the ships, drawing them and their crews towards Africa.

But ships of the era depended on known winds and currents to make a safe return. While a ship could sail *with* the wind at no great effort, it could only make its way back by tacking *against* a slight wind. If the currents of the ocean and the speed of the wind were more than modest, any vessel of the time sailing too far downwind would never find its way home. By the fifteenth century there were many accounts in history of ships that had sailed south along the coast of Africa and not a single telling of one that had ever returned. One source extravagantly claimed more than 12,000 such losses.

Portugal also benefited from a long succession of effective kings. During the key period disputes over succession were settled with relative swiftness and the absence of protracted civil war. There was also an especially close tie between merchants and the royalty, so that commerce and conquest went hand in hand. It was much the same with religion. Profits were as important as saving souls.

Not fully appreciated in considering the motives behind the discoveries is the character of the Portuguese people themselves. The extended struggle to expel the Moors, fought from the north of Portugal to the south, served to unite the people and give them a sense of destiny. Every man was obliged to fight for his king, and many did so, in stark contrast to the practice of medieval warfare throughout the rest of Europe, which relied on knights and mercenary armies. It was Portuguese farmers and labourers who had ensured the nation's independence from Castile. In addition, they had driven the Moors from their land a full two centuries ahead of the Spanish and took great pride in the achievement. During the generations-long struggle the Portuguese were filled with a religious ardour. Expelling the Moors was a holy crusade given to the Portuguese by God. This sense of mission was easily carried over to the explorations, which always possessed a strong religious component.

Because the Portuguese were largely isolated from Western Europe they also developed a high level of self-sufficiency and independence. In one sense it was natural that a nation that routinely considered conquering its much larger neighbour would not be overawed by the prospect of worldwide exploration.

There is also another factor to consider, although it is less tangible. Unlike the doctrinaire Spanish, who were quick to embrace the Inquisition and viewed any deviation from their norm as suspect, the Portuguese were inclined to be more tolerant and accepting of, even intrigued by, differences; this was despite the fact that the Portuguese ultimately followed the path of the Spanish in their treatment of the Jews. There had always been a natural intercourse with northern Africa and the Portuguese people were a blend of many races. Raids by Moors and Berbers, and the mix of black Africans, created a far greater acceptance of other racial groups than was common at the time, particularly in Spain. A large number of Arab words, especially in economics, administration and military matters, remained in the Portuguese language, not to mention the vast number of place names.

As the central region, and later the south, of what is now Portugal were conquered by successive Portuguese kings, the Moorish armies and leadership were driven out, but the populace by and large remained in place, especially from Lisbon south. They generally converted to Christianity and continued their lives much as before. As a consequence, the Portuguese were ethnically more akin to north Africans than were the Spanish, less hostile towards other races.

The large numbers of Moors who remained in Portugal are thought to have influenced the Portuguese, in part by introducing the sexual permissiveness for which the Portuguese became well known. The Moors also possessed superior farming skills, including use of the waterwheel. They greatly improved the cultivation of olives, and introduced cotton, sugar-cane and the silkworm. The intermixing of the racial groups slowly became complete, as did the assimilation of the new ideas and technologies.

This combination of racial stock, location, national identity and purpose, driven by the chronic poverty and the lure of the open sea before them, served to create an explosion in maritime navigation and ship design. Not insignificantly, the Portuguese possessed the desire to know what lay beyond and the courage to go there.

It is no wonder that Camoens wrote of 'the greatness of the race'. They left 'their native Portugal behind them, opened a way to Ceylon, and further, across seas no man had ever sailed before'. The Portuguese captains 'were men of no ordinary stature'. The same could be said of the Portuguese in general.

2

Dear as pepper

Though trade with the East had existed for a millennium, the true source of both gems and spices was unknown to medieval Europe. With their purported curative and aphrodisiac properties, spices were held in near mystical reverence. In particular they were believed to possess rare and beneficial qualities, usually over and above their actual properties and uses. The demand for them was all but insatiable and almost any tale of their origin was given merit. Naturally their powers were thought to have a religious origin.

It was commonly accepted that four great rivers bore both spices and gems from the Garden of Eden into the world inhabited by man after his fall from the grace of God. Following the murder of Abel, by one account, Adam and Eve took their grief to the island of Ceylon, where they wept in sorrow for 500 years, their tears filling a vast lake from which came gems with healing powers. A proverb of the time went, 'Great is the virtue of herbs, but greater is rare stones'. To wear such precious stones was to be righteous, to enjoy good health and to be free of physical harm. There were many tales of pilgrims suffering no harm because they wore gems or consumed certain rare herbs. Such precious stones and spices were costly, not just because of their curative and preventative attributes, but because they were held to come from Paradise itself.

The Garden of Eden, and the origin of gems and of spices, lay somewhere to the fabled East, at the common source of the Tigris, Euphrates, Nile and Ganges rivers. The Nile was reported to encircle 'the land of Ethiopia, and flows into Egypt'.[11] Cinnamon originated in the nests of certain birds, particularly

27

that of the legendary phoenix. In this account both spices and gems were possessed of magical properties.

In medieval Europe the uses for spices and the fantasies concerning them were seemingly inexhaustible. Some were said to increase appetite, a recurring problem because of the bland diet everyone – even the wealthy – was forced to endure. Spices, especially pepper, could disguise the flavour of 'ripe' meat or, as with cinnamon, counter nausea brought on by the pervasive bad water. Soothing balms contained cinnamon, cardamom, cloves, pepper, nutmeg and aloes. But while spices were eventually valued for their purported curative powers and other positive benefits, they were initially sought primarily to be used as aphrodisiacs. The demand for spices had as much to do with the waning sexual powers of the ageing nobility and merchant class as with any other cause.

Spices became a form of currency and were used to pay tribute, often to religious authorities. Camphor was said to possess so many virtues it was impossible to name them all. Cardamom had many varied and valued effects, depending on whether it was taken with vinegar, wine or water. Cloves were said to be good for the liver, stomach and heart, and was used as a cure for coughs and as a fragrance in perfumes and oils. Ginger was a medicine but also useful in preparing meats. Nutmeg and mace prevented vomiting and were said to steady the heart.

But most valued above all the others was pepper. 'Dear as pepper' was a popular expression in France, where a pound of pepper was required for a serf to buy his freedom. In England pepper was used in payment for rent. The Jews in Aix were required to pay their tax in pepper and ginger, as well as wax, in order to preserve their own schools and cemeteries.[12] It was believed to come from somewhere south of the Caucasus, where 'serpents guarded the woods in which it grew'[13] until the thirteenth century, when the monk Bartholomeus Anglicus reported that pepper originated in India. It was employed as a remedy against the sting of poisonous insects, considered effective taken with wine against colds and when mixed with oil became a soothing ointment. Throughout western Europe pepper was added as a spice to food, as much for its medicinal effect for as its flavour. The English, for one, laced their dumplings and sausages with it. But most importantly, pepper preserved meat.

Life in rural Portugal, especially in the Alentejo and south, was always difficult. Indeed, life throughout Europe was harsh and uncompromising, and from it there was little respite. Superstition, often in the guise of religion, was rampant. Tragedy rather than hope was the norm, and countless millions lived short, wretched lives of hunger and brutality. Poverty was so widespread that the prospect of riches fired the imaginations of men, gripping them like a fever.

In medieval Europe the long winters were especially hard on the populace. Even lords suffered from an endless stream of maladies, so that a period of good health was the exception. There was insufficient feed to maintain a large herd of domestic animals for periodic slaughter during the winter, so any excess was killed in the autumn and consumed during the harvest festivals. The winter diet, lacking proper balance and in particular meat, was devoid of adequate nutrition.

One of the most serious problems facing any lord at that time in western Europe was the ever-present threat of a declining population. Attrition, disease, even starvation, exacted a relentless toll on the general populace. In addition to the winter deaths there was often an annual plague – probably typhoid – especially in the large cities. Ceaseless wars and general deprivations could leave a nation denuded and vast stretches of otherwise arable land often lay fallow for years. People were needed to tax, to till the fields and to fill the ranks of the army. Too small a population was a catastrophe for any lord or monarch, and a falling population was often the reality in fifteenth-century Europe.

Such was the Portuguese situation. The Black Death during the fourteenth century had ravaged the nation in successive waves, reducing its population at one point to less than 1 million, bringing with it greater religious extremism. The recurring wars with Castile were also a constant drain on manpower, and lack of workers was a chronic and serious problem throughout the nation.

In addition, the generally illiterate population was uneasy. The mass of labourers in Lisbon were described as 'fanatical, filthy and ferocious'.[14] Although Lisbon was a great metropolis by European standards at this time, its population was only between 50,000 and 65,000.[15] Feeding the restless populace was such a persistent and crucial demand that grain was routinely imported, a constant drain on the economy.

Pepper meant that meat could be preserved into the winter, and meat meant a healthier and larger population. Pepper was a godsend but its scarcity and cost prevented its widespread use. It could be obtained only through the hands of the hated infidels, and never in sufficient quantity or at an acceptable cost. Though its precise source remained a mystery, if a way to India could be found that bypassed the Muslims, many serious problems would be solved. Adding to the allure was this unassailable fact: the nation that controlled an all-sea route to India would be the richest and most powerful in Europe.

Throughout recorded history there had been continuous land trade between the West and East. Along caravan routes stretching in a patchwork across thousands of miles, interrupted by war, revolution and disease but always restored, commerce had continued because it was mutually beneficial. The goods of this trade were generally scented, filled with enticing, wondrous flavours, claimed to possess magical curative powers: in short, spices.

There was an active, though often interrupted, trade between India and Ancient Egypt, where tombs have been found containing spices. Pharaohs of the First Dynasty, around 2900 BC, routinely traded with the region they called the land of Punt, initially believed to be the east coast of Africa but later extended to include India. Legend reports the conquest of the Arabian Sea by a fleet of 400 Egyptian ships sent by Pharaoh Sesostris, who ruled from 2115 to 2099 BC. The clearest signs of a lucrative trade with India were the attempts to construct a canal across the Suez, finally accomplished, or restored by some accounts, by Darius I, king of Persia from 521 to 485 BC.

The Minaean kingdom on the western part of the Arabian

peninsula exported incense it obtained by caravan from the East and traded by sea along the coastline with India for spices. The Phoenicians established a post for sea trade at Aqaba as early as the reign of King Solomon, from 973 to 933 BC. By the sixth century BC there was a regular trade between the west coast of India and the Middle East. Jews, deported to India by the Assyrian kings at the time of the fall of the kingdom of Israel in 555 BC, played a key role in the spice trade.

Alexander the Great quickly grasped the value of pepper when he reached India and directed the creation of trade routes to encourage and develop commerce throughout the empire. One hundred and twenty ships a year set out to India along the sea portions of these routes to collect cargoes of spices, primarily pepper, taking two years to return home and relying on the predictable monsoon to help them in both directions. Sea trade routes extended to south-east Asia, reaching the Han empire of China. Alexandria in Egypt become the gateway for spices into western Europe; one of its portals was called 'the Pepper Gate'.

Despite periodic interruptions, the spice trade flourished during the Roman empire. The Romans established direct contact with India after they occupied Egypt, in essence taking control of the trade that had existed between Pharaoh and India for nearly 3,000 years. After the Greek merchant Hippalus 'discovered' the monsoon winds of the Red Sea and Indian Ocean in the first century AD trading voyages between the Roman empire and India became commonplace. Roman merchants established permanent trading stations on the Bay of Bengal, and Roman products, even Roman subjects, could be found as far away as China and south-east Asia. Roman contact, however, was almost exclusively with the west coast of India, in particular the Malabar coast, which abounded 'in ships sent there with cargoes from Arabia and by the Greeks'. Some time during the first century AD an unknown mariner wrote *Periplus of the Erythraean Sea*. It records:

> They [the Romans] send large ships to the market towns on account of the great quantity and bulk of pepper and

malabathrum [cinnamon]. There are imported here, in the first place, a great quantity of coin; topaz, thin clothing, not much; figured linens, antimony, coral, crude glass, copper, tine, lead, wine, not much, but as much as at Barygaza [Broach]; realgar and orpiment; and wheat enough for the sailors, for this is not dealt in by the merchants there. There is exported pepper, which is produced in quantity in only one region near these markets, a district called Cottonora. Besides this there are exported great quantities of fine pearls, ivory, silk cloth, spikenard from the Ganges, mala-bathrum from the places in the interior, transparent stones of all kinds, diamonds and sapphires, and tortoise shell; that from Chryse Island, and that taken among the islands along the coast of Damirica [Tamil Nadu]. They make the voyage to this place in favourable season who set out from Egypt about the month of July, that is Epiphi.[16]

Imperial Rome imported so many spices from the East that there was a constant drain of tens of millions in both gold and silver. The emperor was forced to issue a decree forbidding the use of gold in such transactions because it was carried out of the empire and never seen again.

Jews played a key role in the spice trade nearly everywhere. The *Book of Conquests and of Countries*, by the Iman of Baghdad, gives as the reason the fact that Jews 'speak Persian, Latin, Greek, Arabic, Spanish and Slav'. They travelled freely from Saipan to Tangier, across north Africa to Cairo then to Damascus, Baghdad and from there to India and China. They exported silks, furs, swords, female slaves and eunuchs. From Asia they returned with aloes, camphor, cinnamon, musk and other valu-ables.[17]

Spices were thought by many in Rome to corrupt public virtue and to be the ultimate cause of the destruction of the empire itself. Nevertheless, the empire's appetite for spices only grew more voracious. Special warehouses were constructed in Rome to prevent the spoiling of spices and they were the source of great wealth. The poet Persius wrote:

> *The greedy merchants led by lucre, run*
> *To the parch'd Indies, and the rising sun;*
> *From thence hot Pepper, and rich Drugs they bear,*
> *Bart'ring for Spices, their Italian ware.*[18]

At Poppea's funeral, the grieving Nero ordered all the cinnamon imported from Ceylon over one year to be burnt.

As the Roman empire spread, so to did the knowledge and use of spices, especially cinnamon, frankincense and pepper. The Germans developed such a fondness for pepper that in 408 they demanded 3,000 pounds of it as a ransom from Rome. The collapse of the Roman empire and the subsequent disorder in western Europe resulted in a 400-year disruption in the steady flow of spices from the East, though a trickle continued.

As normal trade resumed, the route took a different route and moved further north, ultimately reaching Constantinople, where the spice trade constituted the primary source of its wealth and power.[19] There were at one point in Constantinople 103 interpreters of as many languages and dialects, all related to the trade in spices. Europeans returning from Samarkand reported they saw there Persians, Indians and Turks, as well as others with their own shops.

Modest though it was by modern standards, the scale of interconnection in the ancient world was greater than it might have been primarily because of trade, especially in spices. As early as the fifth century Christians were observed living in India along the Malabar coast and by the sixth century they were observed on the island of Ceylon. In 543 the Byzantine emperor Justinian dispatched missionaries to Nubia, were they established a Christian church that lasted until the fourteenth century, and Christianity survived further south in Ethiopia. Individual travellers and merchants made the journey east on a regular basis. In 552 the eggs of the silkworm were smuggled from China to Constantinople by two monks. Indeed, the Far East was so well known that in 628 the Egyptian writer Theophylact Simocatta wrote an accurate portrayal of China. Between 643 and 719 envoys were sent east from Byzantium to seek assistance from the conquering Arabs.

The spread of Islam again disrupted the flow of spices to the West, but in India the conquerors soon became traders, as they did elsewhere. In Egypt in 969 the Fatimite Caliph founded a new city, Cairo, and from then on spices were key to its prosperity. A special quarter of the city was assigned to the spice trade and in 1175 a Western envoy reported seeing for himself a vast quantity of pepper and other spices stored there.

The East was as eager as the West to participate in the trade and the incessant demand for spices influenced events there. In 1072 the Chinese occupied the Moluccas, primarily to gain control over the spices that grew there. The inhabitants of the Moluccas – or the Spice Islands, as the Portuguese called them – soon realized the value of the nutmeg and clove trees and drove the Chinese out, only to be conquered later by the Malaccas, the traditional regional power. Both Persian and Arab traders were visiting the Spice Islands as early as the eighth century and soon afterwards cloves, camphor, sandalwood, pepper and nutmeg made their way west. By 1180, in St Jean d'Acre, taxes were paid in nutmeg. Chinese merchants also traded in spices and, not surprisingly, developed a particular fondness for pepper.

It was in the interest of all those in the East who profited from the commerce to keep the origin of spices secret. The Chinese concocted exotic stories and fables when asked the source. These not only confused the origin of the spices but also added to the mythology surrounding them and enhanced their value.

In the West in the ninth and tenth centuries there was a steady stream of pilgrims back from the Holy Land to Europe who brought with them the spices they had encountered during their trip. But it was the Crusades that were the primary means for assuring and expanding the steady flow of spices into western Europe. Spices that had not previously been known there made their way to the homes of the crusaders, where an immediate demand was created for them.

Between 1099 and 1291 merchants, pilgrims and crusaders by the thousand visited the Middle East. They came from every corner of Europe, from Norway, Wales, Scotland, England, Germany and Flanders to name but a few, and the numbers were substantial. The bishop of Bamberg, for example, led a party of some 7,000. Those who managed to return home were usually enriched by the spices they brought back with them.

. Despite the animosity between Christians and Muslims, an increasingly cosy relationship existed between the Arab spice traders and their Western counterparts. Each dealt in a highly profitable commodity and it was in their mutual interest to assure a steady supply and maximum return on the trade. Drawing on the legacy of Rome and exploiting their fortuitous location, the cities of Italy were best positioned to prosper from the spice trade. The Genoese established a Middle East trading colony by rebuilding the ancient city of Theodosia on the Crimea, which they renamed Caffa.

The trade in spices meant great wealth, luxury and power for those in control of the choke points. Constantinople and Alexandria were the two primary gateways for the flow of spices into the West, and their importance at any given moment depended on politics and religion as times and events favoured first one, then the other.

Once the spices made their way into Europe they created profit at every routing point, though all roads led to the merchants of the Hanseatic League in the Netherlands. In Bruges the merchants from Germany, France, England and Spain exchanged wool for spices. Antwerp, Ghent, Bordeaux, Toulouse and Louvain were all important trading centres because of spices. The Guild of the Pepperers was founded in London as early as 1179, by which time the Corporation of the Spicers was already playing an important role in France. The spice trade in Europe was carefully, and profitably, regulated, the cost of transport calculated to the smallest coin.

By the middle of the thirteenth century the cities of Italy were the centres of the land-based commerce with the Orient and were located at the hub of a network of trade routes leading to the East. They were also the focal point for a system of credit and currency that permitted the trade to prosper. The creation by Genoa, Florence and Venice between 1252 and 1284 of gold coins, which allowed even greater expansion of trade east, was the first in Europe since Charlemagne. The control of trade with the East was the primary source of the immense wealth of these city-states. From the Italian commerce developed regular spice trade routes in Europe. The spice trade was the single most powerful economic engine for producing wealth in medieval Europe.

The price of spices began to rise dramatically in 1300, when the Sultan in Cairo ordered that all such traffic in his region be routed through the city, where he imposed a heavy tax. The Portuguese, who made a careful study of such matters, concluded in the fifteenth century that the ruler in Cairo received revenue from the trade in spices valued at 7.5 million *cruzados* in gold,[20] a fortune almost beyond imagining.

Commerce was not the only means of benefiting from the spice trade. Great profits could be made on the high seas since there was little distinction between commerce and piracy. In 1290, nine hundred Genoese seamen were brought to the Tigris by the Il-Khan Arghun to construct and man galleys for the purpose of raiding the spice sea routes. After a sailor desecrated a mosque, causing a local riot, the men were moved to Basra, where they promptly divided into two rival camps and made war on one another. Nothing came of the enterprise.

In 1324 Jordon of Severac wrote to the Pope from India that just two galleys could severely interrupt trade in the Arabian Sea. A Dominican named William Adam, later the second Archbishop of Sultaniyeh, proposed that three or four galleys manned by 1,200 Genoese should be stationed in the Red Sea and Gulf of Aden to profit from blockading Egyptian commerce. Adam spent twenty months in the Arabian Sea region, nine of them on the Christian island of Socrotra.

In 1315 the Genoese merchants Benedetto Vivaldi and Percivalle Stancone travelled to India, where the former died in 1322. Six Venetians journeyed from Urgenj to Delhi in India on a trade mission in 1338; two of them died *en route* but the four survivors, despite paying substantial bribes to local authorities, returned home with a substantial profit.

The spread of the Mongols throughout Asia during the thirteenth century caused an increase in trade and contact with the

East since the Mongols were occupiers and did not trust the Chinese and other subjected people. The Great Khan commonly used European merchants as emissaries. Andalo da Saignone was sent by him to Europe in 1336 to establish closer ties with the 'Franks' and to request marvels, especially the much prized Western horses, which were larger and stronger than the local breed.

Trade with the East became so routine that in 1340 a Florentine merchant and banker, Francesco Balducci di Pegolotti, wrote that the route from Tana on the Sea of Azov to Peking, via Turkestan and Mongolia, was safe both night and day. He gave detailed instructions on how to reach China, along with accurate information concerning local currencies and custom duties.*

Yet the actual volume of trade was surprisingly small. The three state-run convoys of Venice, for example, are estimated to have brought back just 1,000–2,000 tons of goods of all kinds annually.[21] What percentage of this was solely spices is not known. The items were, however, in high demand and produced a substantial profit. It is no wonder that the hold of a single Portuguese ship, which alone could transport many tons of spices and other desired goods, was such a threat to the Italian merchant cities and the extensive trading centres throughout Europe.

But by 1340 the conditions that allowed improved contact and trade with the East were already deteriorating. In the key Persian city of Tabriz, Venetian merchants clashed among themselves and with the increasingly antagonistic Mongol authorities. In 1335 Mongol rule in Persia collapsed and the local Muslims were aggressively hostile towards Westerners and ethnic Christians. Between 1336 and 1344 the Genoese were compelled to abandon Tabriz and they boycotted trade in the region thereafter.

---

* In 1951, when the city wall of Yangchow, China, was demolished, the tomb of Catherine Vilioni, who died in June 1342, was discovered. The daughter of Domenico Vilioni, her prominent Venetian family had a dominant trade presence in the Chinese city for more than 100 years.

Most significantly, the Black Death was introduced into Europe from the Black Sea in 1348. The resulting decrease in European population, the ensuing decline in its economy and the religious fervour it produced all disrupted trade significantly. Just as Europe was beginning its slow recovery, the Great Khans in China were succeeded in 1368 by the Mings, who promptly expelled the Mongols and all other foreigners.

Constantinople's key role in the spice trade ended in 1453, when the Muslim Turks seized the city and prohibited all commercial trade with Christians. The rise of the Mamelukes in Egypt and of the Ottoman Turks in Mesopotamia and Persia both changed the established trading patterns. The flow of spices was severely disrupted and the cost escalated sharply, at a time when the Portuguese were fully engaged in finding the passage to India.

Despite these obstacles a reduced volume of trade persisted. The Genoese retained control of the Black Sea city of Matrega, located on the coast of Kuban, until 1482 and through it spices continued to enter Europe.

By this time Europe's supply of precious metal was exhausted, leading to an inevitable devaluation of all currencies. Portugal was among the worst to suffer. During the first part of the fifteenth century a single mark of gold (230 grams) rose from 250 *libras* to 251,000 *libras*.[22] The chronic lack of gold and of silver was economically devastating. One consequence was a serious erosion of the income received by the king and other lords, at a time when expenses were rising. The nations involved in the spice trade saw in it a means for acquiring both gold and silver, which were essential in adequate amounts to create a stable currency for financial transactions and the expansion of commerce. Spice did not in itself represent wealth but was a means to wealth and the crucial device for solving the nagging economic problems sovereigns faced. The spice trade was the greatest wealth-producing enterprise in Europe.

During the period immediately before and during the Portuguese discoveries the nation best equipped for world sea exploration was

China, but with a single period of exception the Chinese elected to limit themselves to trading primarily in the South China Sea and Indian Ocean.

During the Ming Dynasty, between 1405 and 1435, the royal eunuch, Admiral Cheng Ho, undertook seven voyages, with fleets of up to sixty-two ships, in part to search of the former emperor, who his successor feared was gathering an army in a foreign land to retake the throne. Another purpose of the voyages was to provide the royal court with exotic creatures, including giraffes, ostriches and zebras. Cheng Ho sailed to India and established trade relations there, then rounded the tip of Africa, where Chinese coins have been found.

But with the emperor's death the fleet was recalled and the Chinese excursions abroad abandoned, though Chinese merchants continued to sail abroad along the routes Ho pioneered and China remained an active trader in the East. Junks (from the Arab *djunk*) were observed at the port in Calicut by Vasco da Gama, but the Chinese had abandoned their brief period of exploration by the time the Portuguese established their presence in the region. Still, many trade goods desired in Europe, and some spices, came from China or from areas under Chinese control and to that extent they were major players in the overall spice trade.

The Chinese junks were five to ten times the size of the Portuguese vessels, exceeding 1,000 tons and with crews of 250. They had early on adopted the centre rudder, one of massive size which made their ships more manoeuvrable. Their battened sails collapsed like Venetian blinds, allowing for relatively small crews and causing less loss of life in rough weather. They used double hulls and watertight bulkheads, adding greatly to the safety of their vessels. They carried herds of animals to be slaughtered at sea and grew herbs and vegetables on board in order to reduce the risk of scurvy. The ships were divided into as many as 300 compartments, which were leased to merchants who stored their goods and lived and worked from them for the duration of the voyage.

The qualities of the Chinese ships should not be overstated, however. Alhough Marco Polo was much impressed with them, his voyage aboard one from China to the Persian Gulf took nearly two years, and almost 600 people aboard ship died.

The establishment of trading colonies related to spices brought Western Europeans into routine contact not just with Asia Minor but also with travellers there who had been to the Far East, exciting great curiosity. As these Europeans dispatched reports home and as they themselves returned, the knowledge of Asia, its customs and habits, grew. Written accounts slowly circulated through the European courts, taking as much as a century to become commonly known. The effect was to produce a strong desire to establish direct contact with the East.

Although commerce, usually related to spices, was the essential ingredient in medieval travel, curiosity and the desire to see the world were no less a passion then than they are now, and had their own impact on the spread of spices and in expanding knowledge of the world. At the end of the ninth century an Arab merchant named Soleiman travelled extensively along the coast of India and then, following the monsoon, continued on to China, which he explored for curiosity's sake. On his return Soleiman wrote an account of what he had seen, called *A Traveller's Tales*. Later this manuscript was expanded with the experiences and observations of another Arab merchant, Abou-Zeyd of Siraf, and the resulting work was called *Two Travellers*. Of particular significance was the accuracy of the geographical descriptions contained in the books. Both works were widely read in Europe and highly influential.

While such accurate information about the East existed, it was mingled with myth and legend. There was no accepted repository of fact on which a scholar or prince could draw to determine the truth from fiction, although such efforts were made. King Roger II of Sicily was fascinated by geography and researched what the Greek, Latin and Arab geographers had written on the subject. He spotted the numerous discrepancies and set about to learn the truth for himself. He inquired personally of travellers from the East, interrogating parties individually,

testing their accounts for truthfulness, and only when the information was agreed did he accept it as fact.

He was joined in this enterprise by a scholar, Shereef Idrisi,
who over fifteen years wrote *Pleasure for the Man who Wants to
Know Thoroughly the Various Countries of the World*. The work was
of particular interest, not just because of the accuracy of its
depictions of foreign places and the corresponding geography,
but because it reported that much gold came from the bed of the
Niger river in west Africa, and that large quantities of other precious metals could be found on the east coast of Africa as well.[23]
In time this would be one of the regions identified as the location of Prester John's mythical Christian kingdom.

The *Book of Marco Polo* was written in 1287, though it took a
century or more to make its way through the courts of Europe,
inflaming imaginations and creating even greater curiosity. Some
fifty years later perhaps the greatest book of travelling ever
known was written, by Ibn Batutah. He had journeyed from
Tangier to Peking, visiting along the way India and even travelling south to Mozambique. Most significantly, he spent time in
Timbuktu on the Niger, which he described as the terminus for
trade and possessed of great wealth in gold.

A Spanish Franciscan friar also went to Guinea, as the region
was known, and wrote of the abundant gold he saw there. He
reported on the caravan trade routes across the north African
desert and how they made possible the commerce from the south
with the port cities of north Africa. In his work, not immod-
estly named *The Book of Knowledge of all Kingdoms, Lands and
Lordships that are in the World*, he described Nubia and Ethiopia,
claiming that the ruler of these lands was one 'Prester Juan', a
Christian, whose subjects were Negroes. The cross, he said, was
burnt into their skins as a sign they had been baptized and over
the kingdoms flew a white flag with a black cross.

Along with these accounts, which were largely accurate
despite the occasional flights of fancy, there was also that of John
Mandeville, whose well-read tale of his thirty-four years of travel
not only described his own extraordinary experiences but also
contained drawings of monsters and the random scatter of gems

to be commonly found in distant lands. Fable and myth were interlaced in his tale, related in a fascinating and highly entertaining manner. Prester John's bed is described as 'made of one sapphire, well bound with gold'.[24] This account did more than any other to establish the legend of Prester John, which was to influence the Portuguese so profoundly, as a wealthy, powerful Christian king, though it did nothing to determine where his kingdom actually lay.

That pockets of Christians existed in the East was known in medieval Europe. The rumours and legends that formed the basis for this belief in this case stemmed from reality. Christians did inhabit lands to the East, though they were not in regular contact with western Europe, and practised a version of the faith, primarily as Nestorians, considered corrupt by the pope. There was a strong desire on the part of the Portuguese to contact these groups and restore them to the True Faith, a desire the equal of that to convert the pagan.

There was also a practical consideration. The Muslims formed a formidable barrier to the East. To succeed in their endeavour the Portuguese were forced to seek a sea route around Africa, the dimensions of which were unknown. Indeed, the highly regarded maps inspired by Ptolemy's in his *Geographia* depicted the Indian Ocean as a landlocked sea and the continent of Africa as extending southward to form a continuous land mass that could not be rounded. The Portuguese understood almost from the first that, if Ptolemy was wrong and they were successful, this would place them out of reach of any help from Europe, surrounded either by enemies or strange people who would have no reason to lend assistance. So-called 'lost' Christians, even of a deviant form, would be natural allies and an invaluable help if they controlled a port where the Portuguese ships could be serviced and repaired. Their existence, and the prospects that went with it, made the feat of rounding Africa and establishing a permanent presence in the East less daunting.

Prester John was the most famous leader of Eastern Christians and became an obsession with the Portuguese since he reportedly commanded a great nation. Medieval chronicles portrayed him as a king–priest who ruled 'beyond Persia and Armenia', though the precise location of his kingdom continued to change with each wave of discovery.

The story of Prester John was first conveyed to the Vatican in 1145 by Bishop Hugh of Gebal in Syria, who drew on a report from Bishop Otto of Freising, in Germany. The thrust of this initial story was that Prester John was descended from the Magi who had visited the Christ Child. He defeated the Muslims in a great battle but had been prevented from joining the crusaders because his army was unable to cross the Tigris river. Still, he remained a demonstrable ally in the East. The basis of this story is probably the merging of certain historical events and personages, capped by a great deal of wishful thinking.

In 1165 a cleverly written though fictional letter reputedly from Prester John was translated into several languages and circulated first at the Vatican then through the courts of Europe, where it was hotly debated. In it Prester John is identified as guardian of the shrine of St Thomas, the apostle to India. In the letter the kingdom of Prester is placed in 'the three Indies', which are described as lands of natural wonders, of immense wealth where peace and justice reigned. He asserted that he intended to go to Palestine with his armies to do battle with the Muslims and restore the Holy Sepulchre to Christian control.

After much debate, in 1177 Pope Alexander III sent a response, the fate of which is unknown. Subsequent pilgrims and missionaries travelling east all searched for Prester John and his kingdom and in so doing established contact with the Mongols, who ruled, among other regions, most of India. By the mid-fourteenth century Ethiopia had become the centre of the search for the kingdom, though its location was imprecisely understood.

The legend of Prester John, the powerful Christian king who desired to make common cause with the European Christians, was a seductive draw to the Portuguese and an essential element in their decision to risk rounding Africa and sail the increasingly extraordinary distances the passage to India entailed. It should not be taken that fact and fiction concerning the East were interwoven in such a confusing and contradictory manner as to confound utterly anyone seeking the truth; rather, there was essentially accurate knowledge of the East and of the way there, and this was generally accepted, confusing as many details were. That way, however, was in the control of the Muslims, as was all commerce from Asia.

What remained completely unknown was the sea passage to India, which nearly everyone agreed must go around Africa. No portion of the world was more filled with legend and fantasy than Africa. Accurate reports ended with the vast expanse of sand that formed the Sahara desert. There was no sense of how large the continent might be or what lay in its waters. Anything seemed possible.

What was self-evident was that the only way east lay south, down the coast of this alien and inhospitable land.

3

The enterprise of Ceuta

Portugal has the oldest fixed borders of any European nation. This fact is all the more remarkable because those borders were established through incessant war with the more powerful Castile. The nation has its origin early in the twelfth century, when Henry of Burgundy and a band of opportunistic knights responded to the summons of Alfonso VI of Leon to assist in his war against the Moors. At that time most of what was to become Portugal was under Muslim rule. In return for his support and conspicuous valour in battle, Alfonso gave Henry his illegitimate daughter Teresa in marriage, along with the northern Portuguese region known as Terra Portucalense, a name derived from the town of Portucale, today known as Oporto. This region included the prosperous county of Coimbra.

Alfonso urged Henry to continue the war against the infidel and empowered him to take as fief such lands south of his new domain as he could seize. By 1109, in campaigns that became known as the Reconquest (*Reconguista*), Henry had conquered substantial territory at the expense of the Moors and was granted the title 'Count of Portugal'. He died three years later and his youthful wife acted as regent for their three-year-old son, proclaiming herself queen in the process. As a consequence Portugal had a queen before it had a king.

Following impressive victories over both the Castilians and the Moors, her grown son declared himself King Alfonso I, ruled for a remarkable fifty-seven years and almost single-handedly created Portugal, independent of any other land. The Moors were not united and continually warred among themselves, dividing central and southern Portugal into small kingdoms which Alfonso found relatively easy prey. City after city, region upon region, fell to his armies.[25] In this struggle Alfonso was assisted by a fleet of crusaders *en route* to the Holy Land, definitively demonstrating the power a navy could play in future conquests. But Portugal was so lacking in skilled seamen that it was necessary to import foreigners to man new ships. Even the first admiral of the Portuguese navy, created in 1307 and deemed essential to the young nation, was not Portuguese.

Although it faces the Atlantic, Portugal was not isolated from the rich commercial life of the Mediterranean. Annual fleets from the Italian city-states stopped on their way north to trade. As early as the twelfth century Lisbon and Oporto were already bustling commercial ports. The historian Fernão Lopes described Lisbon in particular as a city of 'numerous and various foreigners'. These included Genoese, Milanese, Catalans, Lombards, Mallorcans and Aragonese, among others.[26]

Each of the Portuguese kings in succession understood the importance of a navy and took steps that the Portuguese came to regard as of divine origin. King Dinis I expanded the maritime fleet and in 1317 created royal forests at Leiria and Alcacer, in which he directed the planting of the species of trees required for shipbuilding, knowing the forest would not be available for cultivation for more than a century. His attention to naval matters and trade proved so profitable that by the reign of his son Alfonso IV one fifth of the king's revenues came from customs and harbour duties.

In the late fourteenth century King Ferdinand granted that anyone wishing to build a vessel in excess of 100 tons could take the timber without charge from the royal forests. As a spur to commerce, the standard articles of trade at the time, chiefly iron and tar, could be imported free of duty. In addition, no export duty was imposed on the first voyage of these new ships.[27]

It was also ordered that all vessels above 50 tons should be registered. King Ferdinand created an insurance company, the Companhia das Naus, to which all shipowners were required to pay 2 per cent of their gains. This provided a sophisticated measure of security previously lacking. To encourage the use of Lisbon harbour, which already possessed substantial attraction because of its location and safety, the king granted special privileges to foreign merchants, which regularly brought many Italian and Catalan residents to the city. So attractive was the situation that as many as 450 ships were at anchor in Lisbon harbour at any given time, loading and unloading goods.[28]

The Portuguese kings grasped the potential and were quick to engage in commerce themselves. Ferdinand had his ships filled with his own goods before those of anyone else could be loaded. In 1371 the Cortes complained that he had used his power as king to acquire wheat at one rate and then sold it for a twentyfold profit. The following year the Cortes extended its complaint to include criticism of the queen, the grand masters of the religious orders, the bishops and other clergy, knights and government officials for aggressively engaging in commerce in competition with traditional traders, calling these newcomers nothing more than 'merchants and hucksters'. Lopes noted of Ferdinand's revenues that 'they were so great that it is now difficult to believe'.[29] This participation in commerce by these classes was to have a profound influence on subsequent events.

To assist Portugal during the period of the Reconquest were the creation and evolution of the various military orders, of which there were several, although the two most significant were the Order of Santiago and the more powerful Order of Christ. A papal bull of John XXII in 1319 assigned the Portuguese properties of the Order of Templars, which had been suppressed throughout Europe, to the Portuguese and renamed it the Order of Christ. By 1357 it had its headquarters in Tomar. The Order of Christ's special mission was to expel the Moors but also to oppose the enemies of the king, which eventually gave it a singular degree of influence.[30]

The landed aristocracy maintained its position of considerable power in the north, so the orders established themselves in central and southern Portugal. They were granted possession of certain forts to safeguard the nation from counter-attack by the Moors and received the income from these lands. The Order of Christ was especially active in expeditions against Moorish cities in north Africa and later received control of lucrative Madeira after it had been colonized. Membership in the orders eventually became largely hereditary. As the orders represented a potential threat to the king, their hand can usually be found behind every attempt to decrease the king's authority or to influence the succession. In time the kings named their heirs to head the orders as a means of securing their loyalty. Membership and service in the orders was one of the most certain paths to increase the wealth and standing of a family.

In 1386 King John I, Grand Master of the lesser Order of Aviz, which had been founded in 1181 to protect Christian cites from the Moors, and illegitimate son of Pedro I, succeeded to the throne to block the ascent of a hated Castilian, though not without intrigue and a brutal war with Castile. 'Both the virtues required of a king – justice and piety – were combined in his person', the court historian wrote of this remarkable man.

Not long thereafter an event occurred that was to alter permanently the course of Portuguese history. John I recognized that his Castilian enemy was the more powerful and could renew the conflict against him at almost any time. This was especially true as his own forces had taken a huge loss to secure victory. With this in mind he dispatched emissaries to the powerful English duke of Lancaster, John of Gaunt, urging him to act on his neglected claim to the Castilian throne. His wife was the eldest daughter of the King of Castile and had a legitimate right to it.[31] The duke responded favourably and soon arrived at the Portuguese court with an army, wife and two daughters, to seek John's assistance. In return the duke pledged that he would grant Portugal certain frontier cities at the expense of Castile, as well as one of his daughters in marriage.

Politically the younger daughter, Catherine, was the best match, because in time she would be in line to be queen of Castile and the Portuguese were always eager to unite the two thrones, so that the Portuguese maintained control, but King John fell deeply in love with the elder daughter, Philippa, the duke's by a previous marriage to Blanche, the heiress of Lancaster, through which he had obtained his great wealth and title. Although marriage to Philippa brought no added bonus to his nation, the royal advisers could not sway the king from his decision. The pope granted the king release from his vow of celibacy that he had taken on assuming his role as head of the Order of Aviz when just a child, and the fortuitous marriage was made.

There were already close ties between the English and the Portuguese. Englishmen routinely streamed into Portugal, especially the region about Oporto, seeking opportunity. These included textile- and glassmakers, as well as wine merchants. Their numbers were swelled by poets and writers seeking a more temperate climate and a more relaxed lifestyle. The result of this union between John I and the daughter of John of Gaunt was to bind the two countries even closer. The oldest-standing alliance in the world, the Treaty of Windsor, was signed by England and Portugal that same year. In fact, the marriage is believed to have been a part of the agreement.

By all accounts it was a unique and happy marriage, a match equal in love and political cunning. Philippa, described as 'sincere' and 'friendly to all honest people', was also shrewd and usually dominant in matters of diplomacy. During the reign of this remarkable couple the Portuguese court became a centre of learning and one of the most illustrious. The libraries of John I and Philippa as well as of their children were among the most complete in Europe.

It may well have been that fewer of the discoveries would have been made by the Portuguese had it not been for this exceptional family, and it is unlikely they would have opened the passage to India. John I and his wife had six children, anointed by Camoens as the 'noble generation'. Of their sons, one became king, one died tragically in a civil war after having served honourably as regent, another became a saint and the other was Henry the Navigator. Philippa, although she was queen of Portugal, was no less English, and she told and retold to her children stories of the Knights of the Round Table, of gallantry and deeds of heroism. She inspired in her sons a fierce loyalty to one another, a respect for chivalry, *noblesse oblige* and especially a keen sense for their place in history.

The young princes also heard the stories of the struggle of the

Portuguese against the Moors and the exploits of brave knights in battle. Stories of Africa were standard fare as well, with tales of caravans traversing the vast Sahara, bearing gold, ivory, trains of unfortunate black slaves and the skins of exotic animals borne on the backs of camels. Their childhood was filled with lurid tales of savage beasts and primitive, exotic peoples in strange lands. It was a heady brew of the romantic, which fired the imaginations of the oldest three young princes and was profoundly to affect future events.

Whether it was primarily through Philippa's influence, or that of her husband, or of the two of them together, the three oldest sons, Edward, Pedro and Henry, emerged into young manhood united as a team, remarkably free of competition and backbiting, each fired with the ambition to seek his own place in history by following his distinct course. They worked together and could not be pitted against one another, so it was impossible for the often troublesome noblemen to work intrigue. All of these men, but especially Henry, possessed sweeping vision and could see beyond the immediate. Such unity of purpose and foresight was a remarkable accomplishment, and no doubt the brothers themselves deserve credit for continuing such behaviour even after the death of both parents.

Pedro was of an intellectual bent and during his travels in Europe gathered books for the royal library in Portugal. He collected information about Islam and its strengths, reportedly concluding from his research that the powerful Muslims must be outflanked and that Portugal was in an especially advantageous position to do just that. Edward was so studious in his devotion to the classics that he was criticized for not properly preparing himself for his future role as king.

Their father, John I, had repeatedly shown himself to be not just a good king but also an able general and a brilliant soldier. He had proved himself again and again on the field of battle against the Castilians. The oldest sons, now moving into manhood, were eager to make their own mark.

The king's initial suggestion, that they prove their mettle in a special jousting tournament, was rejected by the brothers as scarcely the equal for testing themselves on the field of combat. Instead, they preferred to be dubbed knights on the battlefield, ideally following successful battle with the infidel. The last Moorish enclave in Portugal had been conquered in 1249, so such an opportunity was no longer possible within Portugal. The young men spent the summer of 1411 with their parents in the Moorish palace in the beautiful perfume-scented mountain enclave of Sintra and threw their support behind a secret plan to seize the Muslim trading city of Ceuta on the coast of north Africa, across the Strait of Gibraltar from Spain.

With its palaces and 'large gardens and orchards with many trees' Ceuta was considered to be 'the flower of all other cities of Africa'. It would be the first Muslim city of north Africa permanently occupied by a European Christian nation. The Moors still held part of the Iberian peninsula in Spain; this mission would put the Christians on the offensive in their homeland and was, in their view, the logical extension of the Reconquest.

If it could be taken, Ceuta offered several advantages to the Portuguese. It was the terminus for a lucrative gold trade in northern Africa and as a rich port held the real possibility of significant spoils. It was considered 'the key of the whole Mediterranean Sea',[32] from which the Portuguese could hinder Moorish pirates, who regularly raided the Algarve. It also permitted the Portuguese the opportunity to interfere in the affairs of Castile and Aragon as well as reclaim a city from their eternal enemy the Moors.

The timing could not have been more opportune. The Castilian monarchy was engaged in quarrels with its nobles, the French and English were embroiled in the Hundred Years War and the Italian city-states were preoccupied with rivalries for control of their traditional trade routes east.

In addition, Portuguese attention to and involvement with north Africa had been continuous since even before the founding of the nation. Moors who remained in Portugal had special permission to trade with their brethren in Africa. Fruit from the Algarve was much sought after in Africa and was routinely sold there for gold. Portugal also had an active trade with the Moors in Granada, which had yet to be taken by Castile, as well as direct trade with the Muslims in the African ports. Portugal received cereals, textiles, leather and even sugar from Africa, in exchange for weapons, copper, certain woods and lacquer. Moroccan coins were in general circulation throughout Portugal. So lucrative was the trade that it persisted despite routine condemnation by the Church.

Despite the existence of such mutually beneficial commerce, both Christians and Moors actively practised piracy on one another's ships. So many captives were taken by the Portuguese and the Moors that an ordinance was promulgated in 1388 regulating their ransom. Castile and Aragon had established by treaty their own areas of interest, which did not include Portugal, so as far as the Portuguese were concerned they were free to act as they wished.[33]

The Portuguese discoveries are most commonly dated from 1415, with the assault on Ceuta, though ships of exploration had been dispatched into the Atlantic earlier. But the circumstances of the conquest at the time make it clear that the Portuguese themselves did not know that they were about to embark on the greatest age of discovery the world would ever know. That age developed slowly, a single stage at a time, and when it came to fruition it seemed in retrospect to the Portuguese that the hand of God had been manifest at every step.

People then had no more a sense of living in history than we do today. The future is intangible, the past appears archaic and irrelevant. Life for nearly everyone is consumed with the 'here and now'. They were no less intelligent than we, and in most ways not all that different from us. It was the custom of the nobility to retain chroniclers to record their feats, but these accounts were as much for the sponsors' self-aggrandizement during their own lifetime as for future generations.

At the direction of Alfonso V, Gomes Eannes de Azurara wrote an account of the Portuguese expansion at a time decades before the final outcome was known, so his observations (completed in 1453) are especially salient. When he penned his telling of the Portuguese discoveries he wrote: 'Where could this

chapter begin better than in speaking of the most glorious conquest of the great city of Ceuta, of which famous victory the
heavens felt the glory and the earth the benefit.'

Through creative marriage and dominance in war ambitious
Castile was systematically gobbling up the diverse regions that
inhabited the Iberian peninsula. By 1469 Aragon, Catalonia and
Castile were united with the marriage of Ferdinand and Isabella,
whose mother was Portuguese. The couple reigned jointly from
1474 to 1504 and their union placed Portugal in a precarious
position. It had to maintain the ability to remain independent
and could not afford to leave itself weakened. Through the long
decades of the explorations the abiding concern of the
Portuguese was always Spain.

In 1411 Portugal and Castile had concluded the latest in their
long series of wars and the timing was ripe for such an adventure, so the king did not dismiss out of hand his sons' plan to
seize Ceuta. The royal advisers were favourably disposed, in part
because of a desire to continue the conquest of the Moors, but
also because of the wish to free their shipping from Arab pirates
and the lure of the gold and other valuables to be found in the
north African ports.

Religion cannot be overestimated as a motive, as this was a
continuation of the Reconquest in Portuguese eyes. The medieval understanding and application of Christianity were deeply
embedded in daily life. To attain Heaven required devotion to
the church and reception of its sacraments, especially baptism.
Pagans and infidels were damned to Hell, so even cruel measures
were justified to turn them to God. It was ingrained in the
Portuguese kings and people that it was their divine calling to
continue driving the infidels back to the East. The pope had earlier granted the spiritual dispensations previously given to the
crusaders in the Holy Land to all those who warred against the
Moors in the Iberian peninsula and elsewhere.

It is typical of the Portuguese that the attack would accomplish the twin goals of a religious crusade and an opportunity for
loot, since the sword and the cross in Portugal often went hand
in hand. The combination of the two powerful inducements of

greed and religion is often viewed with cynicism but should be accepted at face value. The Americans went to the moon to beat the Soviet Union, partly for the sake of national pride, partly to fulfil a dream of all mankind and partly to discover. Different motives stirred different people who took part in the endeavour, but all of them were part of the mix. So it was with the Portuguese.

To continue pushing the Muslims back and to bring the word of God to the heathen people was a powerful force, as was the desire of the three royal sons to prove themselves in battle – but so too was the desire for plunder. The wars with Castile were costly and there was no return for the money spent on them. Ceuta, destination for the rich caravans of Mali, was a different matter entirely.

Since antiquity it had been known that west Africa was a significant source of gold. As Genoa and Florence reinstituted gold coins, so essential to the growth of the medieval European economy, the demand for fresh supplies of the precious metal increased dramatically. Access to this gold, however, was barred by Muslim control of north Africa and of the caravan routes to Mali and the Niger region. The point had been made most emphatically by the 1339 pilgrimage of Mansa Musa, the ruler of the empire of Mali. Along his route and in Cairo he lavished such gold that the price was depressed for a generation. On the widely disseminated Catalan *mappa mundi* he is depicted, seated on his throne in Africa, wearing a gold crown, with a gold nugget in one hand, his sceptre in the other. By such means and others, word of vast wealth and wondrous treasures to be found in north Africa and its environs slowly made its way across Europe until, by the fifteenth century, it was widely held.

The sons of John I believed that the taking of Ceuta would bring great wealth to Portugal, as well as being a source of immense national pride. Desire and spirit, however, were not enough. The two requirements of any successful assault on a fortified city on the coast of Africa were an army and a fleet with which to carry it. Portugal possessed neither of the size the enterprise required.

The attack itself carried great risk, not just to the forces immediately involved, but to the nation as well. The army required to defend Portugal from Castile would be on a foreign shore, too far removed to be called home in time for defence. Failure would leave Portugal vulnerable to renewed attack by its eastern enemy. The army could well become stranded in Africa if the fleet were destroyed by the Arabs or by an act of nature.

There were also other considerations. Castile might have an eye on the same prize and would take Portugal's action as a provocation, especially given Ceuta's proximity. The Italian city-states of Genoa and Venice might also have designs on the city, and they were formidable maritime states capable of causing Portugal great harm. In fact, Genoa had captured the city for a short time in 1260 and then returned it to the Muslims for an enormous ransom.

Still, there was much to be gained. Ceuta controlled the sea route into the Mediterranean, which could prove of immense value. Now that there was peace between Portugal and Castile, the latter might even have a similar ambition. Better the Portuguese did it themselves. From Ceuta they could learn more of the mysterious kingdom to the south from which gold flowed. They would be well positioned to learn the source of these fabled riches, and from that only good could come.

There was one other factor. The Black Death, which struck the nation during 1358–9, and the incessant wars with Castile from 1383 to 1411 had created a despondent mood throughout the country. What was needed to restore confidence and national morale was a great victory. What better way than to attack the despised infidel and seize one of his valuable ports?

So in the end King John decided to proceed, yielding, it is generally accepted, to the persuasiveness of his English wife and the passion of his three eldest sons. When the plan was presented to the royal advisers, it was enthusiastically endorsed. Nun' Alvares, an adviser known for his sound judgement, is reported to have declared, 'This plan was not conceived by you [the king] nor by anyone in this world, but was inspired by God.'

Although a certain level of secrecy could be imposed on

preparations, especially during its early stages, it was not possible to conceal the gathering of such a force of arms, and the existence of a new fleet of 200 vessels clearly indicated a sea invasion. In typical Portuguese fashion King John conducted a campaign of disinformation and misdirection. It was essential that his great enemy, Castile, did not feel threatened but also that the Moors were not moved to reinforce and further fortify their ports in north Africa. The Portuguese judiciously leaked that the objective of the invasion was to be the Netherlands. In the meantime, an emissary was dispatched north to assure the Duke of Holland that this was a ruse, that the true objective lay elsewhere.

The Moorish king of Granada, however, was also concerned and sent an ambassador to complain that the merchants in Granada were afraid to carry on with trade as usual because of the gathering threat against them. 'Never was there such discord between your people and mine that they ceased to trade', he said.[34] Again discreet assurances were given.

Young Prince Henry, for his part, was dispatched to Oporto to organize a contingent of troops and see to the construction and refitting of seventy ships. On 10 July 1415 he and his force arrived in Lisbon harbour, the officers and men decked out in their most splendid armour, colourful pennants and banners playing in the breeze from every ship, the blare of trumpets and the blast of cannon announcing their arrival. It was a magnificent sight and patriotic crowds gathered along the shore, cheering repeatedly.

Nearly every summer Lisbon was struck with a plague, and the one that year had already arrived, much to the concern of those responsible for the gathering of the fleet and army. The sailors and soldiers aboard the ships were ordered to remain aboard to reduce the risk of exposure. The plague always struck the poorest with the greatest severity, although no class was ever entirely immune. On this occasion members of the royal court had already succumbed and now Henry learned his own mother was near death. He rushed to her bedside to join his brothers. On 23 July Philippa of Lancaster, at the age of fifty-six, died, surrounded by her family. Her final words were to urge her sons to continue the campaign, to gain honour for themselves and Portugal by the conquest of Ceuta.

The plague, and now the death of the revered queen, were taken by some as an evil omen. There was concern among the captains that fear would spread to the crews, who were susceptible to superstition, and doom the enterprise before it had begun. Despite Philippa's admonition there was talk of delay, but cooler heads quickly prevailed. There could be no procrastination, as the plague would surely spread to the crews and too much had been invested to abandon the campaign because of mere superstition. So the fleet sailed six days after the death of the queen.

The weather stubbornly refused to co-operate and it took the Portuguese invasion force three weeks to sail the relatively short distance from Lisbon to Ceuta. Passage had been brisk until the fleet passed Cape St Vincent, the south-western corner of Europe. But at nearby Lagos the fleet was becalmed for a week. It seemed that God did not look favourably on their crusade. The death of the queen, the plague in Lisbon and now this delay caused a stir among the soldiers and sailors. These events were omens that the attack should be cancelled. Then, when the winds did resume, the fleet was taken by a storm and scattered: another evil sign. But the king and his sons persisted, the ships were reunited and on 20 August the fleet appeared unexpectedly off the coast of Africa.

The storm that had so scattered the Portuguese fleet worked to their advantage. The sultan had received conflicting reports and so took no measures to protect his city. As a result, despite its formidable defences, Ceuta lay unprepared for a determined assault and fell in a single day of savage violence. Once the walls were scaled the Portuguese descended on the hapless inhabitants, as was the practice throughout Europe and the nations of Islam, slaughtering anyone in sight, the princes leading the way. In their frenzy and feverish search for gold the soldiers set fire to stores of expensive silk, tapestries and valuable spices, including pepper and cinnamon. Order was finally restored before the spoils of the victory were completely lost.

Against the hundreds slain by the conquerors, the Portuguese suffered but eight dead. A thanksgiving mass was celebrated within the blood-stained mosque, where King John knighted each of his sons and presented them with golden spurs. Pedro was named Duke of Coimbra and Henry Duke of Viseu, the first time these titles were used in Portugal.

A garrison force of 3,000 men was left behind a few days later, when the fleet returned to Lisbon. Neither it nor the bulk of the army could be risked longer from Portugal. News of the great victory preceded it and the victors received a tumultuous reception as they sailed up the river and entered the harbour. The easy victory following so much apprehension was accepted as God's benediction on the nation. The small kingdom had taken a valuable city from the Moors, something no other country of Europe had managed – not France, England or even Castile. Word spread quickly through the European courts, granting John I and his nation greater prestige than either had ever known.

The slaughter of the populace and destruction of so many valuable stores brought little advantage to the Portuguese. The Muslims reacted by immediately isolating the city. Caravans that had previously traded with Ceuta and were responsible for its wealth were now diverted to other Muslim cities. The Christian Portuguese sat within their prize, isolated in a vast sea of Moorish hatred.

But the conquest served an unintended purpose. In the taking and occupation of the city, the Portuguese were exposed to wealth they had never imagined possible. Within the walls of the city were stone mansions with exquisitely carved woodwork. They had seen for themselves an abundance of silks and spices. Writing some thirty years later, but drawing on interviews with veterans of the conquest, Azurara wrote of the awe these men experienced as they first viewed the amazing wealth of what was, after all, a relatively minor Moorish port city. The impact was profound and vividly evoked even a lifetime after the event.

The princes had heard of the enormous wealth held by the Moors, they had listened to the stories of travellers, but now they saw the affluence with their own eyes, breathed the scent of exotic spices, tasted the luxury that survived the pillaging soldiers. Every tale and fable to which they had been exposed was suddenly credible, no matter how fantastic it had once seemed.

It was all testament to the vast wealth that lay to the south in Africa, riches there for the taking. In Portugal nearly everyone struggled to provide a living. Even royalty lived a relatively spartan existence for the time, certainly nothing approaching the luxury enjoyed by lesser mortals in Ceuta. The fabulous rumoured riches of the Arabs, and of their spice and gold trade, had always seemed as remote as those described in the tales of Sinbad the Sailor. Ceuta casually displayed that wealth and the conclusion was that access to even greater riches could be accomplished, and not necessarily at great cost.

At Ceuta the Portuguese learned firsthand of Timbuktu and the Mali empire of legend to the south, where the gold trade with this affluent region was the principal source of the city's wealth. Absorbing the realization that there would be no trade by caravan for them, as this was controlled by Arabs, they grasped that they must outflank the Moors to gain direct access to the gold, and in doing so would receive a more favourable rate of exchange.

Henry's interest in all things African was especially excited by the conquest of Ceuta, with its riches and exotica. He gathered every scrap of information he could concerning the caravans of the interior, their routes and distribution points, and made a careful study of the merchants and traders of the Niger region. He learned all he could of Timbuktu, of Gambia and the Mali empire. He quickly grasped that if Portugal was to benefit from the riches that lay to the south, it would have to reach the source by following the coast of Africa in ships. He scrutinized the existing charts, especially those drawn by the Jewish cartographers of Mallorca, and compared them one to another in their manifest contradictions. With the exception of a few periods of political unrest, extending the Portuguese reach into Africa and eventually to Asia was to occupy the remainder of Henry's life.

As Europe was chronically short of precious metal, gold was

the initial objective of what would become the Discoveries. India evolved as a destination only later, when the Portuguese failed to find the vast sources of gold they sought and as they developed the means for making the voyage and realized it was within their grasp.

The opportunity to win victories for Christ, and to secure worldly wealth in the process, was a heady mix of God and greed, the perfect elixir to stimulate the Portuguese to even greater endeavours. The motive was not unique to the Portuguese, but it gripped them like no other nation in Europe.

4

Henry and the sea of darkness

It is recorded that of the three princes who won their spurs that bloody day in Ceuta none demonstrated greater courage than Henry, later to be given the title 'The Navigator'. Word of his prowess as a soldier spread rapidly, and Pope Martin V implored him to lead the Christian armies against the infidel Turks. The King of England, the Emperor of Germany, even the King of Castile, each in turn beseeched Henry to fight for them.[35] The young prince declined every request in order to devote himself to a greater cause, which he considered to be divinely inspired.

Even within the span of Henry's long lifetime exploration and discovery became the only practical means for Portugal to expand and prosper. After his eventual passing the situation became even more pronounced with the union of Aragon and Castile. The defeat of the Portuguese army at Toro in 1476 meant there was no possibility that Portugal could ever dominate Spain militarily, while the Treaty of Alcáçovas with Spain three years later gave Portugal an open road to Africa and from there to India. All events combined to point the Portuguese into the Atlantic and south to Africa.

It is unfortunate that the Portuguese historians of the sixteenth and seventeenth centuries turned Henry into a mystical figure, extravagantly praising his artistic ability, his sharp intellect, his courage on the battlefield and his managerial skills. He is portrayed as a tormented ascetic, a nationalist in the service of God, a visionary and martyr who maintained his purity throughout his life and died a virgin.*

---

* Generally overlooked is the bequest in his will to his daughter, though Henry was never married.

The truth, as far as can be determined, is so much better than this stereotype. Henry kept faith with his mother and never contended with his older brothers for the crown or tried to exercise unwanted influence over national policy. It is possible that he chose not to marry in order not to have a legitimate heir who could have vied, or have been seen as vying, to be king. He generally lived far removed from the luxuries of the royal court in Lisbon and thus remained free of royal intrigue and suspicion.

This combination of factors, as well as his own nature, permitted Henry a position of impartiality that was instrumental at key moments in preventing the sort of internecine disputes that typically plagued royal families. This allowed two generations of unprecedented expansion and discovery for the nation. Late in his life Henry still exercised such influence that he was able virtually single-handedly to preserve the peace when it appeared the country would be torn apart by civil war for the crown. Had there been no explorations at his command, Henry would still figure prominently in Portuguese history.

The first Portuguese voyages of discovery along the African coast were launched four years after the seizure of Ceuta. It is assumed that Henry consulted with his two older brothers and that the three agreed to explore southward with the purpose of establishing a trade link with the Mali empire, to discover new lands as opportunity presented itself and to gather intelligence for their crusade against the Moors.

At about this time Henry was named Grand Master of the Order of Christ. From its foundation the order had been given the responsibility of expelling the infidels and that remained its primary objective. This was a great honour to Henry, but even more important for the future of the small kingdom, it meant he received the lucrative income from the order, resources he could use to finance the discoveries. Whether the appointment was simply fortuitous or was intended as a means to give him the revenue and influence he would require for the undertaking is only one of many unresolved mysteries.

United as they were, it is accepted that each of the princes agreed to the role Henry desired to play. In fact in 1428, when Prince Pedro, Henry's older brother, visited Italy, he gathered maps and collected valuable information in Florence, and in Venice was presented with Marco Polo's book. All of these he turned over to Henry.

Considering the conquests within Portugal itself and then the taking of Ceuta, the Portuguese had seized more land from the Moors than France, England or the Italians cities had ever managed. It only made sense to reach the source of riches by sea. If it could be done, Henry was determined to accomplish it.

Such an undertaking over so many years required a man of his determination, character and religious zeal, and by the time of Henry's death the end was within sight. So important was he to Portugal's eventual triumph that, even though he died thirty-seven years before the first voyage of Vasco da Gama, it is unlikely the passage to India would ever have been achieved by the Portuguese had he not been born.

The south-western region of Portugal had been named by the Moors El Gharb and it was the last portion of Portugal from which, in 1249, they were expelled. Across the sea from the Algarve, as it was named by the Portuguese, was the closest possible point of contact with the infidels, so along with his appointment as Grand Master of the Order of Christ, Henry was also given possession of these lands.

Although much less hospitable than the rest of the nation and thinly populated even for the time, the region was ideal for Henry's purpose. An ancient harbour already existed at Lagos, but it lay east of the Atlantic coastline. Instead, Henry cast his eye on the more westerly of two promontories, Cape St Vincent, an unusual rock formation that jutted into the Atlantic and had been the Promontorium Sacrum for the Romans. There Henry ordered the building of a stone complex which he named Sagres. Beneath the rugged coastline was a small bay, where he ordered a town to be constructed. Not far away he built Raposeira, his private residence.

According to Azurara, Henry wished that this seat of

exploration should, among other things, be 'an especial mart for merchants . . . to the end that all ships that passed from the East to the West, should be able to take their bearings, and to get provisions and pilots'.[36] Here Henry faced west across the Atlantic and south to Africa. Far removed from the intrigues of the Portuguese court, no more ideal location could have been possible for his undertaking.

Henry had been educated at a time when the Moorish libraries of Toledo were being or had been translated from the Arabic into Latin. Among the works were rediscovered classics of the Greeks, including the *Almagest*, the Arab version of Ptolemy's *Syntaxis Mathematica*, which made possible new strides in geographical theory.[37] Ptolemy's other great work, the *Geography*, which contained the most complete classical knowledge on the subject, was brought to Europe from Constantinople and translated into Latin in 1410. A revised version, with the addition of Scandinavia, Iceland and Greenland, was soon circulating through the European courts.[38] Much of the information was substantially correct, although Henry was not in a position to distinguish truth from fantasy.

From these and other works Henry read that even in ancient times mariners had reportedly sailed beyond the Canary Islands and that the Egyptians claimed to have circumnavigated Africa in the time of the Pharaohs. The untrustworthy historian Herodotus had written that the Phoenicians rounded Africa in 600 BC with a voyage reported to have taken two years and one that would have covered some 16,000 miles, unquestionably by far the greatest distance that had been sailed up to that time. The best evidence that no such voyage occurred is that it would have given the ancients a clear picture of the true shape of Africa, which they did not have.

For Henry it was not usually possible to determine what of the history was real, what legend, though there was some reliable information. It was known, for example, that in 1291 the brothers Ugolini and Vadino of the renowned Genoese Vivaldi family had attempted to round Africa in two galleys, sailing down the west coast of the continent with the intention of reaching India. They were reported to have passed Cape Juby, just opposite the Canary Islands, and were then lost to history.

The Portuguese had begun their explorations as early as the reign of King Dinis in the fourteenth century. One of his ships had been the first to discover the Azores but their location was promptly lost, though they were later rediscovered and settled. Attention soon switched to the Canary Islands. The Romans had learned of the Canaries off the coast of Africa from a king of Mauretania. In 999 Arabs landed and traded with natives there. Still, by the Middle Ages the Canaries were all but forgotten. During the thirteenth and fourteenth centuries sailors from Genoa, Mallorca and France all visited the islands at one time or another. Portuguese explorers rediscovered them at this time, as did the Spanish, but it was Spain that first settled there and was eventually able to assert its sovereignty.

In losing the Canary Islands, Portugal let a golden opportunity slip from its grasp. The winds from here were seasonably favourable to crossing the Atlantic, a pattern Columbus noted and later exploited after such efforts by the Portuguese further north failed. But more important at the time, the islands were ideally situated for the push south and possessed a fine harbour and resources of fresh water, wood for cooking and produce. Henry grasped that another Canary Islands was required.

During these centuries the discovery, then loss, of islands was so commonplace as to be unremarkable. Typical of what the underdeveloped navigation and mapping techniques produced was Madeira. The archipelago is situated some 700 miles south and west of the south-western tip of Portugal. Genoese seamen discovered the islands, as their location is indicated on a map dated 1351, but often it was not possible to return to such lands because the navigation skills were simply not adequate. The existence of the map bearing the islands of Madeira was not widely known, so they were probably a mystery to Henry's captains.

Maps of every sort, many of them ancient but not necessarily reliable, depicted other islands, both real and imagined. There were the very real St Brendan Isles, but also the Hi-Brasil, or O'Brasil of Irish legend. West of the St Brendans was the island of Antillia, which can be found on a 1367 map. As late as the early sixteenth century mythical islands were still routinely appearing on reputedly reliable maps. These included Mam off Ushant and Brasil, now off Galway. The fabled Septem Ciuitates were placed in the North American continent.[39]

The effect was no less telling, whether or not the islands actually existed. As Samuel Eliot Morison puts it in *Portuguese Voyages to America in the Fifteenth Century:*

> Mythical as they were, these islands had a considerable influence on history; for their presence on the maps in the hands of Portuguese, stimulated . . . ocean exploration in search of something new. . . . There was every reason for the enquiring maritime mind of that era to suppose that more could be found. It is a matter of historical record that such searches were made.

The most widely used map of the time was the product of the Cresques of Mallorca, a family of cartographers who worked at the royal patronage of the King of Aragon. Aragon had been one of the earliest kingdoms in Europe to appreciate the need for better navigation techniques and quality maps. In 1340 it enacted a law requiring all ships sailing from there to possess a map. The Cresques produced a *mappa mundi*, commonly known as the 'Catalan map', which the King of Aragon presented to the King of France. Over the next hundred years it and subsequent versions were widely disseminated and came into Henry's possession. More than a thousand have survived.

This 'Catalan map' was richly detailed, although its features were grotesquely distorted, and contained a tantalizing mix of fact and myth. It was for the time a fascinating read and offered the most comprehensive presentation of the oceans and lands of the known world ever previously gathered on a single chart. The Azores were clearly indicated, and even named, as were six of the Canary Islands. The Atlas mountains were drawn in north Africa with the annotation 'Here pass the merchants who come from the lands of negroes of Guinea.' Three kingdoms of west Africa are named with the legend 'The King of the Negroes of Guinea is the most illustrious and the richest ruler of that land, because of the abundance of gold which one gathers in his dominion.'

Reference was made to Prester John, to the Queen of Sheba, and near the Himalayas was the annotation that 'the Christian King Stephen' ruled. India was identified as beginning at Ormuz, from which both precious stones and spices were known to originate. The names and approximate locations of the cities of China were apparently lifted from Marco Polo's account. The Sunda Islands appear with the annotation 'the Sea of India where the spices are'. Finally there was Sumatra, 'the last island which one meets in the East'.[40]

Cresque Le Jeheu, astronomer of the King of Aragon, a converted Jew renamed Jacomo, subsequently produced three highly respected maps. Following the death of his royal patron he joined the court gathered about Henry at Sagres, where he is reported to have taught navigation to Portuguese officers and continued making maps.

There were among the known maps of this time many disturbing references. A historian of the Berbers wrote of the Atlantic that it was 'a sea without limits, that mariners dared not leave the coast, because they knew not where the winds might drive them, and that beyond that sea there is no inhabited land'. The Arab geographers Aboulfeda and Idrisia wrote that:

> No one knows what lies beyond the Atlantic; no one has been able to discover anything for certain, on account of the difficulties of navigation, due to the darkness, the height of the waves, the frequency of the tempests, and the violence of the winds. However, there are in this sea a number of islands, inhabited and uninhabited, but no mariners dare venture to cross it, nor to sail out into the open sea. They content themselves with sailing as close to the land as not to lose sight of the coast.

At this time a line formed by Cape Bojador in the western Sahara and the Canary Islands north of it was the boundary below which little was known, though myths about the region were abundant. The Arabs had called the region the 'Green Sea of Darkness' from which there was no possibility of return. Legend held that between twelve and fifteen thousand failed attempts had been made to sail beyond it. One European cartographer recorded on his map at Cape Nam 'Here ends the known world.' It is no wonder that the prospect of venturing into the unmapped void south of Cape Bojador was viewed with superstition and fear.

It is unnecessary to speculate as to Henry's motives for initiating his undertaking since Azurara, who knew Henry, recorded them for us, yet historians continue to do so, as if the issue was unresolved. First, Henry had 'a wish to know the land that lay beyond the Canary Islands and that Cape called Bojador, for that up to his time, neither by writings, nor by the memory of man, was known with any certainty the nature of the land beyond that Cape'. Curiosity then. Simple human curiosity as a powerful driving force should not be lightly discounted.

While much was obscure, kingdoms in the Niger region were commonly known to exist and as early as 1350 it was estimated that two-thirds of the world's supply of gold came from west Africa.[41] As Henry's second reason Azurara wrote:

> [I]f there chanced to be in those lands . . . some havens, into which it would be possible to sail without peril, many kinds of merchandise might be brought into this realm, which would find a ready market . . . because no other people of these parts traded with them. . . . And also the products of this realm might be taken there, which traffic would bring great profit to our countrymen.

The third reason identified by Azurara was religion. It was the goal of all Christendom to defeat the infidel, and as Grand Master Henry was specifically so charged. He wished to know more of the enemy, therefore 'the said Lord Infant exerted himself to cause this to be fully discovered, and to make it known determinately, how far the power of those infidels extended.' He sought as well to discover a Christian king or lord with whom to make alliance to 'aid him [in war] against those enemies of the faith'. Henry was concerned as well for the 'the salvation of lost souls'.

The final reason recorded by Azurara, and the one from which all others stemmed, was 'the inclination of the heavenly wheels' – in other words, Henry's horoscope. He was not in line for the throne and needed to do something of worth with his life, so he would have learned with satisfaction that the stars ordained that he 'should toil at high and mighty conquests, especially in seeking out things that were hidden from other men and secret'.

As it developed, the Portuguese explorations along the coast of Africa proceeded in irregular phases, the scope of their effort increasing with each new success. At regular intervals advances in navigation, seamanship, shipbuilding and the emergence of skilled captains made possible the next stage of exploration. In time, the ultimate goal of India became not only possible but probable. It all occurred in a logical progression that gave the entire effort the mystique of inevitability.

So it was for Henry's commitment to his life's work, which slowly evolved during his research and consultations. The plan, as he conceived it early on, was to use his resources as Grand Master of the Order of Christ to push his ships ever south along the coast of pagan Africa, to carry to those primitive peoples the word of God and to bring back to the king pepper, ivory and gold. The ultimate goal was to establish a link with the elusive Prester John and his Christian kingdom. The location of this kingdom, long held to be somewhere in Asia, was uncertain but once the link was made Christian Europe and Portugal would have a powerful ally in the fight against the Muslims. The sea route thus established would become a highway across which the riches of the East would flow through the trading houses of Lisbon, to the glory and fame of both Portugal and the king.

5

The cape of fear

The initial objective of the first Portuguese ship dispatched after the seizure of Ceuta was to sail beyond Cape Bojador, to gather information and, most importantly, to return. If successful, Prince Henry hoped to rid the region of the mythology and dread that surrounded it.

It is difficult today to understand the deep-seated significance this modest cape had for the medieval mariner mind. The African shoreline there is barren with an expanse of low-lying vermilion cliffs, while the cape itself is scarcely discernible. But when Henry sent out that first ship no vessel that had ever sailed below Cape Bojador had returned. The ships had effectively, if not literally, dropped off the face of the Earth.

The west coast of Africa is an especially inhospitable part of the world, as are its ocean waters, and the route to Cape Bojador was particularly treacherous. Powerful *siroccos*, building their strength from deep in the Sahara, blow to sea, impeding the progress of ships. The ocean currents that were so crucial to the sailing vessels of the time were unknown and, because they were not known, were treacherous. Even today the area is not safe sailing and is avoided whenever possible. In addition, there was no protecting anchorage for sailing ships, nor any refuge to which they could readily flee if nature compelled it. If caught in a squall or a powerful, unfamiliar weather pattern, they had no available port. They were naked at sea, utterly exposed to the elements.

There was a steady southward sea current off Cape Bojador. Along with the prevailing summer wind, which blew from the north, this made the trip south relatively easy, assuming the small vessels did not fall foul of unknown currents or a sudden storm. But the square-rigged ships of that time had limited tacking ability and could only just manage to return against both the current and wind. Some were not able to make it at all.

During this initial period more than a dozen voyages to round Cape Bojador were unsuccessful and from the outset there were deaths and lost ships. Those captains who did return rarely sailed below the Canary Islands and the few who actually sighted the cape lost their nerve and turned back. Many of these early captains turned to piracy against Arab ships to bring a measure of 'honour' to their effort. Sailing techniques were simply not up to the effort, nor was Henry possessed of captains with sufficient experience to face uncertainty with confidence and courage.

In those early decades every ship sent out began a figurative clock the moment it left the Portuguese coastline. The supplies were consumed at a specific pace. The crew suffered injury and illness at a less predictable but not less certain rate. The ship itself began to deteriorate at once, slowly at first, but with ever greater speed in the warm waters off Africa. The decline was apparent to every seaman and only served to spread uncertainty and fear.

The fact was that the vessel and crew could last just so many days at sea before either dying or becoming unable to make the return voyage. The captain and crew knew only approximately how much time they had, but they understood with absolute certainty that their time was running out and that their lives depended, at some point, on beating back against wind and current to a safe harbour, which in those earliest days meant Portugal.

It is not surprising then that the first attempts to sail below Cape Bojador were unsuccessful, especially as they were attempted in galley ships little different in design from their Roman counterparts. In the safety and comfort of Henry's estate the reasons given for turning back sounded almost trivial or nothing more than superstition. For someone who spent little time at sea and who was of noble birth, Henry was uncommonly understanding and accepting of the repeated failures of his captains. It would seem that he grasped the true barrier to be mental rather than physical.

Azurara writes:

[T]here was not one who dared to pass Cape of Bojador and learn about the land beyond it, as the Infant wished. And to say the truth this was not from cowardice or want of good will, but from the novelty of the thing and wide-spread and ancient rumour about this Cape, that had been cherished by mariners of Spain from generation to generation.

How are we, men said, to pass the bounds that our fathers set up, or what profit can result to the Infant from the perdition of our souls as well as of our bodies – for of a truth by daring any further we shall become wilful murderers of ourselves?

But being satisfied of the peril, and seeing no hope of honour or profit, they left off the attempt. For, said the mariners, this much is clear, that beyond this Cape there is no race of men nor place of inhabitants: nor is the land less sandy than the desert of Libya, where there is no water, no tree, no green herb – and the sea so shallow that a whole league from land it is only a fathom deep, while the currents are so terrible that no ship having once passed the Cape, will ever be able to return.

The ominous legends and tales of the region were enhanced by the actual experiences of the sailors. They had discovered for themselves that these were treacherous, unpredictable waters with no respite to be found along the barren coastline. There were frequent, unexpected fogs, which engulfed and threatened the ships, the waters were shallow far out to sea and the currents unpredictable. Worse, the storms from the vast desert behind the cape roared far out over the ocean. A red powdery dust settled on every part of each ship, and captains reported that their vessels glowed with an unnatural hue. Although they sailed many miles to sea to avoid the storms, the winds and dust still found them. The sailors were much disturbed by this and the other unnatural phenomena they encountered.

Legend said there were sea monsters and massive whirlpools in these waters, and that no humanity existed, or could exist, in those regions. The sea was said to boil in the heat. The climate became ever hotter as the ships made their way south and only certain bizarre creatures could survive. Nothing grew there, it was claimed. Here also lay the Antipodes, where fierce monsters dwelled. There were also said to be great treasures of gold and gems guarded by ferocious dragons, beautiful women whose provocative gaze could kill a man, and giants who waded into the sea and destroyed any ship passing their way. The reports of returning crews fed into the legends.

With no immediate success along the coast of Africa and tantalizing islands appearing on maps, ancient and contemporary, Henry dispatched ships to search for them. Two of his captains sailed west and discovered Madeira, an island rich in forests, fresh water and fertile land. It was also one of the most beautiful places on Earth and a portent of what wondrous lands lay to be discovered. Madeira was known at least as early as Roman times but, like other Atlantic islands, its location had been lost. The first colonists arrived from Portugal in 1425 and the island was soon sending back to Portugal timber, wine and sugar, which quickly replaced honey in sweetening drinks and food throughout Europe.

Madeira was profitable for both Portugal and Henry, who now had an improved means of subsidizing his voyages. Profits were not limited to sugar. Between 1450 and 1470 the island produced between 3,000 and 3,500 tons of grain, more than half of which was shipped to Portugal.

The settlement of Madeira and, a little later, of the Azores were the first successful European colonizations in the Atlantic and served as models. The Portuguese regarded themselves as pioneers in a New World. The first boy born on Madeira was named Adam, and the first girl Eve. It was an auspicious beginning for the explorations.

But the true destination lay south along the coast of Africa and Henry renewed his efforts there. In 1433 he dispatched one of his proven and most trusted captains, Gil Eanes, a squire in his household and a native of Lagos, with orders to round the cape, but when he approached its waters his crew refused to sail on, claiming they could see the water to the south boiling in the hot sun. It is easy to imagine the frustration Henry experienced upon Eanes's return.

Henry's patience with his captains and crews had finally reached its limit. Azurara recounts the next set of instructions he gave to Eanes:

> [T]he Infant made ready the same vessel and, calling Gil Eanes apart, charged him earnestly to strain every nerve to pass that Cape. . . . 'You cannot find', said the Infant, 'a peril so great that the hope of reward will not be greater. . . . Go forth . . . but make your voyage straightforward, inasmuch as with the grace of God you cannot but gain from this journey both honour and profit.'

Henry was, Azurara assures us, 'a man of very great authority', and Eanes steeled himself not to return without success. He decided to take a new route. Rather than sail to the African coast once he reached the Canary Islands (the usual route these voyages took), Eanes elected on this occasion to remain at sea in a manoeuvre the Portuguese would in time master. There were dangers in staying so far from known land in unknown waters, but there were also advantages. His crew was not subjected to the ominous site of the cape, and in blue water the coastal currents were not a threat to the vessel. Eanes sailed southward for several days until he was satisfied he must be below the cape, then turned east to follow favourable winds towards the coast of Africa.

The coastline that came into view was barren but missing the imposing red cliffs. They were beyond Cape Bojador. A jubilant Eanes laid anchor and led a party of men ashore. He found no sign of human habitation but with satisfaction observed the footprints of both men and camels. There was also the reassuring presence of vegetation, sparse though it was. Eanes plucked a cluster of red flowering plants which he named the Rose of Saint Mary and carried it back to his vessel.

Despite sailing against the prevailing current and winds, Eanes was able to make the return voyage. The boiling water previously reported by crews proved to be only waves breaking on the shore at Cape Bojador. There had been no sea monsters or whirlpools; indeed they had seen signs of man. The caravans of north Africa were well known and Eanes had proved they existed even this far south. He had sailed perhaps 50 miles below the cape but the significance of his accomplishment was astounding. If they could sail beyond Cape Bojador and return, then what other legends were also untrue? Everything became suspect except what the Portuguese saw for themselves.

Henry received the plum-red Rose of Saint Mary as if it was manna from God. When Eanes recounted what he had seen, the prince understood its significance immediately. It was said that 'beyond Cape Bojador the land is desert, there is no water, no tree, no green herb'. The plant he held proved that a lie. 'As you have found traces of men and camels,' he said, 'it is evident that the inhabited region cannot be far off.' He informed Eanes that he was to return, accompanied by another ship, go as far as possible and try to acquire an interpreter from the people he would surely discover there. This time Eanes sailed in a *barca*, a ship small enough to be conveniently rowed if necessary. Some 70 miles further down the coast the captains came upon a river which they named the Rio de Ouro, in anticipation of the gold they hoped they would find up its course. Two men were sent ashore on horseback with orders to secure someone to interpret and give them knowledge of the interior and points south. Their bungled attempts to seize the first men they encountered succeeded only in scaring them off. Unable to find any other people to capture, the captains ordered the slaughter of a large herd of seals at the mouth of the river and returned to Henry with the hides, the first commercial contribution of the voyages of discovery from Africa itself.

That same year the king, John I, died at the age of seventy-seven and with his death came the end of one of the most remarkable reigns of any European monarch. He was buried beside Philippa, and Henry's brother Edward ascended the throne. Edward's reign was to be short and tumultuous, and as a consequence, despite the auspicious African developments, the explorations were suspended for the next five years. Henry had long wanted to return to north Africa as conqueror and had proposed to his father an assault on Tangier, another principal Moorish port. Ceuta had proven to be of little more than symbolic value and was a steady drain on the Portuguese crown. It was hoped the situation could be reversed by taking Tangier. King John had considered this venture too risky, the eventual reward unlikely, and had vetoed it.

Now Henry renewed his argument with his older brother. Although reluctant, Edward granted his approval, even allowing their youngest brother, Ferdinand, to go along to win his spurs as the older brothers had won theirs. Uncharacteristically, and probably over-confident, Henry rushed ahead with an ill-planned expedition. There was none of the elaborate subterfuge of the Ceuta expedition and the Moors were waiting. The port of Tangier was more formidable than Ceuta, so it was necessary to have the army disembark, then mount the attack from landward. Through miscalculation the army became cut off from its ships and then surrounded in the desert by the enemy. Young Prince Ferdinand was taken hostage and the price demanded for his return was nothing less than the city of Ceuta itself.

Ferdinand was a favourite of the king and of Henry. Following payment of a ransom the Portuguese army was permitted to return home, but the king refused to relinquish Ceuta, the crown jewel of the Portuguese monarchy. Broken by the failure and imprisonment of his brother, Edward died the following year. Ferdinand languished in a Moorish cell for five years, beseeching his brothers with an endless stream of heart-breaking letters to negotiate his release until finally succumbing to illness. Henry returned to the Algarve, where he became something of a recluse for the remainder of his life. His younger and beloved brother had trusted him and paid a terrible price for the trust.

For a time after his return Henry was compelled to mediate in politics. Eventually his brother Pedro was named regent to serve in the stead of Edward's six-year-old son Alfonso, and stability was restored. The hiatus from exploration, however, was not wasted. Eanes and another captain, named Baldaia, had agreed that the square-rigged vessels and traditionally designed ships they were using were unsuited for the tasks demanded of them. Since Roman times the single large rectangular sail had been the norm in the Mediterranean Sea and was generally found on a galley. It worked extremely well when sailing with a prevailing wind but made tacking, or sailing against the wind, very difficult even in gentle conditions, and more often than not, impossible. For this reason the galley was equipped with oars, and in fact the first Portuguese explorations took place in such galleys of traditional design.

The two captains fitted a vessel with the Arab lateen sail, triangular in shape, which was more readily manoeuvrable for tacking against the wind and allowed a steeper angle of attack. It meant a ship with such a sail could return more easily against adverse winds. Neither oars nor oarsmen were required. Because of that and the relative ease with which the sails could be managed it required fewer crewmen, which solved many problems for the voyages. Small vessels of this type had sailed the Tagus river for generations, so they were not alien to the Portuguese. This was, however, a new and innovative application for the design.

The new configuration also meant that such a ship was more easily manoeuvrable when close to shore, a decided advantage for the explorations. In tests two masts proved ideal, although later models on occasion had three. The ships were also rigged in a combination of both square sails, which produced the best speed when sailing with the wind, and lateen sails, which allowed for more effective manoeuvrability and tacking.

As they gained experience with the new design, changes were not limited to the sails. The Portuguese were among the first to move the rudder from the side of the ship to the rear, much improving steering. When the vessel was at sea and running with the wind the rudder was locked in place, holding it more solidly on course.

The hull was modified to keep the vessel shallow for the close-in sailing. It also lay close to the water and the stern was wider than the bow, a radical departure from the fixed geometric configuration of European ships up to this time. Rather than remaining round, the hull turned downwards at the keel. This, combined with the locked rudder, permitted the ship to hold its course more firmly in heavy winds. The planks did not overlap, as in the traditional vessel, but following the practice of the Viking ships were butted against one another and placed on a solid oak frame, giving the hull much greater strength. This also allowed ships to be larger. Typically such a vessel was about 100 feet in length and weighed up to 200 tons. This new ship was named the caravel.

The name is thought by some to come from *cara-bella*, meaning 'beautiful shape'. Another account claims the name originates from *carabos*, a sort of lobster.[42] Still another suggests it originates from the Arab word *karib*.[43] Whatever the origin of the name, the ship possessed qualities that made it nothing less than revolutionary.

By 1441 Henry was able to return permanently to Sagres and turn his attention once again to exploration and discovery. The Portuguese had acquired sufficient experience those first years to grasp that, while many difficulties were foreseeable, others were not and had to be overcome as they became known. Until then ships of any size had to receive maintenance in a proper port. A suitable facility was required as well as experienced manpower to pull the vessel from the water, secure it in a cradle, then clean, caulk and seal the hull.

The waters grew warmer as the Portuguese ships sailed further south and barnacles and borers accumulated on the hulls with frightening speed. These were a risk to the safety of the crews since such growths slowed speed to a crawl. Ships also had to land frequently to obtain fresh water and firewood and there were as yet no such places along the African coast. The captains experimented and learned they could beach the caravel and service it far from any port, a remarkable development. Safe landings were still necessary, but now the distance before resupply was needed could be extended.

The ability to preserve and carry food for the increasingly lengthy voyages had to be expanded. Salt, the key preservative of the time, increased thirst. The mainstay of the portable diet was dried salted fish, later cod, which remains today the Portuguese national dish. It was healthy and kept for long periods, but to be eaten it had to be first soaked in fresh water. (On land it is immersed in three batches of fresh water for eight hours each and in any event requires a large quantity of water.) This meant using the supplies of water more rapidly than desired, and in any case water turned rancid if kept in kegs for too long a period. The kegs had to be cleaned constantly but that only delayed the inevitable. Wherever the Portuguese turned they found limits to their desire, problems that simply had to be solved if the explorations were to continue.

Shortly after Henry's return to Sagres there occurred one of the defining moments in world history and, as is often the case, it began inauspiciously. Henry ordered one of the smaller vessels, with a crew of just twenty-one, to be outfitted for a voyage and he placed in command his chamberlain, Antão Gonçalves, still a very young man. The earlier seal hides had proved profitable and apparently Henry wanted to season his chamberlain with a relatively simple task, so Gonçalves was ordered to return to the mouth of Rio de Ouro and collect a cargo of hides and oil. Because of his youth, Henry assumed 'his authority [would be] but slight' with his crew, and little beyond providing the young captain a toughening experience was expected from the voyage.

Gonçalves accomplished the assigned task with no difficulty but, rather than return immediately, he gathered his men and suggested that they might yet do more. 'How fair a thing it would be', Azurara quotes him saying, 'if we, who have come to this land for a cargo of such petty merchandise, were to meet with the good luck to bring the first captives before the face of our Prince.'

His men, knowing of Henry's generosity and desire for interpreters, agreed and that night Gonçalves went ashore with nine picked seamen to search for potential captives. Ten miles inland they came across the tracks of a large party, but it was moving in the wrong direction for their purpose. Even at night the desert heat was intense and soon Gonçalves instructed the men to turn back. On their way, however, they came upon a lone man leading a camel and immediately fell upon him. He put up an impressive fight, given that he was so heavily outnumbered, but after he received a mild wound he was taken. Closer to shore the men spotted a woman older than their captive and took her as well.

Now Gonçalves was in possession of what he knew Henry at this point most desired: locals who could give him the information he needed about this unknown region and who could be trained as interpreters. It is likely the Portuguese had already reached the region once held by the fabled Mali empire but did not know it.[*]

As Gonçalves prepared to set sail the next day he spotted another ship bearing down on his position. It was Nuno Tristão, in command of the first caravel to be dispatched south, under orders to do more than kill seals. The two men were well acquainted from their time in Henry's court. Tristão expressed his pleasure at seeing the captives the young chamberlain had taken. After learning that Gonçalves and his team had spotted sign of a substantial number of people in the vicinity, he argued that in addition to any knowledge to be gained by taking more, it would be profitable to carry off enough of these people so that 'profit will also accrue . . . by their service or ransom'. In other words, he proposed that they took captives to be sold as slaves.

---

[*] The western Sudan had been the centre of three great nominally Islamic empires, wealth made possible primarily by the control of trade routes across the Sahara. The first of these, Ghana, was supplanted by Mali, which flourished from 1203 to 1260. At its peak it stretched to the Atlantic coast east of Gao. Though Mali continued as a separate, albeit greatly reduced, state until 1645, its place as the dominant power was largely supplanted by the Songhai empire, which extended from the Atlantic to Kano, centred on the big bend of the Niger river. In 1471 Songhai subjugated western Mali. In 1591 Moroccan forces crushed the Songhai empire.

This was agreed, so Tristão went inland on foot and, following a skirmish in which his men killed several of the locals, they seized ten as captives. The ships sailed to Cape Blanco, where Tristão conducted another search for captives, this one fruitless. The two captains then decided to return to the Algarve.

Slavery was an ancient institution and little condemnation was attached to it in the fifteenth century, especially as the Pope had explicitly authorized the practice with non-believers. Indeed, the African natives were heathens and 'outside the law of Christ, and at the disposition, so far as their bodies were concerned, of any Christian nation'.[44] Azurara expressed the then commonly held belief concerning black Africans: 'In accordance with ancient custom, which I believe to have been because of the curse which, after the Deluge, Noah laid upon his son Cain, cursing him in this way: that his race should be subject to all the other races of the world.'[45]

Henry expressed his absolute delight at seeing the twelve prisoners, being quick to point out that now they could be turned to the one True Faith. Conversion was from the first, and long remained, the moral justification for slavery. Henry's chronicler commented there was also considerable pleasure taken at the prospect that they would make money from the sale of the hapless captives.

Azurara wrote that:

> Besides the blacks . . . [Prince Henry] got also a little gold dust and a shield of ox-hide, and a number of ostrich eggs, so that one day there were served up at the Infante's table three dishes of the same, as fresh and as good as though they had been the eggs of any other domestic fowls. And we may well presume that there was no other Christian prince in this part of Christendom, who had dishes like these upon his table.

With the introduction of slavery into the equation the money to be made from exploration was readily apparent and the pace of the voyages increased markedly. These first captives were a curiosity in Lisbon and by all accounts were treated as domestic help in the households that bought them. Azurara wrote, 'I never saw one of these slaves put in irons . . . and scarcely any one who did not turn Christian and was not very gently treated.' They were permitted to marry the Portuguese and the offspring of those unions were free citizens. Some were adopted by their Portuguese masters and made heirs. Most of the slaves were granted their freedom over the course of years and in time their blood line was completely integrated.

This is not to make light of the horror the captives faced at being torn from their families and people. They had no choice in the matter and were never able to return home. Humane treatment at the hands of their owners only lessened the impact of their lot; it did not mitigate or justify it.

Although there was a chronic shortage of labourers, Madeira was producing a handsome profit, but when the first African slaves were introduced production improved substantially. Slavery and sugar were a propitious economic mix and the demand for slaves rose dramatically as a result. Sugar was a size-able source of income to the monarchy, and by 1460 Portugal was importing between 700 and 800 slaves annually. By 1498 there were 220 estates on the island and the price of sugar had fallen so far that a limit was placed on its production. The Portuguese were not alone in slave-taking. The Arabs in north and east Africa had already established their own profitable trade in black slaves taken from central Africa and exported the captives to Arabia, Persia and India.

Gonçalves and Tristão had introduced the modern dark chapter of African slavery. For the next 400 years Europeans would be directly involved in the continent's slave trade, greatly expanding it and imposing a degree of uncompromising ruth-lessness. The southern British colonies in America developed an insatiable appetite for a slave work-force, though they were by no means the primary destination for slaves. While the Portuguese virtually dominated the slave trade during that first century, soon Spain, England, the Netherlands, Denmark, France, the Caribbean islands and the American colonies themselves were heavily involved and contributing to its expansion.*

With such substantial profits now apparent, it was certain that usurpers would seek to benefit from Henry's work, so his brother the regent granted to him the exclusive licence to explore and exploit the region below Cape Bojador. In 1444 the first privately sponsored voyage with profit as its sole objective sailed from Lagos with six vessels. The crews raided several villages on Arguin Island, situated between Cape Bojador and the Senegal river, and returned with 235 prisoners.

The ill-fated captives were sold in a meadow just outside Lagos. So great was the enthusiasm of the Portuguese that numbers swarmed down to the shore as the prisoners were landed. Some went out in boats to greet the mariners as heroes. Azurara provides this description of what ensued:

> I pray Thee that my tears may not wrong my conscience; . . . to weep in pity for their sufferings . . . But what heart could be so hard as to not to be pierced with piteous feeling to see that company? For some kept their heads low and their faces bathed in tears, looking one upon another; others stood groaning very dolorously, looking up at the height of heaven, fixing their eyes upon it, crying out loudly, . . . others struck their faces with the palms of their hands, throwing themselves at full length upon the ground; others made their lamentations in the manner of a dirge, after the custom of their country . . .
>
> But to increase their sufferings still more, there now arrived those who had charge of the division of the captives, and who began to separate one from another . . . [T]hen it was needful to part fathers from sons, husbands

---

* Estimates of actual slaves transported are: 3.6 million from south-western Africa to Brazil; 4 million from west Africa to the Caribbean islands; 200,000 to Mexico; 400,000 to what became the United States; 550,000 by Arab slavers from central Africa to the Middle East; and another 700,000 from southeast Africa to the Middle East and Indus region.

from wives, brothers from brothers. No respect was shewn either to friends or relations, but each fell where his lot took him. . . .

And who could finish that partition without very great toil? For as often as they had placed them in one part the sons, seeing their fathers in another, rose with great energy and rushed over to them; the mothers clasped their other children in their arms, and threw themselves flat on the ground with them; receiving blows with little pity for their own flesh, if only they might not be torn from them . . .

The Infant [Henry] was there, mounted on a powerful steed . . . as a man who sought to gain but little from his share; for the forty-six souls that fell to him . . . [he gave to the church]; for he reflected with great pleasure upon the salvation of those souls that before were lost.[46]

The following year the Portuguese constructed a trading post, or factory (*feitoria*), on Arguin Island, the first permanent European presence in west Africa (or Guinea, as the region of Portuguese interest in west Africa was known). Local Arabs began bringing slaves and gold, which they traded for blankets from the Alentejo, leather, cloth* and wheat, as they were chronically short of food. Ten years later a fortress was built there. This factory became the prototype for such trading stations, which in time stretched to the Spice Islands on the far side of the world.

Also in 1444 Tristão reached the Senegal river, where the 'land of the Blacks', as it was known, began. Until this point west Africa had been almost entirely desert, but at the Senegal river there began the tropical forest inhabited by pagan blacks.

The pace of the voyages increased and that same year another captain, Dinis Dias, passed Cape Verde, Africa's most westerly point, and discovered the island of Gourée. The next year Alvara

---

* Cloth was the single most expensive item for European households and was highly desired there as well as by those living in less developed societies. Kings commonly made a gift of their used clothes to royal favourites.

Fernandes reached the Cape of Mists, near the Gambia river. Privately organized and officially sanctioned voyages took place as well, although these were not primarily concerned with pushing the route of discovery southward. They were largely slave raids in already known lands, and in 1445 no fewer than twenty-six ships, in four separate expeditions, set sail for that purpose. The following year fifty-one ships sailed to acquire slaves and in the process also pushed the region of exploration over 450 leagues, some 1,500 miles, beyond Cape Bojador.[47]

After suffering casualties on the increasingly dangerous slave raids, the Portuguese were generally content to remain on the coast and trade with local chiefs and others for gold, ivory and slaves. Certain Jews dared to penetrate inland, and some reached the most remote regions of the Sahara, where they traded nearer the source for the same items and slaves. The Portuguese were asserting a profound influence on the historic trade routes and patterns of this fabled region, interdicting goods, gold and slaves that would normally have been taken to the Muslim ports of north Africa.

Despite ship losses and deaths among the crews, the explorations had until now gone very well for the Portuguese. Madeira was an unqualified success and with the introduction of the trade in slaves the drain on finances was significantly reduced or even eliminated. But now matters changed.

The climate below the Cape of Mists was even less hospitable than anything they had experienced so far, and crews began to die of strange diseases at an astonishing rate. Also, word of the slave raids travelled ahead of the captains and first contact with locals was typically violent, with casualties on both sides. Even before the Portuguese stepped ashore they faced a rain of arrows, followed by combat once they arrived on land. The cost of exploration and discovery, and of exploitation, had risen.

In 1445 two Portuguese captains were killed in slave raids along the African coast. The following year Tristão sailed one of his ships up the Gambia river, as the official goal was still to establish contact with the Mali empire in the interior. As he and his men were preparing to return to the sea, they were attacked by locals, who loosed a swarm of poisoned arrows. Four men died immediately and sixteen others, including Tristão, succumbed a short time later. All were buried at sea. A year later a Danish knight who had come to Portugal to participate in the voyages and make his fortune was attacked along with his men near Cape Verde as he attempted to exchange gifts on the beach. There was but a lone European survivor of the ensuing massacre.

A Venetian adventurer named Alvise Cadamosto left one of the most remarkable and vivid accounts of what was taking place in west Africa during this time. His record includes priceless observations of local customs and draws a clear picture of the relationship between the Portuguese and the locals. He also recounts an incident of the kind that is not commonly recorded, but which no doubt had a significant place in influencing the trade for slaves. The Venetian had sold horses and harnesses in exchange for 100 slaves and came to the attention of the local chief. 'As soon as he saw me, he gave me a young girl of twelve to thirteen years of age, pretty for all that she was very black, and said that he gave her for the service of my bedchamber. I accepted her and sent her to my ship.'[48]

Much of what took place during these years is unknown, as the destinations of ships and what occurred on landings were intentionally suppressed by Henry and later by the kings who wished to maintain a monopoly on their trade. The ships of any other nation that entered the waters were treated as enemies. In addition, access to information was restricted as a matter of state policy. The mariners were forbidden to discuss where they had been, and written accounts of voyages were altered. Charts and globes were carefully guarded or heavily censored. The Portuguese placed an extensive network of spies in the various royal courts of Europe to report back on how much information was leaking. The death penalty was imposed on any subject known to have sent a map abroad or to have attempted to give information to a foreign power. This was no idle threat; assassinations are known to have taken place.

Three papal bulls established a specific maritime area of exclusivity for the Portuguese, effectively giving religious approval for them to take the dominant position with all non-Christians with whom they came into contact. Although they lacked such a sanction, the Dutch and English who followed adopted the same attitude.

The first bull was issued in 1452 and authorized the king of Portugal to attack and conquer Saracens, pagans and non-believers, to seize their possessions and lands, and to reduce the population to slavery; it also granted the king the right to pass ownership of the lands on to his heirs.

The second bull was promulgated three years later and is so specific that it has been called the charter of Portuguese imperialism. It summarizes the accomplishments of the Portuguese to date, and it praises Henry for his devotion and service to God, and for his desire to spread the word of God to the most remote and unknown lands, where he might force non-believers to the faith. It mentions his desire to double Africa and discover the 'Indies', the first record of such a goal in the explorations. Whatever steps were necessary to safeguard these efforts were explicitly justified.

The last bull was issued in 1456 at the request of Alfonso V and Henry as administrator for the Order of Christ. In essence, it recognized Henry's authority for all religious matters within any newly discovered and occupied lands.

Throughout these years royal intrigue in Lisbon continued and, despite an exemplary rein, the regent Pedro was removed by court machinations. Given little alternative other than self-imposed exile, he chose to attempt to take the throne for himself and was slain in battle. Young Alfonso V was now king. Pedro was the last of Henry's brothers and the one to whom he was the closest. His loss would have been very difficult for Henry, especially as Henry allied himself with young Alfonso to prevent a protracted and destructive civil war.

For all the success of his ships and captains, Henry had not lost his passion for military conquest in north Africa. He had been held back only by the apprehensions of John and then Pedro.

When his nephew the new king expressed his desire to attack the Moors in retaliation for the fall of Constantinople in 1453, Henry offered advice and encouragement. In 1458 another Portuguese fleet set sail for Morocco with the 64-year-old Henry among the first to step ashore. Well prepared, the force quickly overcame the defenders of Alcácer-Sequir and the king asked Henry to join him in accepting the surrender. Both were back in Portugal within a week of their departure.

Henry returned to his life as a recluse and remained in the south, either on his estate at Raposeira in the Algarve or at a smaller residence at Sagres. The explorations meanwhile continued. In 1457 one of Henry's captains at last made contact in Gambia with traders from Mali and Timbuktu. He established friendly relations with the local chieftains and when they expressed an interest in Christianity he reported this to Henry, who immediately dispatched a priest.

Henry, Prince of Portugal, Grand Master of the Order of Christ, Governor of Ceuta and the Algarves, Duke of Viseu, Lord of Covilhalm, Knight of the Garter, known to history as The Navigator, died quietly at Sagres in 1460 at the age of sixty-six. For some months he had believed his death to be imminent and had carefully put his affairs in order. He transferred two of the islands of the Azores to the control of an adopted son and arranged for the Cape Verde islands to be administered by the crown. Two other of the Azores were given to the Order of Christ, as Madeira had been some years earlier. He saw to the affairs of the University of Lisbon, the hospital he had built at Tomar, which was headquarters for the Order of Christ, and the chapel he had constructed at Belém near the mouth of the Tagus river.

It is reported that as word of his passing spread, the king 'and all the people of Portugal mourned the death of so great a prince'. Henry had asked that he be buried simply and without ceremony. Consistent with his wish, he was interred with due recognition for his achievements but without ceremony or pomp and placed in the same chapel as his parents, King John I and Philippa, and beside his brothers.

Henry's ships had sailed as far south as Sierra Leone, an unimaginable feat at the time of his birth. It was written of the prince that 'the land and the seas are full of your name; for by continual effort you united the East with the West.'[49]

6

South of Guinea

By the time of Henry's death it had become apparent that the fabled wealth of Mali was just that: a fable. This region of the Niger had been on the economic decline for decades. Expeditions inland revealed a disappointing collection of mud huts and small cultivated fields. One adventurer reported:

> I saw clearly that, though these [rulers] pass as lords, it must not be thought that they have castles or cities . . . Such men are not lords by virtue of treasure or money, but on account of ceremonies and the following of people they may truly be called lords. Indeed they receive beyond comparison more obedience than our lords.[50]

He noted the generally poor conditions under which the people lived and the overall lack of gold or any other sign of wealth.

Although trade opportunities and a source of gold remained primary Portuguese objections, they were no longer the only ones. The idea of circumnavigating Africa to reach the origin of the spice trade had gradually become an important part of the mix. While the prospect was tantalizing, the Portuguese still had no idea how far south the African continent extended, or whether such a passage was geographically possible.

The Portuguese captains had sailed as far south as Cape Verga, some 50 miles below the Rio Grande. Now lacking Henry's interest and drive, the Portuguese explorations stalled. Over the next years there was just a single voyage, which went as far south as Sierra Leone. Here the coast of Africa made a decided turn eastward, and at least one ancient map showed this to be the most southerly point of the African continent. The way to Asia seemed to loom before the Portuguese, but there was no one to lead the way.

Without Henry's influence Alfonso V was more interested in the glory he would gain by attacking the Moors in north Africa than in continuing the explorations and, after his easy victory at Alcácer-Sequir, seized both Arizila and Tangier in 1471. His conquests demanded a constant stream of money, so the merchants in Lisbon continued the prosperous Africa trade, both for profit and to pay the increasingly severe taxes. João de Barros, who had access to contemporary records that no longer exist, wrote in his work *Décades da Asia*:

> At this time the trade of Guiné was already very current between our men and the inhabitants of those parts, and they carried on their business in peace and friendliness, without those war-like incursions, assaults and robberies which happened at the beginnings – as could not have been otherwise with people so wild and barbarous, both in law and customs and in the use of the things of this our Europe.
>
> These people were always intractable. However, after they learned something of the truth through the benefits they received, both spiritual and intellectual, and articles for their use, they became so well disposed that when ships, sailing from this Kingdom, arrived at their ports, many people came from the interior to seek their goods, which they received in exchange for human beings, who were brought here more for salvation than for slavery.

The fact was that a Portuguese merchant looking to barter was more likely to make the journey to Africa than a knight seeking glory, or a priest in search of converts. Captives were processed through the fortress at Arguin Island and most ended their days in the fields of Madeira working the sugar-cane fields, though a significant number were sold in Portugal because of its chronic shortage of labourers. By one reckoning as much as 10 per cent of labour in Portugal was provided by African slaves, although other sources dispute this estimate.

Not only were the king's military conquests expensive, but the cities held in north Africa were a constant drain on the treasury as each had to be manned by a garrison. From time to time the Muslims marshalled forces in an effort to reclaim one of the cities, requiring fresh troops and supplies to be dispatched at considerable cost. In addition, as had been the case with Ceuta, there was no money to be made, as the Moors cut the Christian-occupied cities off from all trade.

With the Portuguese there was always a healthy mix of the merchant in the explorations that compared more closely with the Italian city-states than with Spain, England or France. The increasing profits merchants obtained from the slave and gold trade stimulated interest in expanding the explorations. In 1469 Fernão Gomes, a respected citizen in Lisbon, entered into an agreement with the king for a period of five years, which was later extended for one year. During that time he received a trade monopoly in the lands he discovered below the farthest point the Portuguese had already reached, although some items remained exclusive to the king. In exchange, Gomes agreed to pay 200,000 *reis* a year and to maintain the exclusion he was required to press the point of discovery at least 100 leagues annually.

The men Gomes dispatched exceeded these requirements and pushed the length of new coastline more than 2,000 miles between 1469 and 1474. From the viewpoint of Gomes, who looked to make money from this effort, and Alfonso V, who also stood to profit, the voyages could not have been more successful.

The first went as far as Abidjan, where the captain traded trinkets, metal and cloth for melagueta pepper, woven baskets and slaves. This 'Guinea pepper', as it was known, was more like cardamom than true Indian pepper, but there was a steady market for it. The following year at a point near today's Ghana, the excited Portuguese came upon a thriving local trade in gold. So commonplace was the precious metal in the region they called El Mina, or 'the mine' or 'the Gold Coast', that it was available for little to nothing. For the first time Portugal began to experience an inflow of wealth for which until now they had only hoped.

The king ordered the striking of a gold coin, significantly named the *cruzado* ('crusade'), the first gold coin in Portugal since 1385. This Guinea gold was used to buy manufactured goods and corn from northern Europe and helped to improve the national economy. The gold coins were called *Portugaloisers* throughout Europe for hundreds of years.

In 1472 the coastline of Africa disappointingly turned southward again and proved to be especially unhealthy. The air was hot and sticky, and the contrary currents were warm, causing barnacles and worms to flourish on and in their hulls. Landfall was especially deadly because of both disease and hostile natives, to whom word of the slave trade had already travelled. Indeed, a Flemish ship that dared the coast was wrecked and its surviving crew of thirty-five was reportedly eaten by the locals, much to the delight of the Portuguese when they heard the story.[51]

Still, before the expiration of his lease Gomes had pushed the point of discovery to Gabon, some 100 miles south of the equator. He had become enormously rich in the process and in the final year of the lease was knighted. His new coat of arms bore testament to the means of his wealth. The coat as described by Barros was 'a shield with crest and three heads of Negroes on a field of silver, each with golden rings in ears and nose, and a collar of gold around the neck'. Gomes was also given the surname 'Da Mina'.

In addition to their steady probing southward, the Portuguese also made efforts at exploration to the west, across the Atlantic. Given their appreciation of the true magnitude of the size of the Earth, it is unlikely they were actively seeking a route to Asia, though they were always open to the possibility if suitable islands for resupply could be found. Madeira was proving prosperous, and other lands with similar potential could exist. Legend told of many islands in the western seas and it was only natural, once the Portuguese possessed the means, that they would seek them out. Failures were generally not well recorded, if recorded at all, so we cannot know the full extent of the effort in that region.

However, from the death of Henry until the 1480s royal

charters were regularly issued, granting lordships to certain captains for lands reported to have been discovered or observed at a distance. Expeditions were sent to find these islands, without success, but the belief among those living on Madeira or the Azores fed the continuing expectation of western lands. They heard stories of seamen posted in the crow's nest having seen distant islands; they recovered bits of wood washed up following violent storms; they saw flocks of land birds winging to them from across the vast ocean. Stories of every kind spread among the seamen and navigators, all to one degree or another suggesting the existence of significant lands to the west. When living on Madeira, Christopher Columbus had seen for himself the body of a man of unknown origin and race washed up on the shore following a storm. Some time before 1474 two Portuguese noblemen appear to have reached Greenland or Newfoundland as part of this effort to explore to the west.

One interesting result of the expeditions dispatched into the north Atlantic is a notation inscribed in the mosaic pavement on Lisbon's Avenida da Liberdade. It reads, 'João Vaz Corte-Real, Discoverer of America 1472'.[52]

At the conclusion of Gomes's lease, the king transferred control over exploration and trade in Africa to his son and future king, John. The potential and current earnings were simply too great to allow merchants to skim the cream and, besides, Alfonso V was growing weary of the affairs of state.

From 1475 to 1480 another of the periodic wars with Spain was fought and during these years entire fleets of Spanish ships boldly encroached on to the Gold Coast to exploit trade. This was a source of great concern to the Portuguese, especially since the Spanish were not alone. Intruders from England and Flanders were also routinely spotted. Such was the Portuguese concern that the war-ending Treaty of Alcáçovas addressed these issues. The treaty was to have profound impact on subsequent events, far beyond incursions by Spanish interlopers.

Title to the Canary Islands, which were ideally situated as a provisioning station for the African voyages, had been in dispute by the two nations ever since Portugal and Castile discovered them at about the same time. It is generally accepted that the Canary Islands are the Fortunatae Insulae of ancient times and they were probably known to both the Phoenicians and the Carthaginians. The Roman Pliny described them as a land where wild dogs roamed, and from that came their modern name. The Pope awarded them to Castile in 1344 but the French took them by force in 1462. Spain reclaimed them but the Portuguese continued to dispute ownership, correctly taking Spain's insistence on retaining the islands as an indication that the Spanish had aspirations in Africa.

In this case Spain had been the first to colonize the islands, which was the only true way to hold a claim, but Portugal had planted a colony of its own for a time and undisputed ownership was an issue Spain wanted resolved. Under the treaty Portugal conceded the Canaries to Spain, but in exchange Portugal was granted clear title and exclusive access to the lands it had discovered to date in Africa, and most significantly to 'all the islands which have been discovered, mentioned, or conquered from the Canaries southward'.

The effect was to stop any southern expansion or exploitation by Spain. One consequence was the sympathetic reception Christopher Columbus received from the Spanish court once Isabella and Ferdinand had conquered Granada in 1492. They now had the time and money to turn their attention to exploration but, prevented by the treaty from southward explorations on the way to India, they were prepared to finance Columbus's voyage west. Even if he failed to reach India, Spain could claim any lands he discovered. They also possessed the Canary Islands, from which Columbus would sail. The winds there made his success highly probable.

With the sudden death of King Alfonso V in 1481, his son John, just twenty-six years old, assumed the throne as John II, the sovereign the Portuguese were to call 'The Perfect Prince' (*O Principe Perfecto*). Ambitious and powerful nobles were jealous of their feudal prerogatives and did not welcome a strong king. Alfonso V had slowly dissipated the authority and wealth of the crown by transferring much of it to the nobility. Whenever there was an adverse change, or when the throne was transferred, the nobles were ready to defy the central authority and reclaim lost powers or make a grab for even more. John II took as his first objective crushing the 'nascent conspiracy of the nobles'.[53]

The royal chroniclers naturally present their patron and his ancestors in the most flattering light. John II was a remarkable man and king, but in calling him the Perfect Prince they did not mean that he was a perfect man; rather, they meant that he was well possessed of the necessary attributes required of a successful king. John II openly boasted that he followed the tenants of Machiavelli and imitated the strategies of the unscrupulous Louis XI of France. Despite his great affection for the powerful Duke of Bragança, his brother-in-law, he had him arrested and, following a show trial, had him executed. He personally stabbed to death his wife's brother the Duke of Viseu, in the palace at Setúbal, though there is little doubt of the duke's persistent treacherous conduct. When the queen objected to the killing of her brother, King John threatened to try her for treason if she was not silent. In his drive to secure power, John murdered the bishop of Évora by having him thrown alive down a well and then executed, with or without trial, eighty of the leading Portuguese lords. He not only crushed rivals and potential rivals but also seized their lands and thereby refilled the treasury, which his father had left empty. It was this wealth that made possible the next phase of explorations.[54]

There is a picture of John II written by a highly opinionated Pole who visited the Portuguese court in 1484:

> The King is of medium height . . . He is beyond a doubt the wisest and most virtuous of his people. He should be about twenty-nine years old. And he had with him his heir of nine years, of an English cast of countenance, and him he always kept at his side at table. The king partakes of only four or five dishes at meals, and drinks only well water, without sugar or spices. His son drinks wine with water and

eats the same food as his father, but from a special service
. . . Below the table and at the feet of the king are always
six or eight pages, and one more on either side of him, to
drive away the flies with silken fans.

There are Portuguese endowed with much subtlety . . .
[but] in general the nobility, the citizens, and the peasants
of this country are . . . coarse, poor, lacking in good manners and ignorant, in spite of their pretence of wisdom.
They remind one of the English, who do not admit any
society equal to theirs. The Portuguese have more loyalty
among themselves and also for their king – more loyalty
than the English. They are not as cruel and insensate as
these. They show themselves more sober in eating and
drinking. None the less they are ugly, dark, and black,
almost like negroes. They wear cloaks black and voluminous. . . . In love [their women] are ardent . . . they dress
their hair with no exaggerated adornment and wear scarves
of woollen cloth, or a neckerchief of silk. They allow one
to look upon their faces without hindrance, and also upon
much of their bosoms, for which purpose their shifts and
outer dresses are cut generously low. Below their waist they
wear many skirts so that their posteriors are broad and
beautiful, so full that I say it in all truth in the whole world
nothing finer is to be seen. They are for the most part sensual, fickle like men, lewd and greedy for money. . . . The
women are so dissolute that rarely can one meet a young
girl of 'guaranteed' virtue. To satisfy their desires they suffer
no scruples to stand in their way. Besides all this, both husbands and wives have lovers, and it would be an illusion to
travel among [them] to learn good manners or virtue.[55]

The sexual laxity of Portuguese society, even among the clergy,
was notorious. Between 1389 and 1438 two archbishops, five
bishops, eleven archdeacons, nine deans, four chanters, seventy-
two canons and some six hundred priests received official permission to legitimize their bastard children. This does not include,
of course, the many clerics who never applied for permission.[56]

The Portuguese achievements in Africa were by this time in jeopardy and John II made this his next priority. He ordered interlopers into the gold trade to be stopped, crews to be captured and their vessels and goods to be seized. He solidified the control of the monarchy over the African trade and in 1482 dispatched one of his most loyal officers, Diogo de Azambuja, with a fleet of 12 ships and a complement of 600 men, 100 of whom where masons and craftsmen, with instructions to construct a permanent Portuguese presence in the form of a fortress on the Gold Coast.★

Azambuja selected a suitable harbour just west of Accra in today's Ghana. The local king, Kwamena Ansah, was by now well accustomed to the Portuguese, but could see that this fleet was something very different from what had come before. Arrangements were made to meet on the beach, and when the Portuguese arrived they were decked out in court dress to make the most favourable impression possible. Until now the typical Portuguese had been, in the words of the king, 'ill-dressed and ragged men only'. Clearly these Europeans were up to something significant. By way of greeting the king ordered his musicians and warriors to play and sing, creating a nearly deafening noise.

When Kwamena Ansah heard from Azambuja that he wished to build a 'great house', he argued that it was best to leave matters as they had been. 'Friends who meet occasionally remain better friends than if they were neighbours', he said. But Azambuja was not to be dissuaded and he had the force of arms and numbers to impose his will if it came to a fight. In the end Kwamena Ansah had no voice in the matter. He had profited from his dealings with the Portuguese to date and there was every reason to expect the situation to continue. The alternative was to pick what would almost certainly be a losing fight against a formidable opponent.

Within twenty days the outer wall of the fortress was raised

★ Among these were Christopher Columbus and Bartholomeu Dias.

'to a good height, and the tower to the first floor'. Before long the structure was complete. Azambuja remained for more than two and a half years, losing many of his men to disease – though not as many as expected. During that time he established prices and rules for trade that remained in effect for some years. When he returned to Portugal, he took with him 'much gold', leaving in place a permanent garrison of sixty soldiers, as he had been instructed.

The fortress of El Mina, also called São Jorge, was the first permanent European settlement on the continent of tropical Africa. In time it grew to an ever larger and more imposing size, and it remains today. It diverted the trade in gold from the Moorish caravans at considerable economic loss to them, enriching the Portuguese monarchy an average of 170,000 *dobras* of gold annually for some twenty-five years. Trade from the region was so important to Portugal that the Casa da Mina ('House of the Mine') was established in Lisbon, on the ground floor of the royal palace, to channel goods and gold for control and taxation. It was not unusual for the king personally to observe the unloading of ships.

Tens of thousands of slaves passed through El Mina's barred gates on their way to lives of ceaseless labour and endless night. Besides serving as a portal for slaves and as a trading post, El Mina was invaluable to the Portuguese as a provisioning station for vessels *en route* further south. It remained the focal point of the Portuguese presence in the region until 1637, when it was captured by the Dutch.

The growing policy of secrecy, which marked much of the Portuguese explorations, means that knowledge of the following decades is limited, but some details have been established. John II was eager to renew the voyages, which had been delayed by war with Spain, and the exploitation and consolidation of the Portuguese position on the Gold Coast. Selected for the next effort was Diogo Cão, an experienced captain typical of the sort the Portuguese were now producing with regularity.

These captains were brave, resourceful, skilled in seamanship and navigation, excellent leaders, but most of all they possessed the desire to expand the range of the known world. No doubt some of this eagerness stemmed from the ample rewards they received when they were fortunate enough to return alive, but there was more to it than personal gain. The vision begun by Prince Henry had become imbedded in the effort itself. Captains and seamen were filled with the desire not just for riches but to discover the unknown, to spread the Word to the pagan and to make contact with the elusive Prester John. This was now part of the Portuguese national character.

The Portuguese effort was identified not just by its successes but also by the manner in which it was conducted. The men sent south possessed a commitment to precise observation. They mapped their routes with unprecedented accuracy, producing logs that were readily comprehensible to the next Portuguese captain. They documented the vegetation and animals they encountered, as well as the habits and customs of the people with whom they came into contact. This was not a haphazard effort; it was methodical, as well as being daringly executed.

Cão was a 'man of the people', although he came from a distinguished family line that included Pedro Alfonso Cão, who had served as bailiff for King Dinis, and a grandfather, Gonçalo Cão, who reportedly distinguished himself in the Battle of Aljubarrota in 1385. Cão had captured three Spanish usurpers off the Guinea coast in 1480, which singled him out for special consideration.[57]

For the first time in dispatching an expedition, the ultimate Portuguese objective was clearly spelt out. Cão was to voyage south, but his goal was to seek the passage to India. He bore with him specific instructions and regulations that governed the nature of his exploration. He was to check all possible routes heading east. He was to search for Prester John by sailing as far as possible up major rivers and by establishing contact with the locals.[58] His was to be a systematic and deliberate exploration.

Just a year after John II assumed the throne, Cão left Lisbon harbour bearing new stone pillars (*padrões*) with which to mark key points of his anticipated discoveries. The first taken by Cão was 1.69 metres high and 73 centimetres in circumference, mounted on a slightly larger pedestal. Both the shaft and the pedestal were of a single block of lioz, a coarse marble common in the Lisbon area.[59]

This was an idea credited to the king. Until now the Portuguese had marked their progress by erecting wooden crosses or by carving a message into a prominent tree. These new pillars were intended to be more permanent and conspicuous. Once in place, a wooden cross was placed above them. The pillar itself bore the royal arms, an inscription in Portuguese and occasionally also in Latin, the date, the name of the king who ordered the voyage and the identity of the captain. All four of the pillars taken on his voyages have been discovered.[60]

Cão stopped first at the fortress at El Mina to resupply, then a few weeks later passed the previous point of discovery, just below the equator at Cape St Catherine, taking the time to observe the tree where the southernmost location had been marked. Resuming his voyage, progress southward was tedious since the prevailing current ran towards the north and the surf was heavy. The vessel worked close to shore, as was still the common practice, and only made progress against the prevalent current by the judicious use of a southward wind and favourable land breezes. It was tedious and treacherous going, especially since Cão was in a vessel of older design, not one of the new caravels.

The Portuguese had already surmised that the land in this region was injurious to the crews and conscientiously avoided landfall. This meant that deaths aboard ship required burial at sea, a practice accepted of necessity but distasteful to the Catholic crews, who preferred consecrated ground or at the least earth itself. As the days past, the heavy rains and thick vegetation slowly faded away and for a time the country became nearly arid in character. Cão sailed along a ridge of fine red sandstone cliffs, then a short time later moved away from the coast, seeking more favourable winds. Five leagues out to sea he found his ship surrounded by heavily earth-coloured water that proved to be fresh, the certain sign of a huge river.

Cão turned towards land and entered the mouth of the Congo river, the first European known to have done so. Along its banks his men observed many more natives than had ever previously been reported in one place. Word of the Portuguese had not travelled this far, so the crew were not greeted with violence when they stepped ashore. Although those people resembled the natives of Guinea, with their black skin and short curly hair, their language was different and the Portuguese African interpreters could not make themselves understood. Communication was reduced to hand gestures, which were sufficient for a number of the locals to come aboard the vessel, where they received cloth in exchange for bits of ivory.

The locals made it known they were part of a kingdom whose powerful ruler, Mani Congo, lived several days' march inland. Portugal needed allies along the route to India and Cão's instructions were to make friendly contact wherever possible, and so he indicated his desire for a meeting. He then dispatched black Christian emissaries, probably Africans seized on earlier voyages and trained for such work, with suitable gifts to attempt to establish amicable relations and inform the king of the Portuguese desire to trade. Once his men were on their way, Cão ordered a pillar to be set in place.

Although the guides who went with the emissaries had assured the Portuguese that the trip to their ruler and back would take only a few days, Cão waited several months without hearing from his men. All attempts to learn their fate proved futile, and with great reluctance Cão eventually set sail, turning again to the south.

The most distant point Cão reached was some 400 miles further on, in the southern part of what is now Angola. There he erected another pillar. Written in Portuguese, it read:

> In the year 6681 of the World, and in that of 1482 since the birth of our Lord Jesus Christ, the most serene, most excellent and potent prince King D. João II of Portugal did order this land to be discovered and these *padrões* to be set up by D Cão, an esquire of his household.[61]

Cão then returned to the Congo river to retrieve his long overdue men. The annoyed captain was eager to return to Portugal to report his progress and his discovery of what appeared to be a vast inland kingdom, possibly even that of Prester John or of a ruler who knew his location. When he saw his men were still not waiting, he seized four natives from shore and made it known to those remaining that these men would be returned within fifteen months in exchange for his missing emissaries.

In fact, Cão's messengers had been well received by the Mani Congo and it was his interest in them and what they had to say that had delayed their return. However, according to Ruy de Pina, when the African king heard of what he considered Cão's high-handed methods, he refused future contact with the emissaries and vowed to kill them should his four subjects not be returned. Unaware of the threat, Cão made his way slowly north towards home.

At about this time, and unaware of events in Africa, John II granted the repeated requests of Christopher Columbus for an audience. This was an especially busy time for the king. That same year, 1484, he had appointed the junta to provide him with reliable advice on such matters and to find solutions for the navigation difficulties the Portuguese faced the further from home they sailed. They were initially instructed to solve the problem faced by ships that journeyed beyond sight of the North Star, so the astrolabe was improved by making it possible to determine latitude by taking a reading from the sun. Columbus was present when the more accurate latitude of certain locations along the African coast were reported to the king.[62]

King John was also dealing with a conspiracy and rebellion at this time. The previous May he had executed the Duke of Bragança for treason and only a few months after meeting with Columbus he personally assassinated the Duke of Viseu. Between all the bloodshed the king still found time for the discoveries.

Columbus, who at this time had lived in Lisbon for eight years, was well known to the Portuguese court through his late wife's well-connected family. His oft-repeated proposition that it was possible to reach India by sailing west was not original but was still intriguing. As early as 1474 a similar claim by a Florentine physician, Paolo Toscanelli, had been presented to the Portuguese, and rejected.

Columbus, however, was highly influenced by Toscanelli's argument that the world was small enough to reach Asia by sailing directly west. Such a passage, Columbus believed, would not exceed more than a month. Drawing as he generally did on the Bible to make his points, Columbus was more than a bit of an eccentric, and his science was highly suspect, as the Discoveries had demonstrated that his non-biblical sources were not credible. But although the unconventional Genoan was known to be 'very boastful in his affairs', John II was willing to listen.

At this meeting Columbus argued that six-sevenths of the world was 'known' to be land. Hence, with so much ocean already discovered by the Portuguese, there was surely land to the west. He reminded the king that Alexander the Great had sent the philosopher Onesicritus with a fleet to Ceylon, and that the Roman emperor Nero had dispatched two centurions to Ethiopia to explore the source of the Nile. Above all, he assured the king that gold would come from his successful voyage.[63] His arguments, contrary as they were to what was known, were not persuasive; but even had that not been the case, the Genoan's demands for remuneration were simply outrageous, vastly exceeding anything that any previous Portuguese captain had received. Worse, he concluded his presentation by flatly demanding that King John grant his request.

Columbus was instructed to meet with members of the junta to present his argument. They made short work of his presentation, reaching the conclusion that his words were 'vain, simply founded on imagination'. Columbus was officially informed of the king's refusal in late 1484. By the following spring he was already in Spain on his way to the Spanish court.

Some time before April 1484 Cão entered Lisbon harbour after an absence of a year and a half, the longest voyage yet. His report was enthusiastically received and the young captain was made a *cavaleiro* of the king's household. When the full extent of his accomplishment was understood a few weeks later, he was made a nobleman and given a coat of arms bearing images of the two pillars he had erected on the coast of Africa.

One of the four captives proved to be a nobleman. He soon learned to speak Portuguese and was able to convey detailed information about his people and the region of the Congo river, much to the delight of King John. He was well treated, as were his companions, who were given clothes of silk and other fine gifts.

Political problems, or perhaps the opposition of the royal advisers to any further expeditions,★ prevented an immediate return, but in the autumn of 1485 Cão left on his second voyage, taking with him all four of the hostages he had seized. Also accompanying him was one of the great astronomers of the time, José Vizinho, who was to take measurements of the sun and stars in the southern hemisphere. The invention of new navigational devices and methods was a process at which the Portuguese were demonstrating a remarkable expertise.

Cão may have been joined by a second vessel, commanded by a certain Martin Behaim, identified by Ravenstein as Martim de Bohemia, which suggests he was not Portuguese. Some historians disagree over the existence of this second vessel, the only evidence for which is Behaim's own account, and argue that he did not go with Cão but was on the Guinea coast with a different expedition. In addition to trade goods, Cão took eighteen horses with magnificent harnesses, meant as gifts to Mani Congo. Wherever the Portuguese were to go, their splendid large horses were in constant demand.

★ Opposition to the explorations among the king's advisers became routine, although a number of the objections had nothing to do with the expeditions themselves. Disputes over other political issues were often manifest by opposing something the young king wanted. On the practical side, the Portuguese were enjoying an excellent return on their investment from the gold in Guinea as well as from the slave trade and more mundane forms of commerce. But the route to India remained as illusive as ever and costs to discover it could only mount with each effort.

Once again Cão sailed directly to the fortress at El Mina, where he took on new supplies and fresh water. He then set a course across the Gulf of Guinea, bypassing the unhealthy shores along modern Nigeria and Cameroon and sailing instead out to sea before turning east and heading directly for the mouth of the Congo river. The Portuguese were becoming more experienced at blue-water sailing and, as they accomplished it with greater success, recognized the advantages it offered. The winds were likely to be strong and constant, and there was no danger of attack by enemies or death from disease.

By taking the degree of elevation of the sun at noon a captain could fix the latitude of his vessel when it was out to sea, away from recognized land markings. There was no effective means for determining longitude, and nor would there be for some centuries. For this reason maps of this era generally place discoveries accurately by latitude, but longitude, which was based on guesswork and experience, was often seriously distorted. Since ancient times the theory had been accepted, contrary to the view held by Columbus but no more accurate, that the Earth was balanced by an equal amount of land to water. Since they crossed so much water to reach a new land, explorers, unable to determine the exact measurements, routinely estimated land masses as far greater than was the case.

The Portuguese invented the technique of following favourable winds far into blue water while carefully fixing their location by latitude. As the latitude of the location they were seeking was neared, the vessel was then turned eastward until making landfall, at which time their location from the objective was determined by locating prominent points on their map. This is what Cão did on his second voyage. The shortest distance between two points for a sailing vessel is not a straight line, but rather the route of the prevailing winds.

But it was the often lethal consequences that made such excursions out of the sight of land so daring. In the event of storms there was no time to seek safe harbour. If a ship was damaged near shore, it was possible in most cases to beach the vessel and effect repairs. At the very least, the crew could escape on to land and signal to a passing ship for rescue. Similar damage far out to sea meant certain death for all on board. Morover, extended voyages without fresh supplies were proving hard on the crews, with cases of scurvy beginning to occur.

Before the explorations scurvy had not been widely experienced, though the harsh diet of the poor was so relentless that cases were not unknown on land. But now, as the ships stayed at sea for longer durations to avoid the treacherous coastal currents, the Portuguese were forced to deal with the frightening and deadly disease. Depending on the condition of the crew at sailing – and their state was often not the best – the disease first showed its effects about three months into a voyage if there had been little or no fresh produce during that time.

The disease took several forms, and it was some decades before the symptoms were recognized as representing a single illness. Sailors commonly suffered from discoloration beneath the skin, swollen legs and putrid gums. What affected the conduct of the ship was the prevailing lassitude the crewmen suffered. The slightest effort caused extreme exhaustion. Ill seamen would attempt to stand watch and die on their feet. Because the spirits of the afflicted generally remained high and their death was often quite sudden, scurvy had an especially debilitating effect on the morale of the crew. As the disease progressed to its final stages, those suffering lost their teeth, ulcers appeared throughout their body, scars reopened as if they were fresh wounds, and their bones seemed to dissolve within them.[64] As terrible as it was for the crew, scurvy could, and did, prove deadly for the ship itself. Left to run its natural course, which often could not be avoided, a ship was left without a crew to man the sails or tiller. Although the specific cure for scurvy was unknown, it was understood to occur when crews were denied fresh fruit and vegetables for an extended period. With these not available as the Portuguese pushed southward, more than one of their ships was lost with all hands, probably because of scurvy.

As Cão entered the Congo river 'there was great rejoicing . . . [when] it became known that the hostages . . . were on board his ship.'[65] The natives had doubtless been speculating as to whether the Portuguese would ever return with their country-men. Once on board, they expressed their pleasure at seeing the hostages so well treated. As commanded by the king, Cão released one of the four at once to carry a message inland. When his men were returned to him he would release the other three, as happened within days. Cão also said that his ships would continue on south, but would soon return, by which time the Portuguese would have other matters to discuss with the king and also more gifts besides the horses to present.

Cão was under orders not to waste time and to pursue the passage to India if at all possible. He sailed his vessel out to sea and once again turned south. Along the way he landed from time to time and seized more locals, on the standing order of the king that whenever a native was found who spoke an unknown language he was to be taken.

One hundred and twenty-five miles south of his previous pillar Cão erected another, then continued on. The forest was now interspersed with sandy hills and barren land, occasionally broken by a river or stream flanked by green vegetation. More hospitable than the tropics, it was reminiscent of the desert region in north-west Africa and an indication that the climate would improve as the Portuguese continued their course down the coast.

The coastline continued, however, to head stubbornly south and the ship was forced to make its way against the strong Benguela current. So slow was their progress that it became increasingly clear that the way to India was not to be discovered on this voyage. With supplies running low and fewer places at which to replenish the water supply, Cão was forced to accept the inevitable. At Cape Cross, near Walvis Bay in modern Namibia, on a red sandstone point, unknowingly still some 1,000 miles from the tip of Africa, he went ashore and erected his final pillar.[66] It was a moment of both pride and profound disappointment for the young man, so recently ennobled.

Back at the Congo river, he sailed up to Ielala Falls, the furthest point his ship could navigate. He led a party of men and, bearing special gifts, set out to complete the second portion of his mission. His meetings with the king were cordial, with Mani

Congo indicating his desire to be baptized a Christian and to be allied with the king of Portugal.

Things could not have gone better. The king selected one of the earlier hostages to serve as ambassador to Portugal and requested missionaries to instruct his people, masons and carpenters to build churches and houses, and other craftsmen to teach farming and the other necessary skills to improve the lot of his people. He pronounced, 'The kingdom of the Congo shall be like Portugal in Africa.' Along with the new ambassador, Mani Congo sent the sons of prominent families to become Christians and to learn Portuguese, each of them bearing gifts of ivory and palm cloth. The unsuccessful attempt to establish this kingdom as a new Portugal diverted valuable resources and attention for the next few years.

The expedition returned to Portugal in 1486 or early 1487, after a voyage variously estimated to have lasted between twelve and nineteen months. Somewhere between his meeting with Mani Congo and here Cão is lost to history. According to one account, the captain lost many men 'from the heat', which can be taken to also include fever from tropical disease. Indeed, if Cão did perish on the trip itself, it was probably from disease, as there is no record of hostilities. One account, however, states that he lived long enough to reach Lisbon, but died soon after.

Although the most prized goal of his expedition had eluded him, Cão had still accomplished the remarkable. He had made a good beginning towards establishing favourable relations with a major kingdom in central Africa, and had increased the point of the known world and the route to India by some 1,500 miles. Yet he was apparently discouraged because he had failed to fulfil the most important part of his mission.

It was beginning to seem that the African coastline stretched to infinity. King John, however, was undeterred. He had received information from a mission to the kingdom of Benin which suggested that the land of Prester John was closer than expected, and so the tip of Africa could not lie much further south than Cão's final pillar.[67] Inaccurate though it was, this belief spurred him to action.

One of the conclusions drawn from Cão's successful voyages was that a single vessel, or even two, could not possibly carry the supplies required for the passage to India. Opportunities in southern Africa for resupply were too limited, and the length of the voyage meant a vast quantity of staples had to be taken from the start. Future expeditions would require a small fleet.

7

'. . . To the place where the sun rises'

There was a postscript to the king's meeting with Christopher Columbus, who by this time was languishing in Spain. In 1486 John II was approached by a Portuguese captain, Fernão Dulmo (or van Olm), one of the Flemings who had settled in the Azores, with a plan to sail directly west to discover new lands, in particular the 'island of the Seven Cities' of Portuguese legend. He would outfit himself at his own cost, asking only for suitable 'titles of honour' if successful. This was promised and Dulmo, joined by another captain, set sail in March 1487 with two ships.[68]

As with so many others nothing more is known of this expedition. They left from the Portuguese-held Azores, which meant they had the misfortune of sailing in the teeth of the westerlies while Columbus had the luck to leave from the Spanish-held Canary Islands and benefited from favourable winds.[69] There are suggestions that the expedition returned safely, though without having discovered the American continent.

The true prize, however, lay south. Convinced that the objective was at hand, King John was eager to round Africa and open the sea route to India. He wasted no time after the return of Cão's ship in ordering an immediate resumption of the quest. Within a month he named Bartholomeu Dias de Novaes, identified as a *cavaleiro* of the king's household and superintendent of the royal warehouses, as commander of the next expedition.

There are only suggestions as to Dias's accomplishments before his selection as captain of this important expedition. He obviously enjoyed the confidence of the king as the position of superintendent carried some responsibility. It is recorded that Dias was 'patron' of a royal vessel and had already been granted an annuity of 6,000 *reis*.[70] He is believed to be the same Dias whom John II, then crown prince, had exonerated from payment of the customary royalty on ivory brought from the Guinea coast in 1478. He was also captain of one of the ships sent in 1482 with Diogo de Azambuja to the Gold Coast to build the fortress of El Mina,[71] but neither his age nor any other details of his life are known. It is occasionally asserted that he was descended from the family of João Dias, who had made a name during the time the Portuguese were rounding Cape Bojador, and of Dinis Dias, who discovered Cape Verde, but these claims have not been proved.

No original documents have survived from Dias's expedition and references are incomplete and even occasionally contradictory, but there is much of which we can be reasonably certain. Preparations for the voyage were made in detail, and it was not until ten months after the return of Cão's vessel that Dias set sail on a voyage that was to last sixteen months and seventeen days.

A great deal had been learned from the earlier expeditions and Dias benefited from recent significant advances in both navigation and shipbuilding. This voyage was to be beyond anything that had gone before. Dias was not to land regularly and risk the health and safety of his crew by exposure to hostile locals or tropical disease. Opportunities to obtain fresh supplies would accordingly be limited and so a ship specifically designated to carry provisions was made ready and provisioned. Included with the supplies were three pillars. By this time the techniques for maintaining their ships so far from port facilities were well advanced, and Dias's fleet carried with it ample supplies of spare sail, spars and rigging as well as crews skilled in servicing and repairing the hull.

The chief pilot was Pero d'Alenquer, who was exceptionally close to the king. Although a commoner, he had been given permission to wear garments made of silk, along with the gold neck chain that bore the whistle of his office. So close was d'Alenquer to the king that he could comfortably disagree with him in public. It is recounted that at a dinner with King John and his courtiers, some from other countries, the discussion turned to the merits of the traditional square-sailed vessel, as compared to the modern caravel. The king voiced the opinion that the square-sailed ships could not successfully navigate the far coasts of Africa. D'Alenquer took strong exception and boasted that he could take such a voyage in any kind of vessel, regardless of the size or type of sails. The king pointed out that he and his predecessors had ordered such ships repeatedly to the south and they had all failed, whereupon d'Alenquer insisted he would have been successful had he been given such orders. The discussion became so heated that the king stalked angrily out of the room, shouting to the others, 'There is nothing that a common fool does not think he can do, but when it comes to the crunch he does nothing.'

Later the king met with d'Alenquer in private and explained that he had been seeking to withhold secret information about what could and could not be accomplished with which kind of ship. Few other than the Portuguese had the caravel, but many nations possessed square-rigged vessels and he did not wish it to be known they were capable of such voyages.[72] He had acted aggressively and surreptitiously to stop incursions by Spanish ships and others from trading in Guinea. He had been spreading the rumour that square-sailed, round-hulled ships were not capable of the return voyage from west Africa. His pilot had been putting those efforts at deception at risk.

In furtherance of this ploy the king conspicuously sent ageing Dutch vessels carrying provisions, lime and tiles down the coast of Africa. Once the ships arrived, the crews secretly broke them up so there was no possibility of them ever being seen again, which would give weight to the myth he was creating. The crews were sworn to secrecy and when some were caught attempting to travel to Spain to sell the secret, they were killed on his orders.[73]

Dias was given instructions 'to sail southwards and on to the place where the sun rises, and to continue as long as it was possible to do so'.[74] He was under strict orders to avoid conflict with locals and, whenever possible, to gain their confidence with gifts. He was to command a caravel of just 50 tons, which was matched by another such caravel under the command of João Infante, a knight who had been with Cão. The supply ship was of traditional design and was captained by Dias's brother Pero, who had also been with Cão. Others from Cão's voyage were among the crew, including Alvaro Martins, an experienced pilot. Barros reports that each of the men was an expert in his field. Given the adventure about to unfold, the small caravels were of such modest size that, despite their excellent sailing characteristics, their eventual success was all but impossible. The crew lived and slept above deck, constantly exposed to the elements for a voyage that would last well over a year.

Captives taken previously were again put to use, albeit in a modified role. The two male blacks seized by Cão were on board, as were four females kidnapped at an earlier, unknown time. The women were to be set ashore splendidly dressed in the European style and bearing gifts including samples of gold, silver and various desired spices, which the Portuguese were seeking in trade. They were to proclaim the greatness of the king of Portugal and his desire to communicate with Prester John. It was believed they would be respected, even if a tribal war was raging.[75] It was hoped that word would spread to the elusive monarch, who would then make an attempt to contact the Portuguese king or, at the least, anticipate favourable contact by a Portuguese expedition. As the women were not originally from the regions where they were to be abandoned, it was believed they would return to the coast, where Dias would retrieve them on his return leg.[76]

Dias's three ships sailed in August 1487 and called first at the fortress at El Mina for water and fresh provisions, then journeyed on to the site of modern-day Port Alexander, remaining well to sea to avoid the unhealthy shoreline. There Dias restored to their friends two natives whom Cão had seized. It is believed that he also left his supply ship here, for this was a safe anchorage with plentiful fish. Also relations with the locals were initially good and they had herds of both cattle and sheep for which the Portuguese could trade.

Dias pressed on, landing at the location of Cão's final pillar in modern-day Namibia. Here he placed ashore at least one of the women, then at Cabo da Volta, south of the Orange river, he erected a pillar and released a second woman, whom he turned over to native fishermen. It was a desolate coastline and the wind from the interior was so hot that Dias named this uninviting area 'Hell'. Faced with difficult winds and uncertain, generally contrary, currents at sea, Dias nevertheless resumed his passage along the south-western coast of Africa. The waters of the Atlantic had turned increasingly cold as he made his way south, and the weather was becoming disturbing even to experienced seamen.

Now at latitude 29° south Dias was faced with extremely severe weather. He made harbour to wait out a raging storm, but as the days passed he feared his ships would be beached and damaged beyond repair, so he daringly decided to put to sea and ride it out. He reportedly made several attempts to sail into the wind and was blown back more than once, but finally his two small caravels reached open water and began making their way southward into the violent storm.

This was a very dangerous manoeuvre but a certain sign of the confidence the Portuguese placed in their ships and sailing ability away from land. Barros records that the ships sailed for thirteen days 'with sails at half-mast. The boats were small and seas were getting colder, not at all like the Gulf of Guinea. The seas around the Spanish coast were very rough in stormy weather but these were fatal.' As the ships reached the 'Roaring 40s' they entered extremely treacherous sailing conditions and his crew was in 'mortal fear'. The average temperature here is 50° Fahrenheit or less and would have been very hard on the exposed Portuguese crew, accustomed to warmer climes.[77]

At last the storm mercifully passed and Dias found himself in new waters, unlike any he had previously seen or that had been described. He headed first to the east for several days, sailing with difficulty directly against the prevailing south-easterly winds, seeking the inevitable African coast, but he found nothing except open and heavy seas. The currents were different here and the ocean nothing like it had been, even when standing well out as he had passed the continent of Africa to his east.

Suspecting the truth, almost afraid to hope he was correct, Dias ordered the two ships to turn north. If he was right, they had already passed the tip of Africa.

The two caravels sailed north nearly 500 miles, then on 3 February 1488 spotted the tops of mountains on the horizon and soon entered what is today Mossel Bay. Dias was now 100 miles *east* of the southernmost point of Africa. He surely felt that the expedition had done what it had set out to do, but he needed to make absolutely certain. And if it was true that he and his crew had finally doubled Africa, then the way to India, albeit at an unknown distance, lay before him. The excitement and drama aboard the two ships were overwhelming.

The land around the bay was pleasant green pasture, and from the ships the Portuguese spotted herdsmen quietly tending many cattle. Once ashore, they learned the men spoke no language that any of the interpreters understood. They were also suspicious of these newcomers and refused the trinkets offered as presents.

Dias himself landed with his crew to take on fresh water but as he did so the locals shouted at his men in an attempt to drive them away and even pelted Dias with stones, showing no fear of the armed Europeans. Attempts to hold the locals at bay with demonstrations and threats of violence were not successful. They clearly had no idea what a crossbow was, as one of the locals was killed with a bolt by Dias himself when he approached aggressively, despite repeated warnings. The others quickly drove their herds inland and out of sight.

Once they were resupplied, Dias gave order to continue following the coastline east, though the sailing was very difficult as it went against both the current and winds. Along the coast, the land continued angling ever northward, adding to the certainty of what they had accomplished. After several days the two ships arrived at Algoa Bay, the modern site of Port Elizabeth. Here Dias left the last of his black women, the other having died on board, placing her in the company of two women gathering sea shells. In the vast bay on an island the Portuguese erected a wooden cross. There is no record of any of the black Africans released by Dias ever being seen or heard of again.[78]

Dias sailed on, with his crew muttering and in despair over the extreme distance they had already come. It had been necessary to leave a large part of their provisions in the supply vessel when the two small caravels had taken to the open sea.[79] Barros records that the men were

> very tired and still suffering from the effects of the tempestuous seas they had sailed through. They began to complain and asked not to continue, saying that provisions were running out and that they should return to the supply ship and that the further they went on, the greater would be the distance to sail back to the extra supplies and that they would all die of hunger.

The vessels then reached a point where the coastline made a decided turn more distinctly to the north. Dias had been instructed to consult with his officers on all important matters and so he summoned them and some of the senior seamen for a meeting ashore. He pressed his reasons for continuing to follow the coast and sail on, perhaps even to India itself, the distance to which was unknown. They had two sound ships and the means for maintenance and repair, so there was no practical reason not to continue. The mythical land could be just beyond the horizon. His officers, however, did not agree. They voted in favour of returning.

This placed Dias in an impossible situation for someone not wanting to abandon the passage to India. As an experienced captain he also knew how the story might change later in the comfort of their native land and so required each of the men to sign a document under oath, stating their decision to return.

Then Dias resumed his argument in favour of continuing, pointing out no doubt the vast rewards each would receive if they returned with spice from India itself. To acquire spices they would not even have to reach the fabled land but merely one of its trading ports. A great deal of very valuable information could be gathered as well, for which the king would be very grateful. His arguments were to no avail. The best he could manage was an agreement to sail on for another two or three days and then, unless something was discovered during that time to change their minds, the expedition would return to Portugal.

The two small ships resumed sailing and on the third day reached the vicinity of the Great Fish river, some 25 leagues east of Algoa Bay. The waters were warmer now and a steady current flowed northward. There could be no doubt but that Africa had been rounded and here Dias erected a pillar. In his mind's eye, we are told, Dias could see the distant 'land of India, but, like Moses and the promised land, he did not enter it'.[80]

They returned to Cross Island in Algoa Bay, as they had named it, where Barros records that Dias was filled with sorrow and

> remembered the dangers they had all faced and how far they had come to achieve nothing more because God had not granted the main thing. When they left that place they saw the great and noble cape which had stood there for so many years and it seemed to promise a new world of lands.★ Bartolomeu Dias and his men named it Cape of Storms [*Cabo Tormentoso*] because of the dangers and storms they had suffered on rounding it. However, when they returned to the kingdom, King John gave it another name. He called it the Cape of Good Hope [*Cabo da Boa Esperança*] because it promised the long awaited discovery of India.

This last may come from myth-making, for at least one source records that Dias himself named the tip of Africa the Cape of Good Hope.

At the cape itself Dias erected his last pillar. As he sailed passed it, we are told, he stood at the rail of his battered caravel and 'took leave of it as from a beloved son whom he never expected to see again'. His sense of the moment proved true, for twelve

---

★ Table Mountain was always impressive. Sir Francis Drake wrote, 'this cape is a most stately thing, and the fairest Cape we sawe in the whole circumference of the earth.' Drake's pilot was Portuguese.

years later he drowned at sea, along with his brother, almost within sight of this pillar.[81]

Dias knew that a defining moment in the history of his nation and in his own life had been reached. It was seventy-three years since the conquest of Ceuta when at last the Portuguese doubled Africa. The riches of India, and the power that came with them, were finally within reach.

Nine months after leaving it, Dias and his men rejoined their supply ship. Six of the nine men he had left with it had been killed in trade disputes with the locals. A seventh, who had apparently given the rest up for dead and was extremely weak from illness, reportedly died from joy at seeing Dias and his shipmates. Not surprisingly, the ship was worm-eaten and unfit for the return voyage. The remaining stores were transferred and the ship burnt, as had long been the custom, to recover nails and other metal fittings.

The rest of the return voyage is known only in fragmentary form. Dias is known to have taken aboard the survivors of a shipwreck and to have landed in west Africa at the Rio do Resgate long enough to buy slaves, 'so as not to come home empty-handed'. The governor of the fortress at El Mina apparently turned over to him for delivery to the king the gold he had obtained through trade.[82]

In December 1488 Dias entered the Tagus river after a voyage of sixteen and a half months. Steady attrition had taken a relentless toll on the crew, who were now largely broken in health. When Dias made his report to John II, he expressed his bitter disappointed for not having information concerning either Prester John or India, reporting that the people he had encountered 'along the coast were almost all savages'. Dias presented to the king a detailed colour map of the new region he had penetrated. King John directed that an official map be prepared to include this new information. Inscribed on the chart were the words, 'This is the true shape of modern Africa, according to the description of the Portuguese.'[83]

Interestingly, Christopher Columbus was present when Dias made his report to the king. Columbus had been languishing in Spain, awaiting an audience with the king and queen. Having made no more progress there than he had in Portugal, he wrote to John II in 1488 requesting permission to explain once again his proposed venture. The king granted his request, and so Columbus was in Lisbon when Dias returned. He was allowed to hear his presentation to the king and his advisers, especially as Dias and Columbus had known one another for some years.

Columbus was so impressed with what he heard that he recorded an extended marginal note of the voyage on his personal copy of the *Imago Mundi*, the map created in 1410 by the French cardinal Pierre d'Ailly that was responsible for a measure of Columbus's confusion about the distance from Europe to Asia sailing west. The work presented an Earth much smaller than it actually is. Since Dias now reported doubling Africa, King John had no need to try to reach India by another route and lost whatever interest he had had in Columbus's enterprise. Columbus soon left Portugal, filled with a fresh sense of urgency to find the way to India by sailing directly west.

Dias had discovered 1,260 miles of new coastline and sailed farther than any European heretofore, yet there is no record of the rewards he received, if any. Given the practice begun by Henry, it is difficult to believe there were none, and Dias certainly continued to enjoy the king's favour. He commanded the royal ship *Sao Christovão* from 1490 until 1495, was Grand Captain of the port of Lisbon for a time and still later was commander of El Mina. He also served a pivotal role in preparations for the voyage of Vasco da Gama.

With Dias's return to Lisbon the way to India finally lay conclusively before the Portuguese, yet, for reasons never entirely explained, King John hesitated. At least two more significant events were to take place before the final push and fulfilment of the quest.

One of those was the arrival of Christopher Columbus in Lisbon that stormy March 1493, just over four years later. If John II had seriously considered that Columbus's new lands might be Portuguese, as he said, might not the Spanish monarchs just as well argue that any new Portuguese discoveries were theirs? Almost immediately King John entered into negotiations with the king and queen of Spain.

The predicament existed because the world was round. Asia could be reached both by sailing east and by sailing west – in theory. While King John's junta was confident that Columbus was mistaken as to the true size of the Earth, it was possible that he had found islands and lands that could provide reprovisioning as the Spanish continued their probing towards Asia by going west. The situation was aggravated by a letter from Ferdinand and Isabella to Pope Alexander VI after Columbus's return, asking that 'all discovered and to be discovered lands should be theirs'.[84] Alexander VI was no impartial arbiter. He had been born Rodrigo Borgia – of the notorious family – near Valencia and held long-standing ties to the Spanish monarchs.

At the same time as dispatching emissaries for negotiations John II ordered a fleet to be gathered to seize by force the new Spanish discoveries in the Americas. Eager to avoid war, in June 1494, at the Spanish village of Tordesillas, the Portuguese and Spanish sovereigns entered into a treaty intended to divide the new lands being discovered and yet to be found. An earlier treaty was confirmed, affirming that Granada and the Canary Islands were both Spanish and that John II was king of the Algarve and of his possessions in Africa. The new treaty established a line separating the areas of discovery into two parts. Set at 370 leagues★ west of the Cape Verde Islands and running north to south, the lands east of it were within Portugal's sphere of influence while those to the west were Spain's. The effect of the treaty granted Spain the so-called New World, save for Brazil, while for a time safely placing Asian lands yet to be discovered in Portuguese hands. So complete was the separation and so audacious its breadth that it is said a young boy in Tordesillas coming upon the

---

★ An earlier papal bull, drafted at the direction of Spain, had set such a demarcation line at just 100 leagues west of the Cape Verde Islands. The new line allowed Portugal later to claim Brazil, allowing for speculation it had been discovered earlier.

negotiators taking a stroll stopped them at a bridge to ask, 'So you are the men who are dividing the world?'

But in sending Dias out to discover the route to India, John II had not shot his only bolt. Lack of information had increasingly been seen as the most serious obstacle the Portuguese faced now that the physical limitations were falling before them. If any Portuguese captain was to reach India and return safely, he must know his final destination and have some sense of what awaited him in this alien land. The way must also be prepared to enter into friendly relations with Prester John, for the captain and his men would be far from help and in need of an ally. To accomplish this, John II turned to the most ancient fact-finding device used by mankind: espionage.

8

The spies

At about this time two princes from Ethiopia, alternatively described by Barros as friars, arrived in Portugal and met with an enthusiastic King John. He asked if their ruler was a king or a pope, and whether his name was Prester John. Was his land located in Asia? They told the king what he wanted to hear, since that was the surest route to a liberal reward.

Exhilarated at the prospect of actually establishing contact with Prester John, the king quickly dispatched an abbot and layman to locate Ethiopia and, if possible, India but the pair only got as far as Jerusalem. There, according to Barros, they met with Ethiopian monks on pilgrimage to the city who offered to have the pair accompany them on their return trip. It turned out that the two men were commonly known to be emissaries of the king of Portugal and they were warned by others not to attempt to journey further as they lacked a knowledge of the language and the local customs. The pair considered the wisdom of what they heard, then returned to Portugal to explain why it had not been possible to carry out the king's orders.[85]

For some time King John had been in correspondence with a Venetian merchant who executed commissions for him. The merchant provided the king with much useful information about how the spice trade was conducted close to its origin. In one letter the merchant gave a long account of India, as he understood it, though he expressed regret at not knowing the land's exact location, along with a description of how the spices were dispersed, the profits accrued and where. Although it 'incited . . . his great desire',[86] the information was not of sufficient detail and accuracy to satisfy the Portuguese king.

He deliberated the matter after the return of his first emissaries and decided to send others more suited for the mission he had in mind, men who had loyalty and most of all courage upon which he could rely. Of the two he selected, the one about whom less is known is Alfonso de Paiva, a courtier and native of Castelo Branco. It is reported that he spoke both Spanish and Arabic, and one unreliable source claims that his family came from the Canary Islands.[87] Considerably more, however, is known about Pêro de Covilhan (or Covilhão), the senior figure.

Covilhan was already in service to the king and had an impressive record of performance. He came from the mountains of Beira in north central Portugal and was a man of mature years, about forty, with a wife and children. He had lived several years in Spain and taken an active part in night fighting and skirmishes in Seville. He had distinguished himself at the Battle of Toro, in which both Alfonso V and John II had fought, and had then lived in France, where he was associated with King Louis XI. For one year he served as a Portuguese spy in the court of Ferdinand and Isabella in Spain, reporting on the activities of Portuguese expatriates, always a source of concern to any Portuguese king. He had attended Alfonso V as an esquire until his death, then entered the service of John II. He was dispatched on two diplomatic missions to north Africa, the first at Tlemcen, and is presumed to have learned Arabic at that time.[88] There he signed a peace treaty with the local king and was then commissioned by the Portuguese king's cousin and future monarch Manuel to buy woollen clothing and horses.

In Africa, Covilhan learned the customs, dress and manners of the Moors at first hand and developed extensive knowledge of Arab culture, which extended largely intact from the northwest coast of Africa to the ports of southern India and down the coast of east Africa. Covilhan was possessed of a keen mind and extraordinary memory. John II sent him next to Fez in Morocco. Time and again he had demonstrated his courage and it is unlikely that the young king could have found anyone more ideally suited to his needs. Having made the decision to send another mission east, it was necessary to summon Covilhan from Fez.

In May 1487 Covilhan and Paiva met in secret with their king and select royal advisers, experts in various fields that would be of use to the men. The Portuguese court was filled with spies from jealous European kings, and the practice of secrecy was well in place by this time. At some length John II told the men what he desired of them. They were to travel to distant lands, to see and report back on sights that until now were mostly legend. They were to continue on to India, 'to learn on the spot, whence those spices came, which the Italians imported from Egypt, and to discover whether the realm of Prester John reached the sea, as well as other facts concerning his kingdom'.[89] Once contact was made, they were to convince the Christian king to form an alliance with the king of Portugal against the infidel. Covilhan was also to investigate the spice trade thoroughly, to learn its source, the trade routes, the value of the spices in India and such details as would be of benefit to the Portuguese once the sea route was established.[90]

The king implored Covilhan and Paiva to undertake this vital mission on his behalf. It was essential for him to possess this knowledge and to secure the alliance with Prester John, if possible. Covilhan protested he was not adequate for such a task, fearing 'that his knowledge would not be as great as his desire to serve His Highness'.[91] The king discounted his concerns and proceeded to give the men more detailed instructions. Then he assured them that their wives and children would be well cared for in their absence. He promised each of them rewards 'such as would content his posterity for ever',[92] and, should they die in his service, those rewards would be given to their children and wives.[93]

Covilhan and Paiva were each handed a brass disk that looked much like a medal. Engraved on them in many languages was 'King Dom John of Portugal, brother of the Christian Monarchs'. These were to be shown to Prester John as a display of good faith. The pair were then handed 400 *cruzados*, from which they were to take as much as they needed for immediate expenses; the balance would be transported by a trusted

Florentine who represented the Medici in Portugal.★ When the men reached Italy, they would receive the balance. Knowing the dangers the two would face, they were given precious gems with which to buy their freedom should they be imprisoned. They were also provided with a letter of credit to be used 'when in peril of death, or in need of money'.[94]

Following their private audience with the king, Covilhan and Paiva met alone with the group of select advisers and were given a number of aids for their expedition. These included a navigation chart, extracts from the writings of Marco Polo and John Mandeville, whose outrageous writings still held sway, as well as those from Plano di Carpini and Rubruquis. The bishop of Viseu, who was in attendance, presented the men with a copy of Fra Mauro's map that he had prepared personally. Depicted on it were Egypt, Arabia and Ethiopia. They were to verify its presentation, making notations and corrections as their experiences would indicate.[95]

Finally Covilhan and Paiva received the blessing of the king 'and that of God' and departed on their hazardous mission on 7 May 1487, some three months before Bartolomeu Dias set sail. From that point on all dates can only be estimated.

The pair travelled overland to Barcelona and from there by ship to Italy. Following a short stay they sailed from Naples to the isle of Rhodes, which was under the dominion of the Knights Hospitallers, and there contacted two Portuguese knights who were members of the order. This was the last Christian outpost on their journey, the final point at which they could be certain of a friendly reception and unconditioned assistance. The two knights were intimate with affairs in the eastern

---

★ Although ostensibly rivals, since it was the Italian monopoly in the spice trade the Portuguese were seeking to destroy, the Portuguese actually maintained an active trade and friendly relations with certain trading and banking families in Italy. The Florentines had the best representation in Portugal. Their business relations increased significantly after 1494, when their merchant fleet was destroyed by the Pisans. Trade goods from Italy included fine woollen cloth, leather goods and silk. In exchange the Portuguese provided preserved fish and imports from Africa, including ivory and cork.

Mediterranean and the Middle East, and provided reliable information and advice.

Covilhan and Paiva were advised that it was unwise to proceed further identifying themselves as representatives of the king of Portugal. The Italian cities held a virtual monopoly on trade with the Muslims and were hostile towards any Europeans who entered their region of prominence. It was well known that the Portuguese were attempting to cut them out of their lucrative livelihood by doubling Africa. Any Portuguese would be suspect as agents whose efforts would work against the Italians' interests, and messengers known to come from John II would be assassinated if uncovered.

In addition, the Middle East was under the control of the Muslims, who also profited greatly from the spice trade. They wanted no changes in what had been for centuries a rewarding arrangement with the Italians. The pair would be greeted with suspicion and hostility at every turn. The knights advised that from here on Covilhan and Paiva must travel as merchants and mask their point of origin, both for their own safety and in order to increase the probability of success. The pair procured honey stored in large jars to sell in Egypt, where they could expect a profit. They also obtained new garments consistent with their role as journeymen merchants. They then set sail for Alexandria. There is no record of what national identity they assumed, but it was certainly not Portuguese.

With the fall of Constantinople to the Muslims in 1453, the Genoese Black Sea trading colonies had collapsed and their traders had largely relocated to Alexandria, which was now more prosperous than at any point in its rich history. As the focal point for trade from Asia, India and Africa, quantities of silk and spice, printed cotton and skins, as well as ivory and, of course, slaves passed through Alexandria to Europe, all of it lucratively taxed. Every luxury, and every vice known to man, was for sale in Alexandria. The city had long since outgrown its ancient boundaries as well as the Roman drainage and water systems. By the fifteenth century the port was known for its decidedly unhealthy climate and, once there, both Covilhan and Paiva fell so gravely ill that the town's acting governor assumed they would die and commandeered their supply of honey.

The Mameluke sultans of Egypt may have profited from Christian traders, but Muslims did no more than tolerate them. For purposes of control and to avoid unnecessary contact with them, Europeans were required to live in distinct walled settlements called *fonducs*. These were in place for every significant group of Europeans engaged in trade in Alexandria. Within these enclaves each group managed its own affairs and at night the gates into this artificial world of the *fonducs* were sealed.[96]

The European Christians were permitted to remain in Alexandria only during the time when spice arrived from Asia, but within these enclaves for that period of time they were protected from harassment and arrest by Egyptians authorities, although in the course of their trade they were subjected to every possible insult and humiliation. Christians were for instance required to wear a 5 pound wooden cross on a chain about their necks. Their trade goods were taken for counting and examination, then a tax of 2% was levied on them, and another tax of 1 ducat per person was required as well. Finally the Europeans were literally stripped to the skin and searched, to be certain they had with them nothing that had not been declared and taxed.

After recovering their health neither Covilhan or Paiva drew particular attention except from the certainly disappointed official who had profited from their meagre merchandise. The honey was long gone but after negotiations the men were paid a portion of its value, which they promptly reinvested in other trade goods. The men were taken for what they presented themselves to be, the most modest of traders and therefore undeserving of concern. Had any of the Europeans or Muslims in Egypt understood they were there to gather intelligence for the Portuguese king, to learn the secrets of their mutually prosperous trade in preparation for its ruin, the men would have been dead within moments.

The agents did not move into one of the *fonducs*, where they might be uncovered, but instead travelled on to Cairo by boat.

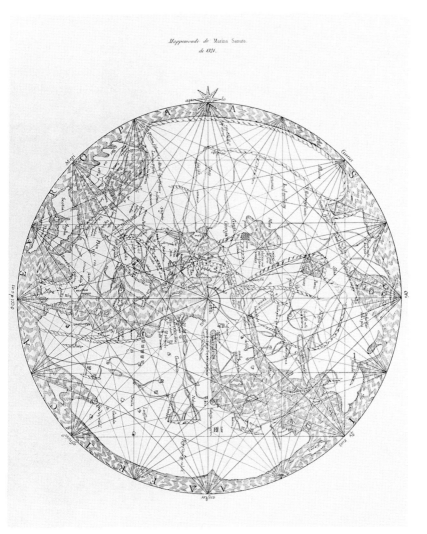

The world as known by Prince Henry the Navigator when he launched the voyages of discovery in the early fifteenth century. This version suggests that Africa might actually be doubled by sea. Others indicate this was not possible

Vasco da Gama would have carried this map with him on the first voyage to India in 1497. It reflects what Bartholomeu Dias had learned upon doubling Africa, but India remained a mystery

Less than 100 years after the voyages of discovery began this was the known face of the world. This map dates from the early sixteenth century and depicts the land discovered by Portuguese mariners

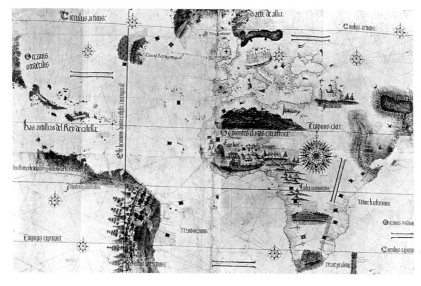

Right: King John I's marriage to the daughter of the Englishman John of Gaunt produced what has been called 'The Noble Generation', those who promoted the 'Discoveries'

Below right: Philippa, daughter of John of Gaunt, married the Portuguese king. She is believed to have been dominant in foreign affairs and made the Portuguese court the most sought-after in Europe

LIS

Left: Prince Henry the Navigator is credited with launching the Portuguese voyages of discovery. He was motivated in part by a desire to outflank the Muslims blocking direct trade with India, but also by the wish to convert pagans to the True Faith. He is shown here with his nephew the future King Alfonso

Above: Lisbon at the time of the 'Discoveries': the harbour often held hundreds of ships from throughout Europe

Right: A reconstruction of Lisbon at the time of the 'Discoveries'. Before the rebuilding of the city's centre in the eighteenth century, the Portuguese capital was more Moorish than European in flavour

Above: The Casa da India was constructed along the Lisbon waterfront to facilitate the offloading of spices. Ships were serviced there as well. The city port was the busiest and most prosperous in Europe

The 'Discoveries' are very much part of contemporary Portuguese life. Reliefs such as this, depicting the surrender of Lisbon by the Moors, are commonplace

Vasco da Gama, from a sixteenth-century manuscript

Vasco da Gama was born and lived as a child in these quarters within the fort at Sines. His father was the town's *alcaide-mór*

This was a much more impressive city than Alexandria, with broad boulevards criss-crossed by narrow, meandering streets. At night, for safety's sake, wooden barriers were erected, closing off the narrow lanes.

Cairo was a vibrant city and the true centre of the spice trade in Egypt. Along ancient streets could be breathed the fragrance of centuries-old spices. The bazaars overflowed with commodities of every imaginable sort. Here the foreign merchants were fellow Muslims but they were trusted no more than the Europeans in Alexandria. Turks, Yemenis, Indians, Persians and Syrians were all required to live within their own designated *fonducs*. Some 10,000 Jews and another 10,000 Coptic Christians were also tolerated within Cairo,[97] along with colonies of Greeks, Italians and Ethiopians. On the busy streets could be seen Nubians and Hindus, trains of slaves and oiled eunuchs.

Even then it was customary for travellers to visit the nearby pyramids and to view the ancient Sphinx as well as the walled garden of Cairo with its forest of balsam trees. The two Portuguese spies presumably did all this, if not for the sake of curiosity then to divert any suspicion. They made friendships among the traders and gathered information in the process. There were countless opportunities for them to collect the kind of intelligence for which they had been sent. It could be argued that simply by remaining in Cairo they might well have gathered sufficient intelligence, but they were under orders to do much more. They had been sent to see for themselves, to learn at first hand.

In Cairo, Covilhan and Paiva discussed how best to proceed. One group of merchants they had befriended were preparing to travel to India. This was too fortuitous an opportunity to let pass, so the pair made the decision to join them. They would have the advantage of travelling with established traders and would learn much by observing and asking such innocent questions as would be expected from any new merchant from Europe. In the spring of 1488 they set out with their caravan, heading first to Aden on the south-west tip of Arabia at the mouth of the Red Sea. From there, they were told, passage to India was easily acquired.

The caravan crawled its way across the desert sands of Suez. They camped at the Well of Moses, within sight of Mount Sinai, and finally arrived at the port of Tor, hardly more than a cluster of hot brick huts. There the men boarded a ship called a *djelba*, made of rough planks bound together with cords of coconut fibre, the sails nothing more than woven grass mats. The ship wallowed in even a mild sea, took on water at an alarming rate and was scarcely seaworthy. They sailed only during daylight, as the vessel was so difficult to steer that otherwise there was a risk of striking rocks. The coastline was uninhabited, except by robbers looking to prey on such ships, so at night it was necessary to seek hidden shelter and establish a guard. It was a time-consuming, perilous voyage, the heat so great it could 'melt a man'.[98]

At Djidda the two spies changed to a ship of superior construction but continued to suffer the oppressive heat. They finally arrived at Aden two months after leaving Cairo. At this time of year the slave sales here were held at night because of the searing sun. Aden, situated near the Arabian Sea, was the gateway to India and Asia. For hundreds of years merchants from India had brought trade goods here, where they were then exchanged with goods from Arabs for subsequent sale in Europe. It was a major portal for the spice trade and had profited enormously over the centuries. Portugal's first emissary to China, Tomé Pires, wrote of it in 1515:

> This city . . . is one of the four great trading cities in the world. It trades cloth to Dahlak and receives seed pearls in exchange; it trades coarse cloths and various trifling things to Zeila and Berbera in exchange for gold, horses, slaves and ivory, it trades Sokotra, sending cloth, straw of Mecca, Socotrine aloes and dragon's-blood, it trades with Ormuz, whence it brings horses, and out of the goods from Cairo it trades gold, foodstuffs, wheat and rice if there is any, spices, seed pearls, musk, silk and any other drugs: it trades with Cambay, taking there the merchandise from Cairo and opium, and returning large quantities of cloth, with which

it trades in Arabia and the Islands, seeds, glass beads, beads from Cambay, many carnelians of all colours, and chiefly spices and drugs from Malacca, cloves, nutmeg, mace, sandalwood, cubebs, seed pearls and things of that sort . . . And in this way it had become great, prosperous and rich. The merchandise of Aden consists of horses, madder, rosewater, dried roses, raisins, opium . . . It is a thing worth seeing . . . although its drinking water has to be brought in a cart.[99]

Again Covilhan and Paiva were able to gather useful information. They learned that in the region somewhere south of Egypt was a Christian king who ruled over a vast land and numerous lesser kings. 'This must surely be Prester John', the men whispered. 'Have we not been told that he is the Emperor of Ethiopia, that he is a Christian ruling over Christians?'[100] But the information was inconclusive. The king's name was not John, they were told, and he was not a priest. Although speculative reports and legend concerning the location of Prester John's kingdom had evolved over the decades, they remained imprecise. The kingdom was reported to be in Asia, then in Africa but also in India. Covilhan and Paiva would have to decide for themselves if the ruler of Ethiopia was the Christian ally they were instructed to seek out.

If they were to fulfil their two-pronged mission, it was obvious that at this juncture they must go their separate ways. They decided that Paiva was to travel to Ethiopia, determine if it was ruled by Prester John, make the appropriate contact and then return to Thebes, near Cairo, where, at a designated date, Covilhan would rejoin him. Covilhan himself would continue on to India to learn all he could about the spice trade, its trade routes and the political situation. The men bade one another farewell in Aden and at this point Paiva disappears from history.[101]

As both the ancient Egyptians and Romans discovered, sailing in the Arabian Sea to and from India is governed by the prevailing monsoon. Being tropical in nature, the monsoon is free from mist, drifting ice and fog. Both the Atlantic and Pacific oceans are open to both poles, and this influences winds and currents, but the Indian Ocean is open only to the south and is bordered by land on three sides, giving its forces a specific and predictable pattern. In general, it lacks the strong currents of the Atlantic, such as the Gulf Stream and its equivalent in the Pacific.

There are also, and most importantly, two monsoons. One, known as the winter monsoon, is dry and blows from India towards east Africa from October to April. The other, the summer monsoon, is wet and blows in the opposite direction from June to September. The two monsoons are not equal in effect and sailors at this time relied primarily on the winter one for navigation.

The Indian Ocean was perhaps the kindest of all seas to sailors, so that even ships of fragile design could safely navigate its waters. Perhaps the greatest threat to mariners were the worms that flourished in its warm waters and relentlessly consumed all hulls except those made of teak, which was known as 'stinking wood'. Oak, from which the Portuguese ships were constructed, was especially succulent to the worms, who quickly turned their hulls into a sieve.

Although the monsoons made the open ocean passage safe and reasonably swift, to sail against the seasonal winds was to risk death. The monsoons also meant long waits on each side of the ocean, which explains the extended length of trade voyages, but the passages were safe and reasonably swift once undertaken.

Some time in August, Covilhan bought passage aboard an Arab vessel bearing horses to India. As most of India was unsuitable for breeding and raising horses, Arab, and later European, horses were much sought after by the nobility for their personal use, but also to employ in their armies. The climate and ceaseless warfare exacted a relentless toll on the steeds, creating an all but insatiable demand for them since replacements could only be had by importation.

The vessel on which Covilhan sailed was a fairly large ship of some 250 tons, though constructed also of crude planks sewn together with fibre. The sails, however, were an improvement, being made of cotton. There was no deck, and the cargo was covered with heavy mats to protect it from the weather while passengers and crew fended for themselves. It was one of hundreds making the annual voyage to south-west India, a veritable fleet of Muslim ships.

It was a long, monotonous month sailing from Aden to the Malabar coast of south-west India. It was hot and humid at sea, the food was often vile, the water foul. At last the crew and passengers let out a cry on sighting Mount Dely, near Cannanore, known for its ginger, where they made landfall. Here Covilhan stepped from the ship on to shore, reportedly 'the first Portuguese [who] trod the soil of India'.[102]

Cannanore was a port of entry for the Hindu kingdom of Vijayanagar, known to the Portuguese as Bisnaga, which comprised the southern tip of the Indian subcontinent, then at the height of its influence and power. From here he made the short journey southward to Calicut,★ which was to India what Alexandria was to Egypt.

Covilhan was now at the epicentre of the world spice trade, in the legendary land of India. More than a thousand ships from every part of Asia stood at anchor off its shore. Among them were the massive Chinese junks with their cargoes of silk, tea, tin and porcelain. One visitor to Calicut at about this time wrote of it:

> Safety and justice reign here! The foreign merchants leave their merchandise in the open market, without even taking the precaution to declare its value, because the customs officials are responsible for its safety. If the goods are sold, they take one-quarter on the transaction; if not sold, then the owner has nothing to pay.[103]

As the trade was controlled by Arabs, who had a large colony, Covilhan was in some respects on familiar territory, but the

---

★ Not to be confused with Calcutta, a city established much later by the British in north-east India in the delta of the Ganges river.

remainder of the city was as exotic and unfamiliar as any place on Earth could possibly have been to a European. Many questions, long unanswered, were finally resolved during his stay here. The origin of individual spices was a key bit of intelligence Covilhan was to learn, as it would tell the Portuguese where to go once they reached the oceans of India and greater Asia.

Through careful conversation and unassuming questions the spy slowly gathered, and recorded, an accurate picture of trade routes and the spice trade. Pepper, indigo, ginger and spikenard, he learned, grew here on the Malabar coast. Cinnamon was imported from Ceylon, not far distant on the other side of India. Cloves, mace, camphor, nutmeg and also pepper came from the Spice Islands, named the Moluccas, and also from Sumatra, Borneo and Java. Musk, rhubarb, aloes and camphor originated in distant China.[104] The trade was vast and complex, probably far in excess of anything he or any Portuguese had ever imagined. India was clearly just one piece of the puzzle and would surely be only a jumping-off point once the Portuguese arrived by sea.

Henry H. Hart, in his distinguished work *Sea Road to the Indies*, writes of Calicut:

> The Hindu city [was] a strange mixture of barbarism and civilization, simplicity and opulence. The dress of the Samorin [the ruler of Calicut] was a perfect example. Naked from the waist up, and barefoot, he wore garments of cloth of gold, and on his fingers were heavy gold rings set with rubies. Surrounded by bodyguards, he reclined on a couch of gold and silver. The perfumed women – always near him – were almost naked. In the streets swarmed an unbelievable crowd of low- and high-caste Hindus, elephants, horses and litters. Coconut palms grew thickly everywhere; temples and the houses of the rich rubbed elbows with the miserable palm-leaf huts of the poor. In tiny open shops half-naked men trafficked in diamonds, sapphires and rubies from Ceylon and Burma, or weighed pearls in tiny scales – and drove sharp bargains in loud

voices. Down on the shore were Arab ships, whose sailors swaggered through the town, seeking to make the most of their shore leave, and about them clustered women, eager to relieve them of their hard-earned wages. Rice was being unloaded from the Coromandel Coast and cinnamon from Ceylon. Boats were in from Malacca, bearing camphor from Borneo and Formosa, lac from Pegu, nutmegs and mace from Banda, and cloves from the Moluccas. Bags of pepper, product of Calicut itself, were heaped high in the warehouses or were being loaded onto the ships of Mecca. And over all the heavy air was filled with the odours of sandalwood and palm oil, cooking and temple incense, the flower of the areca, and the spices lying in the hot sun.

Covilhan also learned the source of gems, including diamonds and pearls. Gold, he noted, was so abundant that it was not accepted in payment; merchants preferred to barter. He found Nestorian Christians, who called themselves Thomas Christians, after the Apostle Thomas.[105] Their rite was strange, as were some of their beliefs, but they were Christians none the less. He inquired after Prester John and was told by these Indian Christians that such a personage had once existed but that his kingdom now lay in ruins. No one spoke of him any longer.

Covilhan had just a few short months to gather the information he needed, all the while presenting himself as a genuine merchant, for the monsoon would change direction and the fleet of ships from Aden would set sail from the coast of India at the beginning of the year. He took passage on a small coasting vessel heading north and landed at various small ports, asking questions, observing, recording what he learned. India, he noted, imported as much silver as it could get and also sought mercury, copper, coral, saffron, printed cloth, rose-water, vermilion, cutlery and some gold. To his surprise he found Europeans, mostly Italians but also Frenchmen and merchants from Bruges, as well as goods from Europe for sale. Most traders, however, were from more distant Asia.

Covilhan arrived at the port and island of Gôa, which would

in time play such a pivotal role for the Portuguese in India, and observed the city-state controlled by Muslims. It was another prosperous centre for trade from Asia, Arabia and the other Muslim states, but especially from Ormuz, situated at the entrance to the Persian Gulf. Marco Polo had written that Gôa was the centre for the Indian trade in horses and he had observed there more than a hundred fine Arab horses.

Covilhan's portion of the mission had been accomplished. In February or March 1489 he sailed to Ormuz itself, the foremost market-place for trade with Asia. His ship was filled nearly to overflowing with spices, porcelain, cotton goods, precious stones, amber and musk. The Arabs at Ormuz were extremely prosperous, and wore splendid white garments bound by golden embroidered belts. About the city was rock salt, which was traded to Ethiopia, where it was a currency, as was pepper.

Less is known about Covilhan's steps after Ormuz. He is known to have sailed along the east coast of Africa through the portion of the Arabian Sea called the Green Sea by the Arabs, where Muslim colonies engaged in a prosperous trade for gold and slaves. It is likely he visited Mombasa, Zanzibar and Sofala, the southernmost point of regular trade, situated at 20° south. Here he learned of a large island not far away, the Island of the Moon (Madagascar), where more Arabs lived and engaged in trade with India.

Covilhan noted that along this coast the locals were black, as they were in Guinea. He surmised that Africa was one land mass, stretching from Guinea to Sofala. This was an encouraging observation. If the next Portuguese expedition sailing from Lisbon could only reach as far as Sofala, it was certain from there to be able to sail to India itself.[106]

According to one account Covilhan returned to Aden, then to Tor and from there to Thebes, outside Cairo, arriving in late 1490 or early 1491. He had by now been gone from his wife and children some three years. After waiting a time he learned that his companion, Paiva, had only recently died while waiting for him. There would be no report of what he had discovered about Ethiopia.

Covilhan was in a quandary. While it was true that he had fulfilled the portion of the mission he had set out on, the instructions from his king had been twofold. He had made no contact
with Prester John, although he had acquired information that
indicated neither he nor his kingdom existed. Before deciding
how to proceed next, two Jewish messengers arrived from
Portugal. One was a rabbi named Abraham of Beja; the other,
José de Lamego, was reportedly a shoemaker. Both were widely
travelled. King John apparently knew of the date and location
for the rendezvous. Since so much time had lapsed, he had sent
these experienced travellers and trusted messengers to relay
instructions and obtain a report.

Abraham handed Covilhan a letter from the king, which
instructed him and Paiva to return at once, if they had completed
their mission in full. If that was not the case, they were to make
a full report to these men, then continue on their mission. The
letter referred explicitly to making contact with Prester John.
Having accomplished so much Covilhan was surely disappointed
at receiving these new instructions, especially as they fell to him
alone.

For some unknown reason Covilhan was also directed to
accompany the rabbi to Ormuz before continuing, while José de
Lamego was to return to Portugal at once. Covilhan gave him a
written account of his journey and of what he had learned.
Believing Dias to be still at sea, he gave a message which the king
should pass along to him. It said, 'If you keep southward, the
continent must come to an end. When your ships have reached
the Indian ocean, let your men enquire for Sofala and the Island
of the Moon. There they will find pilots who will take them to
India.'[107]

Covilhan and Abraham travelled to Ormuz and from there to
Baghdad and other places. Covilhan recorded a detailed account
of his entire journey and entrusted it to his companion. It is generally accepted, and seems perfectly logical, that with this
account he included a map of the lands he had encountered.
Finally, Rabbi Abraham returned to Portugal, bearing also the
new information that had been acquired.[108]

It is not surprising that neither of these written reports has survived and that there is no contemporaneous account of their contents. Such information would have been swallowed whole into the secret recesses of the Portuguese king's junta. It was too vital for its very existence to be known to others. Given that two written reports were made and sent by two trusted and experienced messengers, and that the journey from the Middle East was neither arduous nor dangerous, it is all but certain that at least one of them reached King John's hands. The surest evidence the information arrived is that when Vasco da Gama set sail, his specific destination was not India but the port of Calicut.

Covilhan, for his part, travelled on to Jerusalem and Mount Sinai, where he visited the tomb of Saint Catherine. He returned to Tor and from there went to Aden, Mecca and Medina. At the Strait of Bab el Mandeb at Zeila he learned of the route to Ethiopia and proceeded on it, to arrive at last in 1492 or 1493 at what was the sole candidate to be the long sought kingdom of Prester John. What Covilhan, the first European known to enter the country, saw was surely discouraging. In 1520 a group of locals greeting the new Portuguese embassy was described in this way:

> They are a poor civil people with miserable clothes, and they come into the water uncovered, a black, tall people with thick matted locks, which from their birth they neither cut nor comb, so that they wear their hair like a lump of wool, and they carry pointed oiled sticks with which they scratch the vermin which crawl beneath, because they cannot reach their scalps with their fingers, and scratching their heads is their sole occupation.

Another chronicler wrote:

> The country people . . . kept fields of Indian corn, and . . . come from a distance to sow these lands and rocky ridges which are among these mountains: there are also in these parts very beautiful flocks, such as cows and goats. The

people that we found here are almost naked, so that all they had showed, and they were very black. These people were Christians, and the women wore a little more covering, but it was very little.'[109]

The 'Lion of the Tribe of Judah, and King of Kings', Alexander, was also known as the Negus Negasti. Covilhan appeared at the emperor's court in the mountainous region about Lake Tana on the Blue Nile and presented his engraved brass disk, faithfully carried and concealed all these years. He also turned over letters from the king of Portugal, which Alexander accepted 'with much pleasure and joy'. He assured Covilhan that he would soon send him back to Portugal 'with much honour'.[110]

Alexander, however, was impressed with Covilhan and wished to keep him as a royal adviser. He offered him possessions and honours if he chose to remain. The emperor would also give Covilhan a wife to have children by 'so that when he should return to his own country, he would leave posterity in [Ethiopia], as a worthy memorial of himself'. Covilhan declined, wanting nothing more than to return to Portugal and make his report. But months passed without permission, and to attempt to leave without it meant death.

In May 1494 Alexander was killed in battle and was succeeded by his young son, who died later that year. The former emperor's brother now assumed the throne and flatly refused Covilhan's request to leave. He went so far as to treat Covilhan as a spy, but his reign proved short-lived and his successor was kindly disposed towards the Portuguese traveller. Permission to leave, however, continued to be withheld until at last Covilhan resigned himself to his fate. He was well treated, assumed positions of honour and importance in the court and acquired extensive holdings as well as a new family. In time he was appointed governor of a district.[111] Using trusted Jews as messengers, Covilhan sent many letters to John II. Presumably some, at least, arrived but no record of any of them exists.

Over the years other Europeans arrived at court, and none

was ever allowed to leave the country. Like the Mongol emperors of China, the emperors of Ethiopia preferred to employ the services of outsiders with knowledge of the world, and with no connection to any faction within their own country.

The story of the journey and fate of Pêro de Covilhan is known in large part because in 1520 a Portuguese ambassador arrived at the Ethiopian court. Covilhan met with a friar in the entourage and over time related his fate, and subsequently proved of invaluable service to the ambassador. When he left, Covilhan, his Ethiopian wife and family travelled with the ambassador for two days to the coast. Now in his seventies, King John's emissary had given up any hope of ever going home again. He sent in his place his oldest son, a young man twenty-three years old, to receive the honours and rewards Covilhan had been promised those many years before. He also sent with his son a supply of gold to give to his Portuguese wife, should she still be alive, or to his children if not. The son died, however, of an illness before reaching Portugal.

This is the last known account of the loyal Covilhan. A fellow Portuguese wrote in praise of him that 'the keynote of his character was "obedience".' But more importantly, his determination and willingness to obey had become hallmarks of the Portuguese quest to reach the Indies.

9

Gama of Sines

In 1491 it seemed that John II, the Perfect Prince, had all for which a man and sovereign could hope. He had consolidated the power of the crown and cowed the nobility into grudging, and fearful, obedience; he had extended the Portuguese discoveries into new, and potentially prosperous, lands; and he was pursuing a steady course to attain for the Portuguese the elusive all-sea passage to India that would make his nation the greatest in Europe. When that would occur was in the hands of God, but there was no doubt it would happen. Most of all, King John had an heir, a son to carry on his legacy, a boy to mould and prepare for his accession.

By all accounts the king was devoted to his only legitimate son, Alfonso. This is the same young man described by the earlier Polish observer as being 'of an English cast of countenance', always to be found by the side of his father at the dinner table. Unsurprisingly, John II had dreams of uniting Portugal and Spain, and to that end in 1490 arranged the marriage of Alfonso to Isabella, the eldest daughter and heir of Ferdinand and Isabella of Spain.

Although John II was the first king of Portugal routinely to travel with a bodyguard, having made so many enemies, it was the practice of the king on hot summer days to retire to the shore of the gentle Tagus river and swim. On 12 July 1491 the king was enjoying himself in this way with guests and, as always, had invited the seventeen-year-old Alfonso, married just seven months, to come along. Initially the young man declined, saying he was tired, but later he decided to join his father. His regular mule was not immediately available, so Alfonso rode instead the horse of his squire. As he galloped within sight of his father, no doubt showing off, the horse stumbled, tossing the prince. He was carried unconscious to a nearby house of a fisherman but soon died without regaining consciousness.

An unnamed chronicler wrote of his passing:

> [H]is eyes, once so happy and full of beauty, were in that hour blinded and forever without sight . . . and his sweet mouth, whence had issued so many gentle, tender, and welcome words and from which many had received kindness and happiness, at this moment ceased forever to speak, and his beautiful royal hands, kissed each day for the great and many favours which he bestowed, were in this brief space of time turned to nought. . . . And what sins could such an angelic creature have committed, one of such a tender age, to die such an unhappy and so sudden a death without benefit of confession or of Communion?

Although he was only thirty-six years of age, the king's own health had already begun to decline. The sudden loss of his heir and son, literally before his eyes and in his arms, had a visible effect on him. It was in the steady state of physical decline he had negotiated the Spanish treaties. For an heir he turned to George (*Jorge*), his son by his Portuguese mistress, and brought him into his household to be mentored. There was a precedent, as John I had been the illegitimate son of the king. Queen Leonor, however, would have nothing to do with it. If her own son was not to be king, then certainly the son of her husband's mistress was not about to become king in his place. During what little remained of the king's life Leonor lobbied relentlessly on behalf of her brother Manuel, the Duke of Beja and Master of the Order of Christ. Finally, in the last hours of life, for reasons never adequately explained, John II named Manuel heir.

At the same time, and possibly to give him a measure of protection, John II made George Duke of Coimbra, historically one of the most powerful positions in Portugal. In addition, he named him Master of the Order of Avis and of the Order of Santiago. From these highly influential positions he would be unassailable.

It is perfectly understandable that the belief is held in many quarters that Leonor had poisoned her husband. He had, after all, murdered her brother and threatened her with execution.

So passed away one of the most extraordinary king's in European history. Africa had been doubled and Portuguese vessels had sailed in the waters of the Indian Ocean. Orders for the preparation of the India expedition had been given and the commander named, but the king's untimely death in 1495, not yet forty years of age, and the assumption of an unexpected heir to the throne, placed the matter of the expedition to India on hold.

Manuel was the youngest of nine. Four of his older brothers died young, and the fifth, the Duke of Viseu, was killed by John II. Manuel is described as fair, thin, a light eater, temperate, vain, fond of music and ostentation.[112] His reign was to be marked by unprecedented wealth and fame. Although he was at best an average man, he was placed by circumstances at the pivotal point in Portuguese history. The discovery of the sea route to India and the East set the course of his nation for the next hundred years and utterly transformed the world. Manuel's modest personal achievements are overwhelmed by events that came to him almost entirely by luck. Not without reason he is known to the Portuguese as Manuel 'The Fortunate' (*O Venturoso*).

At the beginning of his reign Manuel pardoned nobles who returned from exile and restored fifty properties to the new Duke of Bragança. Nobles were also introduced into the court circle. In addition, Manuel formally recognized seventy-two families and placed their coats of arms at the royal palace in Sintra. But Manuel was smitten with the royal Portuguese disease of uniting the thrones of Portugal and Spain and set his sights on Alfonso's childless teenage widow, Isabella. There was, however, a price to be paid for the marriage. Isabella consented to become the Queen of Portugal, but only if all Jews were expelled before her arrival for the ceremony.

In 1492 there had been an estimated 80,000 Jews quietly living in Portugal – an accepted, even valued, element of society. Jews made invaluable contributions to science and had long played an important role in the commercial, and to some degree the cultural, life of Portugal. Jews, in fact, had established the first printing presses in the nation.[113] As Spanish oppression and expulsion were imposed, an estimated 120,000 Spanish Jews fled to Portugal.

Portugal initially profited from the influx by extracting a substantial payment for permission to enter. Hundreds of the most wealthy Jewish families were permitted to remain in Portugal, although the rest were forced to leave the country immediately or were imprisoned. The ultimate fate of many was unresolved when John II died. When Manuel ascended the throne, he initially released those who had been too poor to buy passage and it appeared he intended to pursue a lenient policy towards the Jews. Portugal stood to profit enormously from their permanent presence.

But when Manuel sought marriage with Isabella, the daughter of Ferdinand and Isabella of Spain, he abruptly changed course and agreed to a tragic pogrom against all Jews throughout Portugal, a campaign that consumed much of the nation's official time and energy. Manuel began by immediately ordering the expulsion of all remaining Jews. This included the seizure and forced conversion of all Jewish children under the age of fourteen.

Isabella was satisfied and the pair were married. Manuel then relented in part and issued a degree that those forced to convert must remain unmolested for twenty years. He issued other decrees undoing some of the most onerous of his orders, but tens of thousands died or paid a horrible price for the king's marriage, which took place two months after the first ships sailed for India.

During the first two busy years of his reign Manuel was also examining the papers of his predecessor. While digging through a royal chest he came across a letter from a merchant in Venice replying to one from John II. The previous king expressed concern at having gone so long without receiving a report from the two spies he had earlier sent to the East. The merchant had been asked to inquire about them through his agents in Alexandria. In the letter he expressed his regret at not knowing 'where India was'. He went on to encourage the king to undertake its discovery 'by sending ships to conquer it, even if it entailed risking his kingdom and power, for riches and glory awaited him'.[114]

This correspondence created a 'great longing' in the young king to make 'the discovery of India'.[115] He must also have been influenced by those events to which he had been personal witness and been caught up in the great national crusade. Manuel placed the issue before the junta, which did not give its support and instead attempted to dissuade him. They argued that 'the hope was doubtful, while the perils were great and certain . . . [H]e should take into consideration that he might become engaged in war with the Emperor of Egypt . . . that if he should insist on going on as he wished to do, how great an envy he would bring upon himself from the other Christian princes.' The royal advisers cautioned that if the king persisted he risked bringing down on their little nation the wrath of all the great powers.[116]

The ill health of John II, the negotiation of the treaties with Spain, the occasion of the transfer of power, the marriage plans and Jewish pogroms alone do not account for the delay in acting on the success of the Dias expedition. There were other reasons as well. For one, the Portuguese had extended themselves such incredible distances that the Cape of Good Hope assumed a position once held by another projection of African land. It is recorded that 'a new conceit possessed most of the mariners, as had done before touching Bogiadore [Bojador], that there was no sayling any further.'[117] Dias's mutinous crew presumably presented the difficulties they had encountered in the most negative light in order to justify their conduct.

That aside, the ultimate discovery of the sea route around Africa was not universally welcome in Portugal, coming as it did after so many decades of sacrifice. It was not just the royal advisers who had reservations. What riches had come from the Portuguese voyages into the unknown had come only with the loss of many lives and at great effort. Nothing had been easy. Discovery of the cape that opened up the route to India was simply one more obstacle overcome. How many more were yet to be faced? There was no assurance that the next expedition would succeed, or the one after it. When would it end? And at what final cost?

In addition to wanting to marry Spanish princesses, the Portuguese monarchs were nearly obsessed with the idea of continuing the reconquest of the Moors by systematically driving them from north Africa. The eventual objective was Jerusalem and the heady title 'Emperor of the East'. This also must have helped to motivate Manuel to reach India and usurp the spice trade. In doing so he would remove the economic underpinnings of the Mamelukes in Egypt, the primary obstacle to Jerusalem, as well as providing himself with the financial means to renew the conquest across north Africa.

In considering these objections Manuel knew that John II had heard the same arguments and eventually dismissed them. Manuel took the same view and concluded that the drive to reach India had been for too long an objective of the Portuguese people to be abandoned when success was within reach. History compelled him to act. But before committing himself to the endeavour Manuel consulted with the royal astrologer, Abraham ben Zacuto, to determine if the stars were in his favour. Together the pair studied the fate of the proposed expedition. Finally, Zacuto announced that the heavens were at an opportune conjunction. Manuel issued orders for the preparations for the expedition to be resumed.

Shortly before his untimely, and suspicious, death in 1495 John II had selected Vasco da Gama's father, Estêvão, to command the proposed expedition to India. According to at least one account, Estêvão was one of the king's 'most trusted navigators'.[118] He was a respected retainer in the royal court, a member of the Order of Santiago and reportedly an experienced captain. But before the enterprise was organized, both John II and Estêvão were dead. Manuel, for reasons not adequately recorded, appointed young Vasco da Gama to replace his father as expedition captain and so it was that perhaps the most remarkable figure in the Portuguese discoveries and the coming European conquests stepped on to the stage of history.

Vasco da Gama had been in residence at the court for some time and enjoyed the favour of John II, yet one of the mysteries of the selection process was the dogged determination that it should remain with the Gama family. It is a fact the two families were related. Two hundred years earlier they shared a common ancestor, King Alfonso II, though the Gamas claimed their royal blood through Alfonso's illegitimate daughter, never more than a minor footnote in Portuguese blood lines. With so many Castilian queens the Portuguese generally looked with great affection on the offspring of the king's Portuguese mistress, who in her own way was fêted much like a queen and was treated with a respect and adoration no Spanish-born wife of the king had ever received.

The manner in which Vasco was informed of the king's decision is remarkable for its informality, given the magnitude of the enterprise. Gaspar Correa reports that after consulting with his astrologers Manuel prayed daily for inspiration in making his selection and was increasingly persuaded that the choice should remain within the Gama family, as they had claim to it. Members of the court approached Manuel during the gestation period to speak on behalf of their favourites but were rebuffed by the king, who said he had made his decision.

One day Manuel was working at a table issuing various orders when Vasco passed near by in the hallway. The king raised his hand in summons and said, 'I should rejoice if you would undertake a service which I require of you in which you must labour much.' Vasco kissed the hand of his king and said, 'Sire, I am a servant for any labour that may be, since my service is required, which I will perform so long as my life lasts.'[119] It is said that, on learning the mission, Vasco urged Manuel to offer the command to his adored older brother Paulo, but the king declined.

If the only purpose of the expedition was successfully to reach India and return, the logical choice as its leader was Bartholomeu Dias and, given his success at sea and national celebrity, he would have been a popular selection. But Dias had been forced to turn back from India by a near mutiny and his inability to lead his crew at a crucial juncture probably militated against his selection to command a voyage of even longer duration.

Moreover, this expedition was not just another voyage of exploration. What was needed was a diplomat, a man with sensitivity to the demands of commerce and, if necessary, the experience, courage and abilities of a soldier. He had to be equally capable of dealing with the primitive and suspicious chiefs he would encounter in Africa as with the Arab and Hindu princes he would meet in India. He also had to be a worthy representative of the Portuguese king, either as a diplomat or with sword in hand. As is nearly always the case in such situations, he had above all to be a man the king personally trusted.

Given the magnitude of his accomplishment, it is not surprising that so much more is known about Vasco da Gama than about any of the captains who preceded him. He was of average height, had a florid complexion and in later life was given to a certain stoutness of stature. Correa, who lived close to events, wrote that Gama was 'of a very indefatigable disposition, and very skilful in all things'. He described him as 'a discreet man, of good understanding, and of great courage for any good deed'.

Vasco certainly inspired the loyalty of those he led, was not especially gregarious or quick to smile, understood how to command in trying circumstances and possessed a tenacity mingled with a certain flexibility that is often seen in greatness. Given what lay ahead, it is unlikely any other selection to captain this expedition would have succeeded.

The heart and soul of Portugal were in the north, at Oporto, the city from which the country took its name, and in the lands to the north of and around Coimbra, the site of the nation's oldest university and home of the nobles who most consistently vied with new kings for power.

As the origin and seat of the great Portuguese families were north of Lisbon, it is in one sense unexpected that Manuel should have selected a man from a family whose roots lay to the south, from the obscure fishing village of Sines, some 60 miles away; yet in another sense it was a wise selection. Vasco da Gama was not conspicuously allied with any of the families in historic opposition to the king, and the last thing Manuel wanted was for this voyage to bring wealth and distinction to potential rivals.

Sines is situated on a small bay in the Alentejo, the poorest region of Portugal, and the land surrounding the town is not especially fertile. Life was harder here than in the lush north. Situated on a bluff, the town faces the sea and was dependent for its survival primarily on its fishermen. It was, even then, a very old town, with both an ancient castle and church. Life in Sines was simple and had been unchanged for hundreds of years.

The Gama family was neither rich nor aristocratic, but it had a long and renowned history of service to the crown. One note-worthy ancestor had distinguished himself against the Moors in the Algarve in the thirteenth century. Vasco's grandfather and namesake had carried the battle standard of Alfonso V against Castile and held a position of trust with the king thereafter. Vasco's father, Estêvão, had married Izabel Sodre, who came from a noted family with a pronounced English strain. Sodre, in fact, was a Portuguese corruption of the English name Sudley, taken from Izabel's grandfather Frederick Sudley, an Englishman of the family of the earls of Hereford, who had come to fight with the Portuguese king against Castile in 1381. The couple had three sons (one of whom took the last name of his mother) and a daughter. Vasco was probably the youngest of the boys.[120] His date of birth has long been disputed: the latest, and most cred-ible, calculation is that he was born in 1469 or 1470.

Vasco's father was a *cavaleiro* in the household of the influen-tial Duke of Viseu and was for a time the captain and the *alcaide-mór* (similar to mayor) of Sines.[121] In this post he received a modest income derived from local soap-making and later he was granted other small revenues for his increasingly recognized ser-vice in the Order of Santiago, which in this region of Portugal was all but a state within a state.[122]

In the small fishing town where Vasco was probably born and spent his early childhood, he would have spent countless hours with the local fishermen and learned to swim, fish and handle a small boat, as the children do to this day. Such was the habit of all Portuguese sons raised beside the sea, and he would have looked to the ocean for his career.

Vasco grew up during the fascinating time when the accounts of the Portuguese discoveries had become legend and continued to unfold with each new sailing season. From the lips of the sailors he would have heard their tales of terrible storms and vast calms, of shipwrecks and of distant lands and adventures. The common stories were of black men wearing golden rings in their mouths, noses and ears, of cannibals and of hairy, manlike apes. There were also stories of the gold to be had from river beds, of exotic lands and coastlines, of ivory and of slaves. Portugal was a powerful nation, the stories told, and men of courage and commitment could make their way profitably in this new world.

When he came of age, it is most likely young Vasco was schooled in Évora, a town some 70 miles distant, located in the hills north-east of Sines. Évora was Portugal's second city, although it had a population of only 10,000. Like Sines, Évora was an ancient city, founded by the Celts and later occupied by the Romans. The Moorish influence is evident in its historic buildings; even the people are more Moorish in appearance and taller than average for the Portuguese. It was a prosperous region and city, a world removed from the hard life and poverty of the more barren land about Sines.

Évora was also the site of the royal palace built in 1421, and the scenes of royalty, of the court and foreign visitors, could not help but excite the boy. It was also here in the city square that the Duke of Bragança, the most powerful lord in Portugal, had been beheaded by order of the king, and some 22,000 souls, primarily Jews, were murdered in the same square, many of them burnt at the stake.

Vasco's course of study is not known but it certainly included both mathematics and navigation. He was sufficiently accomplished to come to the attention of those in the government at an early age, for neither his family name nor his father possessed such influence. It seems likely, therefore, and there are unsubstantiated accounts, that he demonstrated his worth as a captain and as a leader of men under arms. Ships' crews were tough men, united and controlled only by strict discipline and faith in their captain. Mutiny and insubordination on the high seas were common enough experiences and destroyed more than one captain's career. Moreover, conspiracy and intrigue were the lifeblood of the Portuguese court, which in its own way was as byzantine as any in the Orient, and no man would have received command of the first voyage to India who was not a master of both.

Another intriguing aspect of his selection is that Manuel and Vasco were of the same age, and it is assumed they knew one another in court. Until shortly before he became king, Manuel had not been in line to the throne. That circumstance had only come about because of the accidental death of the young heir and through the incessant lobbying of Manuel's sister the queen, on her husband's deathbed. Manuel's childhood, and the degree of freedom he had to make friends and share in their experiences, would have been far greater than that of the king's son and heir. The opportunities for Vasco and Manuel to have been well acquainted were probably numerous in so small a court, though there is no record of them.

Of Vasco's character there is one often quoted story. The young Vasco and a companion, Diogo Vaz, a squire of the royal household, were walking the narrow darkened streets of Setúbal when the night-watch challenged them. It was presumably cold and Vasco had his cloak pulled to cover his face. This, as well as the late hour, aroused suspicion. When challenged, however, Vasco refused to show his face as ordered, answering, 'I am no criminal', and also refused to give his identity. The watch summoned help and an altercation ensued. A complaint was lodged against both Vasco and Vaz. No final resolution for Vasco is recorded, whereas Vaz was compelled to pay a small fine to have an order for his arrest revoked.[123]

Little is known about Vasco's personality in private matters. He was devoted to his oldest brother and to his family, as is the Portuguese custom. One chronicler from the era describes him as a high-spirited young man. He was also a skilled navigator, probably among the best in Europe, but since other skilled navigators accompanied the fleet it was not for that that he was selected.[124]

Vasco's father, and to an extent Vasco himself, had prospered in the service of the influential Almeida family, though both had been of service to the king as well. This extended family was related to the king by marriage and was well represented in the church hierarchy and within the powerful Order of Santiago, where it was especially influential. It is likely Vasco followed the usual course and worked in the interests of the order in the Alentejo, where there was much to occupy it.[125] He fought in the war with Castile.

The first documented appearance of the name of Vasco da Gama is in 1492, during a dispute between John II and the King of France. A French vessel had seized a Portuguese ship laden with gold returning from Guinea. No state of war existed between the two nations and the ship should have been permitted to pass in peace. The royal advisers recommended that someone should be selected to go to the King of France to take up the matter.

King John was certain that any delegate sent would be ignored, so instead he ordered the seizure of the ten French ships in Lisbon harbour and had their goods stored in the customs warehouse. He then ordered Vasco da Gama, a man identified as one in whom the king 'had great confidence, and one who had seen service in the fleets and in maritime affairs',[126] to sail at once to Setúbal and the Algarve to seize those French ships he found anchored at any other Portuguese port in the region. A second man was dispatched north to Oporto with the same instructions. On learning of these events the King of France ordered the immediate release of the Portuguese ship and all its contents. John II replied in kind. The seizures, including that of Vasco, were handled with such professionalism that no one was injured and absolutely nothing was missing from the French merchandise. This occurred five years before Vasco was named Captain-Major (*Capitão-Mór*) of the India expedition. At the time Manuel was Duke of Beja and in near constant contact with John II. He would have been well aware of his actions and the agents he employed, and a good judge of their competence.

Having received the charge from Manuel, Vasco was now forced to secure a royal pardon for his older brother. Paulo had wounded a judge in Setúbal during a quarrel and at this time was considered an outlaw. 'For love of you,' the king is reported to have answered, 'I pardon him my justice, for the services which I expect from you and from him, he satisfying the parties now that he has his pardon; and let him come at once without making any delay.'[127] Paulo was then named as captain of one of the ships.

There are other aspects to Vasco's selection to consider. The powerful, noble Almeida family had opposed Manuel's succession to the throne and remained in opposition to him thereafter. When John II had failed to elevate his illegitimate son George to succession and named his cousin Manuel, he had appointed George in part Master of the Order of Santiago. The Order could scarcely have been considered loyal to the new king or supportive of his decisions. Why, then, would Manuel select a member of the opposition to lead this expedition?

Part of the answer probably lies in the fact that he was sending it despite the objections of his junta. Picking a captain from the opposition moderated the criticism, and in the end every member of the junta made a significant contribution to the enterprise. Also, for reasons unlikely ever to be fully understood, the smallest of fleets was being sent, causing the likelihood of failure to be greater than it would otherwise have been. Better that failure lay at the feet of the king's opponents, while Manuel could step up to claim credit if the expedition was a success.[128]

Alhough these were likely political considerations, Vasco was primarily chosen for his qualities and prior service to John II and Manuel. The fact that his selection served other purposes was a political bonus.

10

Preparations

As the moment for the final push to India approached, there was a recognition that another leap in ship design was required to make success more likely. The caravel, which had enabled the discoveries, was the marvel of the fifteenth century, permitting the Portuguese to sail farther than any European before – and to return. Northern European seamen, viewing the exotic caravel in the port of Lisbon, considered it much like an alien spacecraft. The success of the caravel had been enhanced by the Portuguese capacity essentially to take their shipyards with them to the most distant reaches of the world.

But for all the Portuguese ingenuity and all their success, the caravel still possessed serious limitations. Because of its small size, often no more than 50 tons, it could not carry sufficient supplies for the increasingly lengthy voyages of discovery. There was also no provision for crew quarters in its design. The captain and his officers had a cramped living space but the seamen were expected to live and sleep on the deck. During inclement weather they sought refuge below, huddling where they could on top of the cargo.

Bartholomeu Dias reported after his sixteen-month voyage to double Africa that a different, larger vessel was required to reach India, as his ships had been too light for the heavy seas and terrible storms of the South Atlantic. In addition, his crew had suffered severely in the cold weather and oceans. He urged that further modification of the caravel be undertaken to make more certain the ultimate success.

Although an adequate complement of healthy seamen was necessary to sail a ship safely such an extreme distance, there was more to it than that. Dias had been faced with near mutiny even

after turning the Cape of Good Hope. If the living circumstances for the crew were not improved, the captain-major of the
India-bound fleet could well face the same fate.

As Grand Captain of the port of Lisbon and as the seaman
with the greatest experience, it is understandable that Dias was
placed in charge of ship construction. He was given instructions
to design ships 'to resist the fury of the sea at the great Cape of
Good Hope'.[129] Some historians report, however, that he did
not assume these duties until after Vasco da Gama had been
selected to lead the expedition and that Dias worked under
Gama's direction from the first.

Two new ships were constructed from timber felled in the
royal forests of Leiria and Alcacer. They were not beauties.
Three-masted, the ships were larger than the traditional caravel,
with square-rigged sails, a flat bottom for working in close to
land, a square stern and peaked bow. A lateen sail was installed
to the mizzen to aid manoeuvrability. Under full canvas they
presented 4,000 square feet to the wind. Displayed on each massive sail was the crimson cross of the Order of Christ.[130]

Heavy planking 'two fingers thick' was placed on the sides of
the hull for added protection in the event of combat. Towers
were constructed at the front and rear to provide fortresses for
defenders in the event of being boarded. These were so high that
the forward one was used as a fourth mast to allow the spread of
a square spritsail. From the highest mast, some 110 feet above the
keel, was flown the royal standard while the captain's scarlet flag
flew from the crow's nest some 70 feet up. On the bow was the
figurehead of the ship's patron saint carved from wood and
painted in gold leaf.[131]

At 100 to 120 tons the new ships were not especially large,
though the ton measurement used then was roughly twice that
of today. (By calculating the amount of goods stored in the two
new ships one source has concluded the vessels were between
250 and 300 tons by modern measurement.) Although the
voyage was to be of an unprecedented length, relatively small
ships were still judged as the best choice to allow safe navigation
in shoal waters and rivers. The new ships would be slower than

the caravels but would offer far greater comfort to the crews. Additional wales were added along the sides to reduce rolling. Special care was given to the ships' bottoms in an attempt to reduce fouling from barnacles and borers. The wood above the waterline was painted black, probably with some sort of tar to serve as a protective.

In an unusual innovation for the times the vessels were constructed as exact replicas, to enable the replacing of parts from one to the other in distant seas if necessary, and, as had long been the Portuguese practice, every ship carried an extensive selection of spares. So different was this new ship from what had gone before that it was given the new name of nau (*não*).

Although the voyage was possible, it was only just so, the technology barely permitting its accomplishment, and there was more to consider than the actual sailing feat. Vasco da Gama's voyage was expected to last up to three years, and for most of that period he and his crew would be far beyond the reach of any help, sailing in waters, anchoring in ports, in the control or under the influence of mortal enemies. Not only were the winds and currents alien and a constant threat, but every port would be occupied by an actual or potential adversary. Any ship they encountered would destroy them if at all possible. Any misjudgement on Vasco's part would mean death for his crew as well as for himself.

This was not meant to be an armed intrusion, but weapons were nevertheless essential to the expedition's success, and so every ship bore a full complement. Each of the naus carried twenty guns, the heaviest of them made of wrought-iron staves held fast by iron hoops. There was also a wide selection of bombards, matchlocks, crossbows, axes, spears, swords, javelins and pikes. Officers and men brought with them thick leather jerkins, breastplates, armour and helmets of a quality and quantity as their station and circumstances permitted. If it came to a life and death struggle in a distant sea or port, the Portuguese would not go down easily.

It is generally agreed that the names of the new ships were *São Gabriel* (under Vasco's command) and *São Rafael* (under Paulo).

Acquired for the voyage was the *Berrio*, which was probably rechristened the *São Miguel*, a swift caravel with lateen sails and, at 50 to 59 tons the smallest of the tiny fleet. Young Nicolau Coelho, considered by the Gamas to be a brother, would command it.

Given the projected length of the voyage, it was not possible for the three primary ships to carry sufficient supplies for the duration. As a result, the fourth vessel was a large supply ship of standard design, weighing between 120 and 300 tons, though it would be manned by a minimum crew. It was commanded by Gonçalo Nunes, a trusted Gama family retainer. In a fair wind the average speed of the fleet was between $6\frac{1}{2}$ and 8 miles an hour.[132]

Given the substantial size of the second fleet sent to India,* the Portuguese capabilities and the significance of this expedition, the small number of vessels involved has always been hard to comprehend. By any reasonable assessment only the most wide-eyed optimist would expect success from such limited resources. Dias had barely made it back home, limping into the port at Lisbon with a depleted crew, and he had not even reached India, let alone faced the threat of the hostile Muslims known to dominate the waters there.

For this and other reasons great care was taken in the selection of the crew. As was the custom established by Henry the Navigator, the new captain-major was given a free hand in preparations. Everything he requested was given to him. During these months the king and Vasco consulted at all hours of the day and night, which suggests that if a close bond did not already exist between the men it was almost certainly formed during this exciting period.

Vasco carefully selected the crews, each of whom was to be paid 5 *cruzados* a month. They were offered an additional 2 *cruzados* if

---

* Pedro Alvares Cabral sailed in March 1500 with 1,200 men and thirteen ships. Nicolau Coelho, just returned from India, was captain of one of the ships. Tragically, Bartholomeu Dias, who captained another vessel, was lost during a violent storm in the South Atlantic, reportedly within sight of his furthest pillar.

they learned a craft during the wait for departure, a gesture that was well received. The men were instructed in rope-making, smithing, ship servicing, carpentering and other skills that would be useful on the extended voyage. Contributing to the eventual success of the mission was the fact that a number of the crew had been with Dias. Experienced pilots were also selected, among them the legendary Pero d'Alenquer, who had navigated Dias's ship. The pilots received fresh training in navigation and were presented with nautical instruments of every kind to assist them.

Between 170 and 180 men eventually comprised the tiny armada.* With one notable exception, all were volunteers. Sailing ships of this era required a certain number of skilled seamen and the near constant attention of all of them. The simple act of weighing the anchor required at least ten men, with many of the others aloft loosening canvas, while others set lines. Maintaining a heading in violent seas was especially dangerous, and the men worked high above the deck without safety lines or nets. A seaman falling overboard was all but certain to drown.

There were among the crewmen surely sets of brothers. A father and son combination is not unlikely. Given the length of the voyage, the dangers jointly faced, the forced quarters and the Portuguese family style of food preparation and consumption, a strong bond of loyalty and fast friendships were the inevitable result. Every loss on the voyage would reap an intense emotional toll. For all this, it is likely Vasco had a difficult time winnowing the vast numbers of those wanting to sail down to the select few.

Each ship had a master and a pilot, an assistant pilot, a mate, a boatswain, at least twenty able seamen, ten ordinary seamen, two boys, bombardiers, trumpeters, an 'officer of justice', a purser, a barber-surgeon, a priest, artisans and servants.[133] In addition, each carried six *delgradados*, condemned prisoners taken from the cells and offered the opportunity of a pardon and reward for faithful service – assuming they survived. This was apparently

---

* As with many details of this voyage, there is disagreement as to the details. The precise number varies from 148 to 180, depending on who is doing the writing; the higher figure now appears the most likely.

Vasco's idea, which the king gladly granted. *Delgradados* had been used in the past, typically banished to the west coast of Africa, where they 'went native' and supported themselves as middlemen between the African chiefs and the Portuguese traders.

Vasco's *delgradados* were to be put ashore at the most dangerous and uncertain situations, or left behind as appropriate to work at building goodwill for the Portuguese at a crucial port. These condemned men were not necessarily hardened criminals. One is described as having been imprisoned for killing another man in a dispute over a woman. They were to conduct themselves with great effectiveness.

Also included in the crew were three interpreters, one of whom had previously lived in the Congo, another who spoke both Arabic and Hebrew, and a third, identified as 'an African slave', who had once been a prisoner of the Moors and also spoke Arabic.

Preparations and the equipping of the fleet were the preoccupation of the capital city and of the nation. Special oversized ovens were constructed in Lisbon and a vast quantity of sea biscuit (hard tack) was baked. Loaded aboard the ships was a more than adequate supply of wine, as indispensable to the Portuguese as beer to a German. Each man was allowed one and a quarter pints of the spirit a day. In addition, the seamen received a daily allotment of one and a half pounds of biscuit, one pound of salt beef or half a pound of pork, two and a half pints of water, vinegar and olive oil. On fast days they were given half a pound of rice, cod or cheese to replace meat. To break the monotony of the diet, sardines, prunes, onions, beans, flour, mustard, garlic, sugar, almonds and honey were also stored. Whenever possible, of course, the diet would be supplemented with fish caught from the ocean or fresh game acquired at landfall.[134] For all the shortcomings of the diet, most seamen on the expedition were likely to eat better at sea than they did at home.

Although the Portuguese employed the most advanced methods of the time, the primitive means of storage available placed a limitation on what foodstuffs could be taken on such a long voyage. The hard tack would begin to deteriorate, for example, after the first year. Salt was the primary preservative and so a generous quantity of water was necessary, both for drinking and for cooking. Unfortunately, water had a tendency to turn bad in wooden kegs and was the most serious concern to any captain.

For their personal use captains and officers brought fruit preserved in syrup, dried raisins and nuts. In addition, as was the custom, the captains had with them their personal silver dishes and cutlery, crystal cups, gilded glass bowls, linen, carpets, and all the necessities and luxuries to make life as pleasant and bearable as possible.[135]

Vasco was quartered in the tower (sometimes called a castle or citadel) rising on the quarterdeck. The ships officers lived in the room below his and in the forecastle. The crew made their quarters in the space immediately below the gang boards, a considerable improvement over the situation endured during previous voyages. Each of them was assigned a locker and they were allowed to bring their own personal trade goods for barter once the fleet reached India. They slept wherever was convenient, on deck or below it.

No special provision was made to combat scurvy. Its cause was only vaguely understood and the cure was known to be found in fresh food, especially fruit and vegetables. The Portuguese had no idea of what to take to prevent it or how to preserve it if they had. Journals of the Portuguese captains are filled with the tremendous suffering of the seamen and of the horror of the dreaded disease. But like unknown whirlpools, unexpected currents and contrary winds, scurvy was just one more adversity to be faced and overcome.

Manuel took the extraordinary step of ordering that the names and addresses of wives or parents of the crew be recorded and deposited in the Colonial Office of Portugal. In the event of deaths, of which many were anticipated, the family members would receive the deceased man's pay. Also meticulously maintained was an account of every cost for the expedition.[136] He ordered 100 *cruzados* to be paid to every married man sailing, to be left with his wife, and 40 *cruzados* to be given to each single man, presumably for his mother. Vasco and Paulo were each given 2,000 *cruzados* to assist them in buying what personal items they might need, while Coelho was provided with 1,000.

Vasco, his captains and pilots, also received the very latest in navigation and astronomical aids, as well as mathematical tables of declinations to fix position, which the junta had been improving at a remarkable pace. The compass had first appeared in western Europe during the twelfth century and quickly proved invaluable. By the time of the final passage to India it had become the most important navigation instrument. In design a needle was fixed to a pivoted card which bore the points of the compass, painted in various colours. The card was housed within a round bowl, lit by a small lamp. This was placed in a hooded box, which was set on top of a stand where the helmsman could easily see it. On each vessel was also a lodestone, which was used periodically to remagnetize the needle, if required. A supply of extra needles and entire compasses was also available.[137]

The astrolabe, which probably originated with the Arabs, was still new to Europeans and few were skilled in using it. The device was employed to measure the altitude of the sun and stars, and to fix one's position to the north and south. It was eventually replaced by the more superior sextant. An astrolabe was specially constructed and presented to Vasco, but did not prove as effective as in future voyages because the small ships of his expedition rolled in all but the calmest of seas, which made accurate readings nearly impossible.

Although most of its members opposed it, the junta now decided to support the expedition, and every member made a contribution to aid the scientific outfitting. Vasco was provided with a copy of Ptolemy's *Geography*, along with extracts from the writings of Benjamin of Tudela, Marco Polo and Nicolo di Conti.[138] Presumably Vasco received at least some of the information received from John II's spies, though clearly little in detail.

Vasco is believed to have been given a copy of the *Ephemerides* of Regio Montanus and most certainly the *Almanach Perpetuum* of Abraham ben Zacuto for use in solar observations. Zacuto had been professor of mathematics in Salamanca, Spain, and had come to Portugal in 1492 seeking refuge. He was named

Astronomer Royal, served as the king's astrologer and was commonly regarded as the greatest mathematician of his time. He gave each pilot a chart depicting the names and direction of the winds, which were portrayed in contrasting colours. In addition, the armada possessed tables of traverses used by ships in long tacks to assist in the potentially confusing zigzag course it entailed.

Although Vasco took with him the very latest in instruments and the most complete information available, the science of navigation was still in its infancy and he did not possess many of the basics that future captains would take for granted and consider indispensable. There is no record, for example, that anyone in the fleet possessed a quadrant.

Stored within the ships was everything that logic and prior experience dictated would be required. Each vessel carried six anchors, since these were often lost during storms. At the waist of each ship was a light yawl and a longboat, both of which could be rowed by a small crew when in port or near shore. The holes of the ships were divided into three compartments on two decks. On the upper deck, to the rear, was the supply of water, stored in wooden casks, and additional rope. Shot, gunpowder, firearms and weapons were kept amidships. Forward was the additional spare equipment and food supplies. A tremendous quantity of spare tackle, sails and nautical equipment of every kind was also provided to each ship. The health of the men was of paramount concern and each vessel carried a large supply of drugs.

In the lower deck the compartments held more provisions, plus assorted merchandise, presents and trade goods. These included a wide selection of wool, necklaces, chains and bracelets, and hand basins as well as swords, daggers – both plain and engraved – ornamented spears and shields, as well as the traditional glass beads and the usual trade items. Later historians reported the ships carried both gold and silk, jewels of gold and princely gifts to 'be presented to the kings and lords of the countries where they might land – and a small quantity of every kind of spice'.[139]

The reference to spices is accurate, but there were no 'princely gifts', as the most startling aspect of these stores lay in the actual selection of trade goods and articles to be used as gifts. The traditional interpretation has been that until now the Portuguese had been dealing with tribes along the African coast and had grown accustomed to bartering successfully with cheap items, but they surely knew better than to see these as legitimate goods for trade in India.

For generations Europe had received costly spices from Asia. The Portuguese knew they were valued there, as they were in Europe. It took gold and silver to buy pepper, cinnamon, cloves and the other desired spices. In addition, Europeans had heard frequent lavish stories of the vast, incalculable wealth of Asia and India. Woollen cloth, striped cotton, sugar, honey, coral, glass beads, red hats, trousers, bells and tin jewellery were simply not going to be adequate, yet for the most part that is what Vasco was given. The reasons for such a profound error in judgement – one that was to cause no end of difficulty – are unlikely ever to be established.

In every other respect Vasco was provided with the very best Portugal had to offer to make the expedition a success. No expense was spared, so there must have been a reason why he carried the trade goods he did. Accepting that this was not a serious miscalculation, which the methodical manner in which the explorations had taken place would indicate it was not, then there would have been a logic behind it.

One factor may have been that Vasco was not expected to succeed. The incredible distances Dias had covered were known, and he had still been a long way from India, even at his furthest point. Although the precise location of the subcontinent was not yet established, by the time of Vasco da Gama's voyage the Portuguese had a much better idea of where it lay. They could make a rough calculation of the increased distances involved and make a determination as to the likelihood of success. Given the technology, there were legitimate concerns as to whether the voyage was even possible. Why send valuable trade goods or a large quantity of gold and silver on a mission so likely to fail? Better to use them once it was established that they were capable of making the voyage, and returning.

The selection also suggests the nature of the people with whom Vasco was expected to contact. No advanced civilizations had been encountered thus far in the push to India, and it appears the planners doubted any would be on this voyage either.

Finally, the trade goods taken indicate that this was still primarily viewed as a voyage of exploration rather than of commerce. While the eventual aim was to establish a trade mission and bring back a profitable quantity of spices, the primary purpose of this voyage was to discover the way to India, and return with that vital knowledge. Goods that would be of use *en route* were considered more important than those to be used for barter in the event of the ships actually reaching India.

During the lengthy preparations Manuel and Vasco continued meeting on a nearly daily basis. Correa records that:

> Vasco da Gama gave an account to the king of all that he did, and always talked to him of the things which he desired; and the king told him to do what his heart prompted him . . . and that in the countries at which he touched, he should take great precautions for taking care of his health and life upon which depended all that had been done, and that remained to be accomplished; and, according as he saw fit, he was to make peace or war, and to make of himself a merchant or a warrior, or one cast away or who had lost his way, and he was to make himself an ambassador . . . And all that he said to him thus was nought, because it seemed to the king in his heart that Vasco da Gama would know much the best what to do; for each time his heart received greater satisfaction from him.[140]

Vasco reported to his sovereign that 'his soul was in readiness, and that there was nothing to detain him from embarking at once'.[141]

All was now prepared. Carried aboard the *São Gabriel* was the carved image of Santa Maria, whose presence was meant to grant the voyage good fortune. When all else was in readiness, placed within the holds of the ships were three stone *padrões*, similar in design to the pillars Cão and Dias had used, but specially prepared for this voyage, to mark the more distant points to which Vasco, his captains and crew sailed. The last of them was to be planted on the shore of India, as remote from western Europe then as the planet Mars today.

11

Volta da Guiné

By that summer of 1497 the four ships destined for the first passage to India had lain at anchor in the tranquil fresh waters of the Sea of Straw (*Mar de Palha*) at the port of Lisbon for many months. New sails and rigging were strung across the masts and a veritable ocean of supplies had been stored deep within the holds. Pennants snapped in the breeze and bright fittings glittered in the summer sun.

Preparations for the impending voyage had consumed nearly every aspect of Lisbon's commercial life. In the numerous *tascas* along the wharf seamen, soldiers, merchants and labourers gathered over cups of wine, speculating endlessly about the imminent expedition, while in the courtyards and meeting halls of the Portugese nobility there had been talk of little else. Hundreds of other ships, from nations of Europe and throughout the Mediterranean, were also anchored in the busy harbour and not one of those crews was unaware of the adventure about to unfold.

The weather remained temperate and as yet the yearly summer plague had not shown itself within the city. With the coming of the annual wind from the north it seemed that at last the small fleet would finally sail.

For nearly a century the Portuguese had been directed towards this moment. From the day the young Prince Henry had first seen for himself the wonders of conquered Ceuta and his mind's eye had grasped the possibilities for his people, the course of the nation had been set. These had been decades of success but also of failure, of high expectations as well as profound disappointments. Countless lives had been lost, and on occasion the meagre resources of the nation had been stretched to their limit to maintain the push to India by sea. The departure of these ships was recognized by the Portuguese people and the monarch as the single most momentous event in Portuguese history since the creation of the nation itself.

Saturday 8 July was selected for departure. In acknowledgment of this enormous undertaking no ceremony to mark it was omitted. The 28-year-old Vasco da Gama, Captain- Major of the four-ship fleet, and his officers were directed to present themselves before the equally youthful Manuel to request formal permission to set sail and to receive the royal instructions.

With nearly 200 men about to depart on such a treacherous voyage, their extended families and circle of friends meant that much of the populace was personally affected. Emotions were running high, not just at the prospect of success and wealth, but also from the certain knowledge that, even should the expedition be a resounding success, many – even most – of these men would die in the effort. Given the large number of ships that had previously set out, never to return, and the enormous distances and difficulties to be overcome in this effort, even the most optimistic possessed deep concern for the fate of Vasco and his crew.

On 7 July, Manuel received Vasco and his captains in solemn ceremony. Assembled about the sovereign were the most important nobles and other personages of the court, including the highest members of the clergy, all arrayed in their finest ceremonial attire. The crowd both within and without was also bedecked in a bright patchwork of dress. For all the gravity of the gathering there was also a festive mood to the occasion among many of those present, or at the least an effort to make it seem so.

Vasco, his older brother Paulo, their devoted friend the young Nicolau Coelho and other high-ranking officers of the expedition all wore their finest armour. Helmets, breastplates and the elaborate hilts of their swords were polished to a bright lustre. One by one they were escorted forward, introduced to the king and court and then stood at attention. When all were in place, Manuel, regally attired in the fashion of the Portuguese monarchs, delivered prepared remarks.

He recounted how he had received the benefits of the efforts of past kings in driving the Moors from Portugal and also by way of exploration and conquest. He said that he had pondered the next step for the greater good of his nation. 'I have come to the decision that no other is more proper for this my kingdom – as I have debated with you often – than the search for India and lands of the East.' The purpose of such a search was to spread the word of Jesus Christ and thereby obtain their reward in heaven, 'but in addition [to acquire] kingdoms and new states with much riches'.

Manuel reminded all those assembled that the Italian city-states had become wealthy and powerful through their monopoly on the trade in spices. It would, he pronounced, 'be an [act of] ingratitude to God to reject what He so propitiously offers us, and an insult to those princes of lauded memory from whom I have inherited this quest, and an offence to you who have shared in it if I neglected it for [too] long'. For these reasons he had ordered ships to be prepared, which now lay in readiness.

Continuing, Manuel said:

> And I have in my mind how Vasco da Gama, who is here present, has given a good account of himself in all matters which were entrusted to him, or with which he was charged. I have chosen him for this journey, as a loyal cavalier, worthy of such an honourable enterprise. I hope that Our Lord may grant he may perform such services for himself and for me that his recompense may be as a memorial both for him and for those who may aid him in the work [to be] performed in this voyage, because with this confidence and with the knowledge which I have had of all [of them] I have chosen them as his co-workers, with the intention that they obey him in all things which pertain to my service.

He charged the men to work together co-operatively, so as to overcome more easily the dangers they were certain to face. 'And that through you this my kingdom may share the benefactions.'[142]

With that, Vasco knelt and in the solemn hush that ensued kissed the hand of his sovereign in thanks for the great honour that had been given him. The silk banner of the Order of Christ was presented by an official. Vasco placed his hands on it and then pledged his oath of fealty in a clear, loud voice for all to hear:

> I, Vasco da Gama, who now have been commanded by you, most high and most powerful king, my liege lord, to set out to discover the seas and the lands of India and the Orient, do swear on the symbol of this cross, on which I lay my hands, that in the service of God and for you I shall uphold it and not surrender it in the sight of the Moor, pagan or any race of people that I may encounter, and in the face of every peril of water, fire or sword, always to defend and protect it, even unto death. And I further swear that, in the pursuit and the labours of this quest which you, my king and lord, have ordered me to undertake, I shall serve with all fidelity, loyalty, watchfulness and diligence, observing and enforcing the orders which have just been entrusted to me, until such time as I return to this place where I now stand, in the presence of your Royal Highness, with the help of the grace of God, in whose service you are sending me.[143]

Vasco accepted the banner and was then given a copy of his orders, a letter of credence and correspondence to princes with whom he might come into contact, but most especially to the fabled Prester John and to the Zamorin of Calicut.* Then Vasco and the members of the expedition remained at attention as Manuel and his entourage exited with great dignity and ceremony.

In procession, by one account accompanied by the king himself, Vasco and his men solemnly marched towards the nearby

---

* The formal title of the local Hindu king. The origin of the title is unresolved. According to one account it is a corrupted version of words that mean 'King of the Coast'. Another says it means 'Sea Raja'.

harbour. Another account places Vasco on a horse. The great crowd greeted the men with both cheers and tears. In deference to his older brother Vasco had directed that his vessel, the *São Rafael*, would serve as flagship and so the banner of the Order of Christ was raised over it, snapping in the freshening breeze.

The men boarded the ships to the steady tattoo of the drums and the flourish of trumpets. Each vessel was adorned with colourful banners and fluttering pennants. The ships were soon moving slowly, carried by the modest wind and current of the Tagus river towards the ocean. Along the shore an enormous crowd was gathered, waving gaily at the ships, which fired their bombard cannons in answer and sounded their trumpets in fanfare. The vessels passed before the excited crowd in line for the short journey to Belém, where they dropped anchor.

Here a long generation ago Prince Henry had built a nationally revered chapel dedicated to all who took to sea. An order of nuns maintained a nearby hospital, where they nursed seamen carried ill or dying from ships just returned from distant voyages. Vasco, his brother Paulo and Coelho, still attired in their armour, went back ashore and passed through the throng that was awaiting them, swelled by the numbers who had followed the ships on horseback and by carriage. Others travelling on foot continued arriving throughout the night.

It was customary for departing Portuguese seamen to offer prayer to St Mary of Belém within this small chapel, and so the three principal captains assumed their places, possibly accompanied by others of higher rank who would sail, and knelt during the long night, joined by the priests of the nearby monastery. The men confessed and tended to their devotions, each man offering prayers in words immortalized by the great Portuguese poet and author Luis Vaz de Camoens:

> . . . *Oh, Mighty God, be Thou our watchful guide.*
> . . . *To weigh our anchors from our native shore –*
> *To dare new oceans never dared before –*
> *Perhaps to see my native coast no more.*[144]

At sunrise on Saturday 8 July Manuel arrived at the chapel, whereupon the three captains joined their sovereign outside. Now ashore were most of the crew, deeply tanned, barefoot, in the distinctive attire of sailors wearing red caps, bidding farewell to family and friends. As the moment arrived, the women drew out black mantles, which they placed across their heads and about their shoulders and began to conduct themselves more as mourners than well-wishers. By one account a spontaneous chorus arose from the crowd as Vasco and his men emerged from the chapel – so young, so brave.

> Ah, miserable mortals! See to what a fate such ambition and greed are rushing you headlong! What more dreadful punishments could be visited upon you if you had committed the most heinous of crimes? What far distant and measureless seas you must penetrate, what merciless and mountainous waves you must brave, and what dangers threaten your very lives in those faraway lands! Would it not be wiser for you to face death in whatsoever fashion [it may come] here at home than to launch forth into hidden places far from your fatherland, and to find graves in the salt depths of the sea?[145]

It is unlikely such a joint outcry took place, but the sentiments were surely held by many of those present. Whatever words were spoken from the crowd to Vasco moved him deeply and this most disciplined of men, on the greatest day of his life to this point, shed tears which he quickly wiped away with his bare hand. He then turned to escort the king into the chapel for the final Mass. At its conclusion the bells of the chapel and the nearby monastery pealed, announcing to the throng that the long-awaited moment was at hand.

Outside, the officials and dignitaries gathered themselves for the short procession to the shore. The rector of the chapel went first, followed by the priests and monks with bowed heads and hands clasped before them, walking at a measured pace, chanting in unison with each step. Next were the acolytes, swinging ornate censers emitting a pungent blue smoke that swirled about their skirts and floated into the crowd. Then came those bearing crosses, then more dark-robed priests joining in the chant, the crowd murmuring its response.

Next was Vasco da Gama, clasping a lit taper, his breastplate and helmet glistening in the bright summer sun. He moved slowly, looking neither left nor right, his head erect. Behind him fell the officers and men of his fleet in lines of two, each also carrying a lit candle. The smiles were gone, as were for the moment the good wishes. Every face was grim. Women wailed at the sight of their loved ones moving to the ships, others threw themselves on the ground in anguish, certain they would never again see a son, brother, husband or lover.

At the beach the rector paused and then knelt, joined by all in a great sweeping wave as everyone present knelt in place. The crowd grew silent. The priest held a general confession and then, in accordance with the papal bull obtained long before by Prince Henry and applicable to all those who died in the conquest or discovery of distant lands, he granted plenary absolution to the men of the expedition who might lose their lives. All rose and with deliberation Vasco gave the order for the crew to man the waiting ships. There was a final moment for an embrace, the grasp of hands, the meeting of eyes.

Near the shore the young king addressed the crew, jointly and individually, giving them his blessings and good wishes, then took his leave as the crew entered the waiting boats. The sunlight reflected off the sparkling river, the oars of the small boats dipped in bright flashes. It was recorded that the surface of the water, 'appeared in no way like the sea, but like unto a field of flowers'.[146] In short order all were aboard their respective bedecked ships.

To the rhythm of a timeless sea chant the mariners drew the anchors from the muddy bottom of the river. The massive new white sails, adorned with the enormous crimson cross of the Order of Christ, were unfurled and billowed with the breeze. The ships moved slowly at first, then more swiftly towards the open sea. The king himself boarded a small boat so as to accompany the ships as far as reasonable, calling out repeatedly his good wishes and blessings.

On deck the seamen crowded against the bulwarks or hung from the rigging, every man attempting a final view of loved ones, who waved bright scarves or bare hands and called out a final farewell while the officers and captains crowded atop the two castles for the same purpose. For a moment Paulo attempted to pass the royal standard to Vasco so that he would have the honour, but the younger brother refused and indicated Paulo should proceed. The royal standard was again raised, to the blast of a trumpet fanfare. The drums sounded in a steady martial riff, joined in turn by pipes, flutes and tambourines. Numerous small craft trailed the departing ships as far as possible until at last, their sails filled with the hearty wind of the open sea, the vessels pulled ever more swiftly beyond all reach.

All eyes were fixed on the ships until they were out of sight, but none more firmly than those of Manuel, who from his boat watched the departing fleet as if mesmerized and did not stir until there was nothing left to see but the vast blue ocean before him, stretching across the world to India.

An invaluable source here is the *Roteiro*, an account maintained for most of the voyage by an unnamed member of the crew. Of this day of departure the author – whose identity has long been the subject of historical dispute – wrote, 'May God our Lord permit us to accomplish this voyage in his service. Amen!'

It is safe to assume that, given the momentous nature of events and the ceremony surrounding their departure, few aboard the four ships slept that July night after they had left the Portuguese coast behind. This first twenty-four hours were likely to be the safest of the voyage and the one time when the men could come to terms with what lay ahead, and what they had left behind.

The two freshly built ships had a pleasing smell about them that would not last long. The newly hewed oak and pine emitted the fragrance of the trees from which they were taken. The not unpleasant odour of pitch and tar was interspersed. The rope and canvas for the sails both had their own sweet aroma. No crewmen had relieved himself below deck, as they later would, against orders; the ever present rats were too few to be seen; the provisions were still fresh and appetizing. In time the two naus would show their age and become as weather-beaten and sour in smell as all ships did, but on this day of departure they were surely a delight for any seaman and a source of enormous pride for the Gama brothers. They captained what at the time were the two greatest ships in European history.

Sailing with the fleet bound for India, or possibly joining it shortly after departure, was another ship, captained by Bartholomeu Dias, who was transporting men and supplies to El Mina, where he was to assume command. It is not known what role, if any, he played in the departing ceremonies, nor why this particular moment had been selected for him to leave. What thoughts passed through his mind as he gazed at the other four ships and contemplated the mission ahead of them, the secrets to be uncovered, the mysteries to be witnessed for the first time, the incomprehensible rewards to be garnered for success, will also never be known.

Following a week's peaceful run the small fleet sighted the Spanish-held Canary Islands. Here they altered course to come in close to the coast of Africa, where the crew cast lines and caught fish for their pots. Sailing on the night of the 16th, near the Rio de Oro, they were engulfed by one of the thick fogs that appear so unexpectedly off this part of the African coastline. The next morning Vasco discovered his ships had been scattered. None of the others could be seen. Standing orders called for them to rendezvous at the Cape Verde Islands, so Vasco ordered the *São Gabriel* to set course.

Four days later the look-out on the *São Rafael*, which was sailing alone, spotted two vessels bearing down on her. These were the fleet's stores ship and the vessel commanded by Dias. The three ships united and on the evening of 26 July overtook Vasco, who on expressing his great pleasure at seeing them ordered bombards to be fired and trumpets sounded. He had been warned that his two greatest dangers were the scattering of his ships and mutiny, so he would have been very relieved to be reunited with the rest of his ships.

The next day the entire fleet, including Dias, dropped anchor in the harbour of Porto da Praia on Santiago, the largest of the Cape Verde Islands. The crews were granted leave ashore while the ships were serviced and fresh stores of water, meat and wood were collected.[147]

Next Vasco turned his fleet to the east, along the coast of Guinea. As his ships came upon favourable winds, ones for which he was probably searching, he gave the order to follow them and turn south by west, filling the enormous sheets of canvas over his ships with the prevailing wind. At this juncture Dias parted ways and with a final gaze at Vasco's fleet sailed on to El Mina. Escaping both the South Equatorial and Benguela currents, the fleet was carried along by the wind, veering slightly at first but then relentlessly ever west as the pattern permitted.

The decision to take this untested course to the Cape of Good Hope was almost certainly made before Vasco's departure, despite the speculation of some historians. It is all but certain that from the time of Dias's return the Portuguese dispatched ships into the central and south Atlantic to search for islands and lands more favourable than the coast of West Africa for reprovisioning the ships on the anticipated voyage to India and to chart the ocean currents and prevailing wind patterns. Columbus's discovery of substantial lands in the Atlantic would have been just one more impetus to such an effort.

First Cão, then Dias, had demonstrated that Portuguese ships could safely travel long distances far out to sea and that such a route was faster and easier on the crew than bumping along the unhealthy and unpredictable waters of the African coast. Provision for Vasco's daring manoeuvre had surely been made during the preparations. The final decision would have been his, as was the Portuguese custom, and dependent on what he discovered south of the Cape Verde Islands, but it is all but certain that he did not act in isolation in making such a potentially reckless decision, one described as 'an act of superlative audacity'.

Soon the four ships had turned south, steadily eating up the miles on the route to India, carried along as well by the power-ful Brazil current. They were taking the great circular course from Europe to Asia, the route still preferred by sailing vessels. It carried them an estimated 600 miles from the coast of Brazil, then ever southward, well out to sea but parallel to the coast of South America.

They were in waters never before sailed by man, and every horizon offered the prospect of a fresh discovery or unknown danger. They found no islands, spotted no landfalls, encountered no other ships. They were removed from all sight of land and all human contact. This would have been one of the worst situa-tions considered, although by no means the worst imaginable. Vasco had gambled that some point of land for provisioning would appear, but knew that one might not, and he would be called on to make this great sweep into unknown waters with only the provisions on hand. He could only estimate how long it would take.

Although it is reasonable to assume there were occasional gales, and although some of the ships suffered light damage, weather conditions remained generally favourable throughout this leg of the voyage and the crews of the four ships fell into a steady, reassuring routine. The main meal was taken at midday and was prepared by the seamen themselves. They would have eaten in working groups, as remains the Portuguese custom. The evening course was little more than a snack followed by the quiet hours, which were filled with the haunting melodies of fado accompanied by the strings of the mandolin. At night each ship marked its location with the reassuring glow of a lantern. Living accommodation for the crew was better than any had experi-enced before, so these were the good days.

As the weeks passed, the familiar North Star dropped below the horizon, to be replaced by the Southern Cross. For many this was a new experience but others had seen it before and would have spoken reassuring words. Although these were new waters, not every event was unanticipated or a threat. It was long, monotonous sailing, but each sailor knew it to be risky. August passed, then September.

Volta da Guiné

At the tropic of Capricorn the ships began to veer east by south-east, following the wind and sailing into the favourable south Equatorial Counter Current. They entered the tempestuous Westerlies, the weather now colder, the waves heavier, the winds more robust, but made good time. The ships were becoming increasingly rank and the once fresh water was turning foul now. Frequently it was poured from kegs into vats and left to air as contaminants settled before it was marginally fit for use. The fresh victuals were long since consumed and the diet was now mundane.

Concern for their fate would have been a constant discussion among the seamen. Not everyone would have had faith in the daring course they were taking. Yet there was no threat of mutiny; no captain turned his ship back; there was no call for harsh measures by Vasco. If any testament to his leadership is needed, it lies here.

Having begun this course on 3 August, they spotted seals and whales along with coastal seaweed on 27 October. These were strong, and reassuring, indications of land and intermittent soundings were now taken as the ships proceeded cautiously. At 9 o'clock on the morning of 4 November land was sighted. The ships drew near to one another and the crews exchanged shouts of exaltation and relief. Every man about the ships knew they had just accomplished something remarkable, and now that land was at hand they could rejoice in the achievement. The officers turned out in their finest clothing, banners and standards were raised aloft in a colorful canopy and the ships fired their bombards in salute of the Captain-Major.

The ships then slowly tacked in closer to landfall. Vasco's pilot, the legendary Pero d'Alenquer, had been in this region with Dias but was unable to identify the shore ahead. Given that Dias's ships had not been within continuous site of Africa, this was not unexpected. The ships sailed south, keeping within view of the coastline, and three days later they spotted a broad bay. D'Alenquer was sent by boat to sound the waters and soon pronounced it suitable. It was named St Helena Bay.

The ships had deteriorated in their time at sea. Their smell was now so foul that ocean winds were required to make them bearable. Vasco ordered the vessels to be cleaned inside and out, the sails mended and all necessary repairs begun. The ships were also to be careened on the beach, their bottoms scraped, cleaned, caulked and then resealed. The surviving water supply was not only low but was almost completely foul and undrinkable. Crews were therefore dispatched to refill kegs from a nearby stream and to secure such fresh meat and edibles as could be safely located. Dias had met with violence in this region, so the Portuguese were on the alert.

It had not been possible aboard ship to take the kind of precise readings of the sun's angle that Vasco desired, so he went ashore with his pilots. A tripod was erected on top of a hill and with his astrolabe Vasco and the pilots made careful observations. The determination was that the fleet had originally struck land some 100 miles north of the Cape of Good Hope.

Vasco had sailed an estimated 3,370 miles over a period of more than three months, without spotting a single landmark to assist in navigation. To have maintained discipline and the unity of his ships was remarkable, especially considering that Columbus began facing the prospect of mutiny after just three weeks out of sight of land. Navigation readings aboard the ships had been taken under difficult circumstances at best. To have landed so close to his chosen point was astounding and ranks as one of the two greatest feats of seamanship in world history, beside the world circumnavigation by the renegade Portuguese pilot Ferdinand Magellan (Fernão da Magalhães).

12

'Foam upon the wave'

The immediate objective for the Portuguese – India and the region of the Indian Ocean – was no more tranquil than Europe at the time, and the Muslims living there were no more united in the brotherhood of their faith than were the Christians. The situation on the subcontinent was further complicated by the existence of a diverse as well as substantial Hindu majority and numerous rival kingdoms, both Muslim and Hindu, none strong enough to dominate the others. The relations of the region were volatile, creating a chronic tinderbox that almost any internal or external force could ignite without warning or foreseeable consequence.

In describing commerce in this region the tendency has been to refer to it as a 'Muslim lake' and to use such phrases as 'Arab dominance' or an 'Islamic world-economy'. The reality was too complex and subject to historic conflicts to justify such a description. The political and economic structure was aggressively eclectic, lacking any central control.[148]

This area of land and sea was also a world of its own, as ignorant of the Europeans as they were of it. A few of the Muslim merchants along the coast of India knew the Portuguese were attempting to reach their market directly by rounding Africa, but there was no consensus that they would succeed, expectation of their imminent arrival or agreement on how to deal with them if they ever arrived.

India itself and the land about the Indian Ocean were a mix of disparate ethnic groups and rival economic forces. Although Islam united the traders and merchants to some degree, it was not the dominant force in all areas, nor even in many places the leading mercantile group. And peace between Hindu and Muslim was always tenuous.

A number of non-Muslim trading groups thrived, including the Gujaratis, Tamils, Telugu Chettis, Syrian Christians, Jews and even for a time Chinese from Fukien.[149] The Muslims themselves did not act in unison but vied constantly for advantage, attacking and betraying one another as circumstances provided the opportunity. The Muslims of southern Arabia viewed their brethren of east Africa with contempt, believing they had joined the True Faith solely for commercial advantage, considering their observation of the Prophet's admonishments to be superficial.

This opinion was not limited to the Muslims along the African coast. The Arab navigator Ahmid ibn Majid recorded a view widely held when he wrote of the Malay Muslims:

> These are bad people, who do not know any rule; the Infidel marries the Muslim, and the Muslim the Infidel woman; and when you call them 'Infidels', are you really sure that they are Infidels? And the Muslims of whom you speak, are they really Muslims? They drink wine in public, and do not pray when they set out on a voyage.[150]

About the coastlines of western India, southern Arabia and eastern Africa that bordered the Indian Ocean were numerous rival port city-states that dominated ocean-borne commerce. Some were independent, others were subject to control by larger ports. Each possessed associated trader settlements and the ports themselves were often allied with one another. These included Cochin, Calicut, Basrur and Gôa in south-western India; Ormuz, Muscat, Shihr, Aden and Mokha in and immediately around Arabia; Mogadishu, Malindi, Mombasa, Zanzibar, Kilwa, Sofala, the Comoro Islands and northern Madagascar in east Africa. They prospered from port duties, the customary 10% levy on imports and from a local monopoly in the trade of certain spices, ivory and slaves.

This cultural and commercial *mélange* was the consequence of centuries-old developments, some of which were still unfolding when Vasco da Gama and his alien ships suddenly appeared off the coast of India. From the seventh century to the end of the ninth Islam unexpectedly exploded, spreading through Egypt and then sweeping in a great wave over Arabia, across Persia and into the Indus river region. By 1400 it extended through all but the southernmost portion of India and along the east coast of Africa as far south as Kilwa.[151] In this region of Africa, Islam was limited to the coastal area and was primarily the religion of the Arab ivory and slave traders, though some of the local population also converted.

Muslim settlements along the coast of east Africa had generally been established as the results of conflicts on the Sinai peninsula. In the seventh century the inhabitants of Oman revolted against the caliph and in defeat were forced to flee, settling near Patta. Following a conflict in AD 739 another group settled on the Benadir coast. A second wave of refugees joined them in the early tenth century, also establishing Mogadishu and Brava as Arab and Muslim communities.

In AD 975 the son of a sultan left Persia for some unknown reason with seven ships and a large number of colonists. They settled in Mombasa, Pemba and Quiloa. One of his ships went as far south as the Comoro Islands. With this, Arabs had essentially taken or occupied the historic land of Punt. The Arabs referred to the region as Zanj, their word for native, and from it comes the name Zanzibar. Arab expansion stopped at Sofala in modern Mozambique, at about 20° latitude, just across the strait from Madagascar.[152]

The ultimate region of Arab expansion was scarcely greater than it had been for the Romans, although they established trade routes to the Far East of a much greater magnitude. They initially dominated the waters demarcated by a rough triangle formed by Djibouti, Colombo, Zanzibar and the Comoros, and called this region the Sea of Lar. The eastern portion of the Indian Ocean was known to them as the Sea of Harkand. They appear not to have used a single name for the entire expanse of ocean.[153]

Throughout the Indian Ocean Arab traders were responsible for the spread of rice, coffee and sugar-cane. They also introduced the Chinese inventions of paper, the saddle and stirrups, the compass and gunpowder. They brought to the Chinese the astrolabe, so essential to long-distance blue-ocean sailing.

In this region of the Indian Ocean the Arabs traded for spices, silks and precious stones, exchanging for them linen, woollen cloth, cotton, carpets, wrought iron, silver, coral and, of course, horses. The Arab *dinar* replaced the Roman *aureus* and the Persian *dirhem* as the coin of trade. The area assumed legendary significance within Arab culture and is the location of Sinbad the Sailor's adventures.

Muslim trade and the Arab voyages were not restricted to the Indian Ocean. They established a 'route to China', sailing with the prevailing winter winds from the Persian Gulf to the Indian Malabar coast. From there they rounded the tip of India and Ceylon, then sailed to the Nicobar Islands, where they acquired new provisions. Some ships went from here to Sumatra and Java, while others sailed to the island of Tiuman, then to ports of the Champa kingdom, on to Hanoi and finally Canton in China.

The voyage from Basra took six months. The layover was also six months, as was the return trip, making a total of eighteen months. The Arabs had established a colony in Canton in AD 758, some eighty years after their first expedition. In 878 there was a massacre of both Arabs and Jews in Canton and thereafter the Arabs were content to trade with the Chinese from a base in Malaya while the Jews sent expeditions to China throughout the tenth century.[154]

Among the major commodities traded throughout the region were black slaves taken from east Africa. Countless cargoes of slaves were transported into the Middle East and to India, many of them carried as far east as China, a traffic that continued until the nineteenth century. Trade in slaves had always existed in the Indian Ocean, but it was the Arabs who became its great specialists and perfected its operation. Their methodical exploitation of native Africans led to at least one uprising, in Basra in the ninth century.[155]

The history of the Indian subcontinent is generally recorded by recounting the nearly endless stream of invasions through the

north-western mountain passes from Central Asia into the Indus
river region. The most significant is the series of invasions by the
Aryans, but other groups that followed also left a permanent
mark on Indian history and its culture. Afghano-Persian nobles
ruled the vast Indian population, first in the north and then later,
for a time, in the south as well, leaving a residue of their culture.

From earliest times Indian society was defined primarily by its
social and cultural institutions and especially by its division into
a rigid class structure. At the bottom was the general tribal
group; next was the warrior class, from which the *rajan* or tribal
chieftain was selected. Then there was the priest class, who as
early as 1000 BC were identified as Brahmins. This traditional
Indian cultural model was to endure no matter who conquered
or ruled, or for how long.

The first expansion of Islam by force into India came from the
Middle East in AD 711, when an Arab expedition entered the lower
Indus Valley in north-west India. This area was under the control
of the caliphate of Baghdad for a time, then was ruled by two independent Muslim rulers. Other portions of India, Baluchistan,
Seistan and large parts of Afghanistan, all areas that traditionally
had come under Indian influence, fell to Islam. Once established
in these regions, the Muslims had a base of operations from which
to attack India proper.[156]

The great Muslim push into India began in the late tenth century, when Maymud of Ghazni, ruler of a Turkish state in
Afghanistan, executed a series of seventeen devastating raids
against the declining Pratiharas to plunder and seize slaves. As a
consequence a substantial expanse of north central India passed
under Muslim control, with Lahore as the capital.[157] In the
twelfth century the leader of a new Turkish dynasty established
just north of Kabul, Muhammad Ghuri, raided in force into
India. He quickly defeated the existing Muslim rulers and then
moved south and east, looting and conquering as he went.

The Muslim incursions enjoyed such success in part because
of the endless wars among the Hindu states, which had so weakened them, but also because arrogance and contempt for all
things foreign had become institutionalized in Hindu culture

among the élite. Alberuni, a scholar in the Muslim court at the time, penned the most extensive description of India written by a non-Indian before the arrival of the Portuguese. He recorded that:

> The Hindus believe that there is no nation like theirs, no kings like theirs, no religion like theirs, no science like theirs. They are by nature niggardly in communicating that which they know, and they take the greatest possible care to withhold it from men of another caste among their own people, still much more of course, from any foreigner. Their haughtiness is such that if you tell them of any science or scholar in Khurasan or Persia, they will think you both an ignoramus and a liar.[158]

Such self-imposed isolation from new thought and innovation left the Hindu states vulnerable to foreign conquerors.

The Muslim armies – with their superior military structure, equipment and above all tactics, based on cavalry armed with light bows – proved no match for the enormous plodding Indian armies made up of ill-trained massed infantry supported by ponderous elephants. Their highly disciplined horsemen charged straight at an enemy, stopped abruptly, wheeled their horses so that the head did not obstruct their view and aim, and then unleashed a murderous volley of arrows into the opposing ranks. They withdrew as quickly as they appeared, only to attack unexpectedly in the same manner elsewhere, wreaking damage on the opposing ranks far out of proportion to their own losses.

At the Battle of Tarain, north of Delhi, in 1192 the power of the Rajputs was broken primarily by the destruction wrought by 10,000 mounted archers. Ghuri then advanced east into Bengal, where his forces sacked the capital.

The inability of any conqueror, indigenous or foreign, to take or hold India is primarily the result of its geography. Few regions on Earth are as divided by nature as the Indian subcontinent. Penetration southward by armies was extraordinarily demanding because of the difficult terrain and the numerous adverse rivers, often swollen by the monsoon. South India is separated from north India by the Vindhya mountains, the formidable Narmada river and a vast barren, inhospitable zone.

A region extending from Gujarat on the west to Orissa on the east alone contained four enclaves largely isolated from one another and creating a formidable barrier to any lord seeking to unite the country under one rule. Large parts of India were so inaccessible that even basic knowledge travelled at an incredibly slow pace. To the south disease, which flourished in the more tropical land, was a debilitating plague on every army or attempted occupier and ultimately as devastating as any opposing force of arms.

One persistent problem faced by the nobility of India was the modest surplus produced by agriculture, much less than was the case in Europe. Rulers depended on this surplus to support themselves, their courts, bureaucrats and armies. In India the margin was razor-thin. Although ostentatious wealth was the norm for kings and royalty, it came upon the backs of a far greater and much poorer population than that of Europe. It was, accordingly, more precarious and hence maintained with greater brutality.

Indian history has been dominated by the *chakravartin,* a lord who attempted to conquer the known world.[159] The personalities and accomplishments of the seemingly endless stream of rulers throughout India are virtually unknown. When a strong ruler died, the empire and capital very often died with him. Almost nothing remains save their names, uncovered by archaeologists. In few parts of the Earth did rulers and kingdoms arise and flourish only to be swallowed whole within short years.

In the Vishnu Purana, a Hindu religious text from the seventh or eighth century, the petty rulers of India's numerous small kingdoms are mocked for believing, 'This earth is mine, it is my son's, it belongs to my dynasty', unaware that 'they themselves are but foam upon the wave'.[160] On a grander scale, an invader from the north could emerge from unknown regions, establish an empire and then pass into obscurity within the span of a single lifetime.[161]

Although they may have arrived with different beliefs and practices, what remained was assimilated by the entrenched and resilient Hindu culture.

The chief function of rulers was the collection of taxes and the imposition of their will by force of arms. A Chinese Buddhist pilgrim visited India in the seventh century and reported that the subcontinent possessed no fewer than seventy kingdoms, divided into a 'web of conflicting sovereignties'.[162] Decentralization, though, had little affect on the life of the average person. He still paid taxes to his local ruler, no matter how large or small the kingdom in which he found himself.

Adding to the difficulties of rule, the land was also occupied by groups separated by a cacophony of languages, racial groups and religious beliefs. Intolerance was no less common in India than it was in Christian Europe and was just as often used as an instrument of royal power.

The introduction of cavalry warfare by the Muslim invaders initially changed the balance of power in India, but their methods were quickly adopted, re-establishing an equilibrium of sorts. The change meant, however, that the modest agricultural surplus could be even more effectively appropriated. This was made necessary by the new armies, which depended so heavily on swift – and far more expensive – mounted cavalry. Generally, horse-breeding was not effective in India, which meant horses had to be imported at great cost from Arabia and Persia.[163]

By the thirteenth century, with Delhi as the capital, Muslims held the entire north of India, from the mouth of the Ganges in the east to the headwaters of the Indus in the west, and as far south as Gwalior just below the Chambal river.[164] When their empires had run their course for a time, regional states emerged, each with a similar pattern. As far as was possible, the Muslims attempted to centralize control, as was their model elsewhere, but they largely failed because of the traditional difficulties faced by all conquerors in India. Interestingly, Hindus and Muslims shared a uniform court culture, for even when the Muslim invaders arrived they adopted the existing ruling protocol.[165] At the core was a lavish royal centre towards which streamed the greatest measure of wealth. Direct royal authority diminished with distance from the court, so that at the outer region the influence of the adjoining state could be felt. There was intense competition among these concentric states and their borders were in a constant state of flux.

Because of the difficult geography and for other reasons over 100 years passed before Muslim armies advanced to southern India, yet these events were the turning-point for both the Muslims and Hindus.[166] The greatest expanse of Islam throughout India occurred under Muhammad Tughluq during the fourteenth century. Drawing on previous success, he ruled a largely consolidated empire that consisted of nearly the entire subcontinent with the exception of Kashmir, Orissa and certain remote areas in Rajasthan.

The most lasting affect of the Muslim invasions was the establishment of a permanent Muslim minority within the subcontinent; this constituted the first time invaders had not been assimilated by the Hindu culture. The Muslims came to recognize that the Hindus would not accept Islam *en masse* and reluctantly accepted an accommodation with the indigenous population. Where conversions did occur, they were typically the lowest Hindu castes seeking to escape their social stigma and this was only one more reason for the Hindu majority to disdain contact with Muslims.

In general, Muslims also held themselves apart from the conquered majority. The Muslims tended to be concentrated in Delhi and when they lived in other cities they resided within a fortified compound surrounded by a hostile Hindu majority. In time practicality dictated that the Hindus be granted the *de facto* status of *dhimmis*, which had originally been intended for Jews and Christians only. Beyond the immediate sphere of royal power tax-collecting generally remained with the Hindus rulers, who were left in place so long as they paid tribute to the Muslim government. In an area about 100 miles in radius from their capital the Muslims maintained immediate control and all Hindus were reduced to abject poverty wherever possible, to take from them the means of revolt.

For all this, one of the most impressive aspects of Indian society was its ability to continue to feed itself and to support the nobility, despite a substantial and growing population. The subcontinent's population at the end of the fifteenth century is estimated at 100 million.

The reality was that India simply could not be bent to the will of any one conqueror. The invasion of Timur in the late fourteenth century and his sacking of Delhi, with the wanton slaughter of the entire Hindu population, only served to speed the decline of the Muslim rulers in their increasingly diminished states.[167] By one estimate the Muslim invaders slaughtered as many as 10 million Hindus, but in the end they did not conquer for long.

By the late fifteenth century and early sixteenth, five independent sultanates had been established in north and central India, the strongest of which was Delhi. Although their sultanates were reduced in size, the Muslim rulers were great builders, constructing entire cities and erecting forts, mosques and tombs. They were patrons of Islamic culture, which remained dominated by Persian culture and literature.

By the time of the arrival of the Portuguese three centuries of conquest and intermittent rule by the Muslims was still visible throughout most of India. Regardless of who ruled in a particular region, two cultures and religions, Hindu and Muslim, existed, each within its own constraints. Although there were areas of interaction, as far as possible the two cultures remained distinct and uninvolved,[168] even though in the Muslim courts certain Brahmins were employed while in the Hindu states Muslims served a key role in trade.

The southern tip of India was the least frequently conquered region of the subcontinent and, if seized, was generally held but a short time. The 'Far South', as it was known, had a distinct history of its own from which evolved its own unique culture, though antagonism existed among regions, primarily between the highland and coastal lowland. Initially trade and the source of wealth came from pearls, shells and gems, including diamonds. Because of its proximity to the trade routes with the East and the Middle East the trade in spices assumed the dominant role and greatly enriched the south, although, as was the case throughout India, the rewards were primarily enjoyed by a handful at the top. The trading ports and the duties derived from them had been another source of wealth for the rulers since time immemorial. King Solomon, it is believed, sent ships every three years to south India bearing precious metal, ivory, monkeys and peacocks.

In the absence of a dominant Muslim power two areas of Hindu authority asserted themselves. One was in Rajasthan and the other, significantly for Vasco da Gama and the Portuguese, emerged south of the Krishna river (also known as the Kistna river), occupying all of the far south of India, from where it fiercely resisted the Muslims.

One of the natural barriers of the subcontinent is a line that roughly follows the southern edge of the Rayalaseema region, which is the northern border of the Teluga language. It was here that the wave of Islam conquest was finally stayed, and here that a Hindu empire not only survived but flourished for 200 years. It was named after its capital, ambitiously called Vijayanagar, 'The City of Victory'.[169] During the decline of the Delhi sultanate the Vijayanagar empire arose as one of the strongest military states in all India.

At the time of Vasco da Gama's arrival the Vijayanagar empire was just entering its most powerful, albeit short-lived, period of supremacy. The empire was founded in the mid-fourteenth century and from the first created an elaborate mythology to establish a religious legitimacy for the new kingdom. An inscription establishes that Vijayanagar was actually founded by King Ballala III.[170] This Hindu kingdom fought successfully against both Muslim sultanates and other Hindu kingdoms to establish itself as the first dominant power in all of southern India. Their most consistently powerful opponent was the Bahmanid kingdom to their immediate north. Many wars were waged with that sultanate for the rich land between the Krishna and Tunghabhadra rivers. Vijayanagar fell in the mid-sixteenth century, succumbing at last to the combined pressure of the northern sultanates and independent chieftains, but in its time it flourished from the spice trade.

The capital city of Vijayanagar was located in a largely barren region yet was one of the largest and most magnificent cities in the world. Seven concentric rings of formidable walls, running some 60 miles, surrounded the inner city. Outside them, driven into the hard ground close together, were stone spears the height of a man, designed to break any cavalry charge, impale war elephants and obstruct massed infantry in their attempt to get to the first wall. Along the northern walls ran the broad and swift-flowing Tunghabhadra river. Within sight were numerous temples, while the city itself stretched into the far distance, a sea of tan masonry interspersed with bright pennants, stone watch-towers and gaudy pavilions.

The land area within the walls was enormous. Cultivated fields, homes and lush gardens occupied the area between the first and third walls. Streams flowed in meticulously charted stone-lined channels. Here were the suburbs with markets and shops which grew increasingly numerous towards the centre. There the market-place was lined with arcades. Hundreds of thousands of visitors streamed through the streets, to barter, to seek favour or opportunity. So rich was the empire, so opulent this capital, that silk was more commonly seen than cotton. The women, described universally as the most beautiful on Earth, wore their gold jewellery with ostentation, and both gems and jewels were sold in the open so effective was the security.[171]

At the royal centre, conducting himself as a Persian ruler, the king, or *raya*, held court within the House of Victory, a vast hall supported by forty pillars. Here also were the palace and administrative buildings. The royal palace was constructed from exquisitely carved, gilded wood, interspersed with marble. The rooms within were adorned in mother-of-pearl and gold leaf. Surrounding the palace were many temples, flanked by impressive buildings. All around were statues of gods and goddesses and across from the House of Victory stood stunning pavilions, designed in such a way that each presented an entirely different view when the previous one became stale.

In the mid-fifteenth century Abd al-Razzaq travelled from Ormuz to Calicut on a horse-trading expedition and there acted

as the ambassador of the Timurid ruler. He was invited to journey to the Vijayanagar court by the ruler and recorded his first-
hand observations. He noted that there was a substantial west
Asian trading community in the capital city and this was only
one of many such trading groups. The trade in war horses was
jealously guarded by the rulers since the animals were essential
to maintain military dominance.[172]

An account of the military power and ostentatious wealth of
Vijayanagar's Bahmanid neighbour comes from one Athanasius
Nikitan, a Russian merchant who spent some months there in
1470. What he recorded was mirrored in the Hindu Vijayanagar
empire to the immediate south.

The size of the Indian armies, Nikitan records, was enormous, especially by European standards. The great bulk of the
troops, however, were marginally trained infantrymen. The key
component was the cavalry, with their expensive, imported war
horses. Nikitan estimated the size of the sultan's army, both cavalry and infantry, at 1 million men, armed with both 'long mus-
kets' and 'heavy guns'.

The sultan was 'a little man, twenty years old, and in the
power of the Khorasani [i.e., Afghano-Persian] nobles'. He rode
his horse during celebration sitting 'on a golden saddle, wearing
a habit embroidered with sapphires and on his pointed headdress
a large diamond; he also carried a suit of gold armour inlaid with
sapphires and three swords mounted in gold'.[173]

Before the sultan marched a gigantic silk-clad elephant,
clutching in its trunk a gold chain with which it swept away the
masses to clear a path for the sovereign. The sultan's brother followed, resting on a bed made of solid gold, covered in velvet, set
with precious gems and held aloft by twenty men. Next was the
chief minister and mentor to sultans, also reclining on a bed of
gold pulled by four horses in gilded harness. About and behind
the lords was a great mass of cavalry in full armour, accompanied
by hundreds of young female dancers and singers, many of them
nearly naked but all bearing a shield, sword, lance or bow. To the
rear were 300 heavily armoured war elephants holding a 'citadel'
containing six soldiers armed with guns. Attached to the massive

tusks of the elephants were extended, enormous swords.[174] There was no doubt in Nikitan's mind that he was witnessing a sovereign who ranked above all others, '*the* Muhammadan sultan of India'.

The Vijayanagar empire derived a substantial portion of its income from the taxing of trade, though control of the distant trading ports was tenuous. Although not especially large, Calicut, Vasco da Gama's destination, was the most prosperous trading port in the empire, yet because of the difficult terrain of the Western Ghats separating them it was largely independent of direct control from the capital. It selected its own leader, the Zamorin, and with its highly skilled professional soldiers was too formidable an opponent to be totally subjugated. It took, for example, two strenuous months to journey from Vijayanagar to Calicut, a passage that would have exposed an invading army to countless opportunities for defeat.

The Zamorin was the eighty-fourth of his line, and of middle or advanced age. He worked to achieve lasting control over a collection of petty chieftains whose domains extended throughout central and northern Kerala. Abd al-Razzaq observed that the Zamorin was unimpressive in appearance and wore very little because of the oppressive heat. He was tolerant, even solicitous, of the Arabs who controlled most trade in his port. The Zamorin was very much concerned with matters of trade and security was intense. In fact, much of the ruler's reputation was based on the level of security he provided to traders.

> In that city [Calicut] security and justice are such that wealthy merchants who sail the seas bring many goods there from Daryabar. They unload them from the ships and store them in lanes and the bazaar as long as they wish without having to worry about guarding them. The *diwan* watchmen keep guard and patrol them day and night. If they make a sale, one fortieth is taken in alms; otherwise no duties are imposed on them. It is the custom of other ports to seize as windfall and plunder any ship headed for one port but driven by God's destiny to take refuge in another.

Innovation and continuous modification of ship design made possible the Portuguese discoveries. These are some of the ships they used, shown on a contemporary manuscript. The caravel at the top with a lateen sail was nothing less than revolutionary

This painting of the simplest of caravels still captures the elegance of its design

This reproduction of the *Nina*, used by Christopher Columbus on his voyage to America, is an accurate depiction of the Portuguese caravel

Above: A nineteenth-century rendering of King Manuel bidding farewell to Vasco da Gama on the first European voyage to India. It was the culmination of a Portuguese effort that lasted nearly a century and cost the lives of countless seamen

Left: A later impression of Vasco da Gama's small fleet under way. The first voyage to India lasted two years. The two surviving ships sailed a distance equal to that of a circumnavigation of the world at the equator

A rather dramatic rendering of Gama's first meeting with the Zamorin, the Hindu ruler of Calicut, India's leading port in the spice trade. Because of Ga-ma's voyage the king of Portugal would become the richest monarch in Europe

Left: Traditionally believed to be a portrait of Dom Vasco da Gama shortly before his death, this picture is now suspect. Gama's age at death has been more accurately placed at fifty-four or fifty-five but this appears to be an older man

Below: After returning from India, Vasco da Gama married well and lived for a time in Evora. Eventually he bought this residence in Sines, where he lived the remainder of his life between subsequent voyages to India. The dwelling offers a commanding view of the town itself

Portugal introduced the modern chapter of black African slavery. The slaves were sold on the beach in the Algarve. They usually worked in the fields beside other Portuguese labourers or household servants. In time most were freed, though this was just the first phase in the introduction of plantation slavery and all the misery that went with it

King Manuel ordered the construction of the Mosteiro dos Jerónimos in the place from which Vasco da Gama's ships sailed for India. It remains Portugal's lasting monument to the 'Discoveries'. The river has since changed course and the gardens in the foreground are where his ships were anchored

This monument to the 'Discoveries' was erected in celebration 500 years later. Every key participant is depicted. The monument is located at Belém, the site of departure for the fleets

However, in Calicut, no matter where a ship is from and where it is headed, if it docks there, they treat it like any other ship and subject it to no more or no less duty.[175]

There is a story told of the integrity of the Zamorin in Calicut. A Chetti merchant from Coromandel returning to the Red Sea following a trading expedition found his ship overloaded with gold. He deposited a large treasure chest in the stone cellar of the Zamorin and departed, the story goes, with little optimism. When he returned he found the entire treasure awaiting him. In gratitude he offered the Zamorin half, which was refused, the ruler observing that he had done nothing more than was expected of him. The merchant went on to found the bazaar in Calicut.[176]

The Portuguese, and the Europeans who followed in time, were more developed in technology, in the construction and use of ships, in their realization of the significance of sea lanes and especially in the building and use of cannon than were either the Muslims or Hindus. The lack of unity hurt India enormously when it came to resisting the encroachment of the Portuguese, for disunity was something the Europeans understood and knew how to exploit. They also profited from the conviction shared by nearly all rulers in India, articulated by Bahadur Shah, King of Gujarat, that 'wars by sea are merchants' affairs, and of no concern to the prestige of kings'.[177]

As the Portuguese were to discover to their great delight, no kingdom that used the Indian Ocean possessed a single ship of war. The merchant vessels were lightly armed, if at all, and of much more fragile construction than the Portuguese ships.

Such was the world Vasco da Gama and his crew were about to enter. India was a self-contained universe, confident in its military dominance, arrogant in its cultural supremacy, essentially unaware of and utterly unconcerned with any nation beyond its shores.

13

'You will have to conquer'

As Vasco de Gama and the navigators completed their readings on the coast of southern Africa the seamen were busy cleaning and refilling water kegs. Other crewmen explored the immediate area while a few wandered atop the nearby sand dunes to view the interior. They spotted two Bushmen busy with a small torch smoking bees from a hive so they could harvest the honey. When informed, Vasco ordered the pair to be surrounded and captured peacefully in the hope he could learn something of this region.

Unlike the slaves the Portuguese had been taking for a generation, these Bushmen were short and tawny-coloured. They wore the skins of animals rather than woven cloth and covered their penis with a 'war sheath'. They carried olive wood spears, tipped by a brown horn strengthened in fire. They were accompanied by a pack of dogs which to the Europeans looked much like those in Portugal, with the same reassuring bark. The Bushman diet consisted of seal and whale meat, gazelles and roots. This pair, it transpired, was preoccupied and caught by surprise, although one managed to struggle loose and flee.[178]

As for the other, none of the interpreters could communicate with the terrified man. Seeing this would get him nowhere, Vasco had a cabin boy and black sailor take him aboard the *São Gabriel*, where he was seated at the captain's place, fed the best food available and reportedly ate with gusto. The experience calmed him and the three managed to communicate a bit by sign language. Vasco gave instructions for the Bushman to be dressed from the slop chest, given small bells and glass beads, and then had him sent alone to his village with a request to bring others of his tribe back the next day.

That morning some fifteen of the Bushmen appeared and readily accepted the offered trinkets. But when shown a selection of spices, pearls, gold and silver, they demonstrated complete ignorance. Two days later, just after the Portuguese had taken their meal, between forty and fifty locals appeared, and again relations were friendly. The sailors bartered for souvenirs, as seamen of all ages are inclined to do. A single copper coin secured ornaments worn in the ears and fox tails attached to a handle, which were used as fans.

Contact between Europeans and distant people was always fragile and likely to turn suddenly from peace to violence. To reassure the Bushmen that the Portuguese had come in peace Vasco instructed his men to carry no weapons of any kind. One of the men-at-arms, Fernão Velloso, a loud and boastful sort, announced that he would like to return with this group to their nearby village to see how they lived. Vasco hesitated, knowing how tenuous all this goodwill was, but when his older brother Paulo urged him to allow it, he let the man go. Velloso set off in high spirits, the entire group laughing and chattering as Vasco returned to his ship.

Nicolau Coelho was ashore with men, gathering wood and collecting lobsters, which were in abundance. The Bushmen with Velloso soon spotted a seal, which they killed and decided to cook on the spot. Perhaps they were having second thoughts about letting this stranger know the location of their village, because when the meal was finished the Bushmen told Velloso he should return to his ship and go with them no further.

While this was transpiring out of sight, Paulo decided to hunt one of the small whales that came in close to shore and set out in a small boat (*batel*) with two of his crew. He had the ropes of his harpoons tied to the boat's bow so that when one of his men speared a whale it dragged the boat after it as it swam quickly for the open ocean. The Portuguese were caught by surprise and had neither an axe nor a knife with which to cut the line. The men precariously clung to the boat, which was in danger of capsizing at any instant. As they reached the sea the whale suddenly veered back towards the shore, where it went to the shallow bottom and lay still. Taking advantage of this interlude, the men were able to untie the rope and immediately rowed to their ship. The scene had been good sport to the seamen on board the ships who had witnessed it, although more than one thought it a foolish way for men to drown.

Vasco, unaware the Bushmen had stopped to cook a seal, was by now quite concerned about Velloso and began pacing the deck of his ship, casting frequent looks in the direction the group had taken. Suddenly there was Velloso, running for all he was worth, shouting and gesturing for help. Coelho was in the water by this time, returning to his ship, when Vasco called out for him to hurry ashore and retrieve Velloso. Coelho's men were well acquainted with their shipmate and thought this was just one more of his pranks and so they rowed their boats slowly.

The situation on shore was deteriorating by the moment. Two Bushmen raced from an angle to head Velloso off while others appeared behind him in hot pursuit, armed with bows, arrows and stones. Coelho's boats suddenly leaped forward in the water. The two Bushmen tried to seize Velloso, who fought them off with his fists even as he scrambled aboard one of the boats.

The boats moved out of immediate danger while Coelho tried to determine what had happened and restore peace. The instructions to all the crew had been very specific about maintaining friendly relations with the people they contacted, if at all possible. The situation, however, continued to deteriorate and as the natives gathered in force Vasco climbed into a longboat and joined the scene. Just as he arrived stones and arrows were unleashed at the Portuguese, three of whom were lightly wounded. When Vasco stood in his boat and attempted to restore calm, they turned on him and he took an arrow in the leg.[179]

Vasco ordered all boats back to their respective ships. On shore the Bushmen continued shouting and gesturing with hostility towards the Portuguese. The lesson learned over the long years of the discoveries was that such an assault must be greeted in kind. Other Portuguese were likely to find themselves in this very bay – indeed Vasco himself might have to put in here on his return voyage – so the situation could not be left as it was. If the locals weren't to have friendly relations with them, then they should know fear. Vasco ordered a team of crossbowmen to row ashore with a full complement of arrows and instructions to retaliate against the Bushmen.[180]

There is no record of the source of the dispute with Velloso, nor is it known how many, if any, Bushmen were killed or wounded by the armed force. The injuries to the Portuguese were apparently not serious, but had the arrows been poisonous Vasco da Gama would be a footnote in history.

The Portuguese took an important lesson from this experience. The author of the *Roteiro* records that 'all this happened because we looked upon these people as men of little spirit, quite incapable of violence, and had therefore landed without first arming ourselves'.[181] They were not to repeat what they saw as a mistake.

After eight days in St Helena Bay, Vasco ordered his small fleet to set sail. Two days later, with jubilation, they spotted the Cape but when they attempted to round it they encountered a strong wind blowing from south south-east and were unable to make headway. Time and again Vasco ordered the ships to turn into the gale, only for them to be forced back and compelled briefly to seek shelter against the coast. Even the largest of his vessels was too small to face the formidable winds, currents and heavy seas of this region where the Indian Ocean and the south Atlantic tempestuously meet.

The weather deteriorated and the crew suffered terribly in the attempts. The ships were struck by such powerful waves there were fears they would break up. Battered by the winds, with massive waves crashing across the decks, the seamen, frightened, unable to cook meals, cold and wet, began to grumble among themselves. The repeated attempts were so perilous that the crew begged Vasco to break off his efforts. At one point a group crowded about the Captain-Major and implored him to turn about. They said he was responsible for them and had no right to force them into such a terrible death as the one they were certain to now face. Vasco mounted a stand and shouted that 'double the Cape he would, even if it meant trying again and again'.[182] He ordered the men back to their places and renewed the assault against the heavy seas and fierce winds.

Finally, at noon on 22 November, the ships turned the tip of Africa. Trumpets were sounded and the crew broke into a spontaneous dance of joy. Now hugging the coastline, the ships made their way slowly east. Three days beyond the large curvature of the coast, running low on water, they sailed into Mossel Bay and dropped anchor.

Had there not been a shortage of water, it is unlikely Vasco would have put in at this location. He had been warned this was where Dias had experienced problems with the locals and had killed one with a crossbow. There would surely be ill will towards them, so the Portuguese were in a heightened state of readiness.

Vasco ordered the ships to approach land only in an area clear of any brush so that the landing party could not be caught by surprise. A large number of locals, identified as Hottentots, were observed on the beach behaving in what appeared to be a friendly manner, which came as a welcome surprise. No women or children were in view, however, and those greeting the Portuguese were primarily older men. Vasco instructed the shore party to wear armour and to be well armed, then went ashore with them.

Before allowing the boats to beach Vasco tossed tinkling bells to the Hottentots, who danced in pleasure whenever they caught one. Satisfied, Vasco and his men stepped ashore and in the next few minutes traded more bells and red caps for ivory bracelets which the locals took from their arms. Not wanting the Hottentots to be in a position to overwhelm his much smaller force, he insisted they approach in small groups. This first contact went well but Vasco had already witnessed how quickly, and unexpectedly, such occasions could turn to violence.

Once the Hottentots had moved off he gave the usual orders to lay in such fresh supplies as could be found and for repairs to be made on the battered ships. He had the remaining stores on the supply vessel transferred to the other three ships, then ordered it to be broken up. Any wood that could conceivably be of use in repairs was preserved and much of the rest was taken as firewood; the remainder of the ship was burnt on the beach so that nails and other metal fittings could be recovered. There now remained only the two naus and the smaller caravel.

Two days after landing some 200 locals were seen approaching the ships, driving before them a herd of cattle and sheep. Barter was obviously to be increased. Boats went ashore and Vasco and his men were warmly greeted. A number of *goras* (a native pipe) were produced and the festive crowd broke into song and dance. Vasco ordered trumpets to be sounded aboard his ships. A short time later, satisfied with the state of affairs, he returned to his own vessel. The festive mood was infectious, so he instructed his musicians to play a suitable tune. As the sailors began to dance, to their astonishment the Captain-Major joined in. Once the dancing and music were finished, a fat ox was bought for three Portuguese bracelets, providing the officers and crew with dinner. 'We found him very fat,' the *Roteiro* reports, 'and his meat as toothsome as the beef of Portugal.'

Later that same day another group of Hottentots arrived with cattle. They had with them their women and children, which the Portuguese found reassuring. They too played music and danced, though the women, children and young men with weapons remained a short distance away, crouching in the brush. As the first ox had proved so satisfying, Vasco sent ashore Martim Alfonso, who had experience with the locals in west Africa, to see if he could acquire another. The situation began to deteriorate almost at once.

First, the Hottentots took Alfonso to a nearby water source and gestured that it was out of bounds to the Portugese. Although no mention is made, it is likely they had been filling their kegs here. When Alfonso indicated he would like to acquire one of the oxen, the locals drove their livestock into the brush and trees, indicating forcefully that there would be no trade. Watching from aboard his ship, Vasco became suspicions and gave orders for Alfonso to return. He then gave orders for a heavily armed party to go ashore, which greatly excited the

Hottentots. The purpose of the armed men was to demonstrate that the Portuguese had the power to inflict harm if they wished but that they chose to be peaceful. When their presence did not seem to have the desired effect on the agitated herdsmen, however, Vasco ordered two of the ships' bombards to be fired for show. The thunder of the cannon startled the Hottentots, who ran about in a panic before finally running off as fast as they could, driving their herd ahead of them.[183]

Vasco now directed that the first of the marker pillars should be erected. A large wooden cross was constructed out of a mizen-mast and was placed on top of the stone pillar to create an impressive presence. Their own white sails bore the crimson cross of the Order of Christ, and the symbolism of the pillar could not have been lost on the local population. It was as if a brand was being placed by these newcomers on the land. The Portuguese were either unaware of the message they were sending or did not care.

The fleet set sail on 6 December, thirteen days after arriving, but as the ships were clearing the bay a group of Hottentots surrounded the pillar and broke both it and the cross into pieces, much to the anger of the Portuguese.

The weather was now working against Vasco and the ships made little progress. After they had sailed just a short distance the wind failed and the ships were forced to drop anchor. Grumbling among the crew had not entirely disappeared. Two days later they were again under way and on the 12th encountered 'a great storm' that seemed to blow 'from all parts'. Worse, at times the wind ceased, trapping the ships within the troughs of the huge waves, great volumes of water washing over their decks. The sailors strapped themselves to the ships to prevent being swept overboard, and more than one gave himself up as lost. It seemed at times as though the ships themselves were breaking up, and heavy kegs of water broke loose, crashing below deck, causing great havoc.

The *São Miguel*, the caravel captained by young Nicolau Coelho, was separated from the larger naus and for a time feared lost, but when the storm mercifully abated the ship was spotted in the distance. An unsuccessful attempt was made to attract its attention, but the winds worked in their favour and drove the ship back to them.

On 16 December the Portuguese passed the pillar Dias had left to mark his farthest point. They were now in the Agulhas current, which flowed against them, and progress was extremely difficult. These were uncharted waters and thus inherently dangerous. For four days the ships sailed well out to sea to escape the current and beat against strong winds, tacking repeatedly in an attempt to make headway. On 20 December, despite their best endeavours, they discovered to their chagrin that they were back where they had started on the 16th. Finally the wind changed in their favour and they were 'able to overcome the currents which we had feared might frustrate our plans. Henceforth it pleased God in His mercy to allow us to make headway!'[184]

On Christmas Day 1497 Vasco named the land they were slowly passing 'Natal', the Portuguese word for Christmas. They were now advancing in waters no European had sailed before. At such times uncertainty and doubt were at their strongest. Commitment to such voyages of discovery was always firmest among the captains, partly because they stood to gain so much from success but also because they had been specially selected for their persistence, so necessary to explore the unknown, to push on in the face of risk.

Two historians record a suspiciously fanciful account of what occurred next. At this point in the expedition Nicolau Coelho discovered a plot among some of the crew but also, most disturbingly, among the masters and pilots of the vessels. When the *São Miguel* and the *São Gabriel* drew close enough for the captains to shout to one another, as occurred quite often, Coelho was able to deliver a carefully worded message urging Vasco to clap the masters and pilots in irons. The Captain-Major understood Coelho's meaning but concealed it until he could arrange a ruse whereby the pilots and masters of the other vessels joined him, along with their nautical instruments and charts. Presumably he told them he meant to establish a firm fix on their position and to update all charts in order to reflect their new discoveries.

Once the men were on board he suddenly turned on them.

'I do not require master or pilot, nor any man who knows the art of navigation because God alone is the master and pilot who shall guide and deliver us in His mercy. His will be done', he shouted along with, presumably, a few other well-chosen words. 'Henceforth let no man speak to me of putting back. [. . .]If I fail to achieve that for which I have come, to Portugal I shall not return.'

Vasco placed the men in chains and then, in their presence, flung their instruments and charts into the sea, pausing to let the full impact sink in. Only the Captain-Major now possessed the means of navigation and the essential charts to see them safely home.[185]

Vasco's initial orders were that the men should be kept in chains until they had reached Lisbon and there face the king's justice, 'if they do not die before that'. Later, he allowed the men to rejoin the crew with the knowledge they would be put in chains once Portugal was sighted. In the end the men conducted themselves so well that Vasco relented and promised to intercede on their behalf before the king.

There is no mention of this incident in the *Roteiro*, and other usually reliable sources also exclude it, but then other events known to have occurred are also not mentioned in them. If it really did occur, it was as audacious a decision as any captain far from safe harbour ever made, and it resolved once and for all any thought of turning back.

To escape the unfavourable current Vasco ordered the ships to be put well out to sea. They were very low on water once again, which suggests that on each of the two previous stops they had been unable fully to restore their supply. Although it was summer, each sailor was receiving less than a pint of water a day for drinking. For cooking they used sea water, which would have been very unsatisfactory as most of the provisions had been preserved with salt. The ships had been continuously at sea since 6 December. Some repairs had been made while under way but these were inadequate. Vasco ordered the ships to approach the coast and on 11 January they dropped anchor at the mouth of a small river in southern Mozambique.

As longboats from the ships were rowing to shore, a large group of black Africans, identified by historians as 'Bantus', gathered on the beach to greet them. Tall and well-built, they much more closely resembled the Africans with whom the Portuguese were most familiar and were quite different from the Bushmen and Hottentots with whom they had previously been dealing.

Martim Alfonso, joined by an unidentified Portuguese (probably one of the *delgradados*), was sent ashore to make this initial approach. The pair made promising contact with someone they took to be a man of influence. Vasco sent this 'chief' a jacket, a pair of red pantaloons, a Moorish cap and a bracelet, which were well received. Alfonso and his companion were invited to spend the night at the chief's nearby village. On the way the chief donned the new clothes and, as they passed, people clapped their hands in approval at the gifts while the chief beamed with delight. When he reached his village he paraded about it while the villagers came out to express their delight.

Alfonso and his companion were fed millet porridge and chicken, and housed in the chief's straw hut. Throughout the night men, women and children approached the Portuguese to stare at them as if they were a marvel, smiling and often clapping as a sign of their approval.

The next morning the chief ordered two men to accompany them back to their ships and presented them with fowls to give to the Captain-Major. By the time the men reached the landing place for the longboats a crowd of 200 locals was trailing in their wake. Back on board, Alfonso reported to Vasco that the region was heavily populated, that the people were farmers, that they used long bows with iron-tipped arrows and spears, that they wore armlets and anklets of copper, and that some of the men carried daggers in ivory sheaths. Alfonso also noted that they carried sea water to their village and evaporated it in pits to gather the salt.

Vasco expressed his approval that matters had gone so well and proclaimed that they would name this country the Land of the Good People (*Terra da Boa Gente*). Relations remained so friendly that the locals assisted the Portuguese in transporting their kegs as they filled them with water. Vasco would have remained longer but, after just five days and with their water supply not yet satisfied, a favourable wind came up and he ordered the ships to set sail immediately. By this time the ships were in such a poor condition that the pumps had to be manned night and day to keep them afloat.

By late January the passing coastline was becoming thickly wooded with tall trees. On the 25th the ships anchored at the mouth of the Quelimane river, a tributary of the Zambezi, a land in which the Portuguese were to establish a lasting presence. They were now nearing the southernmost region of Arab trade along the east African coast. The locals were also Bantu, and both male and female wore only loincloths because of the constant humidity and heat. Although the young women pierced their lips in three places and inserted bits of twisted tin into the openings, the Portuguese men found them comely.

The country proved to be marshy, with many large trees. There was an abundance of fruit, which formed a regular part of the local diet. In dug-outs the locals brought the fruit and other food out to the men as gifts, then welcomed them into their village to fill their kegs. 'These people', the *Roteiro* notes, 'took much delight in us.'[186] Paulo's ship, the *São Rafael*, had sustained damage to its mast and the crew set about repairing it.

Until now Vasco had been lucky. With a crew healthy on departure, scurvy generally took about three months to show its first signs. The Portuguese had reached Africa after about that time but in their previous stops they had not been able to access the fresh fruits needed to ward off the illness. Now some of the crew began to experience swelling in their hands and feet and inflammation of the gums, which made it hard for them to eat. Paulo, 'a man of gentle disposition', had personal supplies of medicine, which he shared liberally with those afflicted, visiting them each day and seeing to their needs, conduct for which he was widely praised.[187]

The gums of those afflicted swelled up over the teeth, and their breath was foul. Sailors used their knives to cut away the flesh, then rubbed their bleeding gums with urine, a treatment repeated again and again as the effects of the disease progressed.

Word of the Portuguese presence spread and a few days after their arrival two 'lords', as the Portuguese took them to be, arrived from upriver by boat. One wore a cap with tassels embroidered with silk, while the other had a headpiece of green satin: both indications that they came from a more advanced region. Their manner was arrogant and they held themselves aloof, looking with disdain on the gifts they were offered by the Portuguese. There was still no truly effective means of communication, but one of the pair made it known that he came from a distant land and, since he had seen large ships such as these before, he was not impressed. Vasco took this and the silk and satin as a sign that they were approaching their destination.

These men ordered grass huts to be prepared for them on the riverbank and remained a week engaging in modest trade. Finally, they vanished back upriver in their dug-outs. The ships remained for thirty-two days and the health of the crew was partially restored during the stay, although there were many deaths. The ships were once again careened as these waters were especially debilitating on the hulls, which had sprung leaks and become overgrown.

Each ship was towed into shallow water. The cargo was then shifted to one side of the ship, so that it leaned over on its side. Tackle was used to pull it over even further, then scaffolding was built over the exposed underside. The accumulation of barnacles and other marine encrustations was meticulously scraped away. A boiler for heating pitch was set up and the seams of the hull were caulked with pitch, oil and oakum, after which the bottom was painted. The process was then repeated for the other side of the hull. The ship was relaunched and then the inside was carefully scrubbed and the cargo properly stowed.

Vasco directed that another pillar should be erected, again crowned by a large wooden cross. He then held counsel with his senior officers and instructed that from here on, whenever they made contact with the Moors, they were to make the point that these three ships had become separated from a much larger fleet which was expected to rejoin them any day. He was concerned that, when they faced the kind of formidable enemy he was certain the Moors would constitute, his ships might be seen as easy prey.[188]

On 24 February, with repairs complete, the three ships set sail. They were now well into the adverse Mozambique Channel and were only able to make some 300 miles by cautiously sailing during daylight and seeking anchorage at night. The lack of a pilot knowledgeable about local conditions had become a serious problem and endangered the voyage. They sighted islands on 1 March and the next day encountered sailing vessels from a nearby port on Mozambique Island. Taking them for Muslims, the seamen offered to show the Portuguese the way into the harbour. A number of them came aboard Coelho's ship, where they ate and drank their fill before going back to their small boats well satisfied.

The Portuguese gave thanks that they had at last entered 'a region of navigation' because it meant they were drawing ever closer to their destination. As night approached, the Portuguese made their way tentatively into the harbour channel. Coelho's vessel went first as it was more manoeuvrable and shallower of draft. In the gathering darkness he struck a shoal and broke the tiller. He was able to get the ship free, however, and move it into deeper water some 'two bowshots from the village', where he dropped anchor. The other Portuguese ships quietly assumed positions with him while carefully taking in the scene before them.[189]

They were within sight of the port village, 'a large town of houses covered with thatch', from where a number of small boats came out, the men aboard playing a tune of welcome on their *anafils*, an Arab trumpet. Clearly the newcomers were being greeted as fellow Muslims and the Portuguese did nothing to dissuade them from their false impression.

The Portuguese had now entered land under the control of the Muslims. Here were Arabs, an Arab–African mix and converted locals. The language spoken was a sort of bastard Arabic, and the complexion of the people overall was generally lighter. Strung along the east African coast was a chain of Swahili city-states that included Kilwa, Mombasa, Malindi and Pate. Each had achieved a certain level of prosperity and cultural accomplishment, though the degree to which they adhered to Islam varied considerably. The region had close ties to India and Arabia, both economically and politically. The culture was primarily Arabic with a strong Persian influence, which was not surprising given how these port communities had first been established. The Swahili society was firmly established through generations of both marriage and concubinage with the indigenous Bantu women.[190]

Until now the tribes with which the Portuguese had come into contact were insufficiently motivated or united, or lacked adequate technology genuinely to oppose them. This, however, was an entirely different situation and Vasco recognized it at once.

Whatever measure of fanaticism the Portuguese held against the Moors* was fully reciprocated by the Moors' hatred for all things Christian. No longer were the ocean currents and winds Vasco's chief enemy. His ships had entered the mouth of the lion, a circumstance every man aboard the ships had anticipated since before they had left Lisbon and one that many of them had already experienced.

The most profitable export from this region was slaves. There was little production, except for modest iron implements needed locally and some woven cloth. Along with slaves, gold, ivory and ambergris were also shipped to India, Arabia and Persia in exchange for pepper, cloves, ginger, pearls and gems. The reason the Arab presence extended no further south, it is believed, was that their more fragile ships could not withstand the strong currents the Portuguese had just overcome with such effort.

This and other ports in the region were generally prosperous.

---

* 'Moor' was the universal term used by the Portuguese whenever they came into contact with a Muslim, just as 'Frank' was the common term used by the Arabs to identify any European.

Foreign, though Muslim, vessels visited routinely engaging in the mutually lucrative trade. Instead of the simple wrappings the Portuguese had seen before now, the people wore flowing robes of striped or white linen or cotton, with a head covering of either cotton or silk, depending on status.

Anchored near by were four Arab dhows, which Vasco and his men examined with keen interest. They were surprised to discover the planks were not held in place by nails, but were sewn together with stout cord. Both the decking and the sails were of matted palm leaves. Once contact had been established with the sailors aboard these vessels, the Portuguese immediately recognized their navigational aids and charts as equal or even superior to their own. Arab ships of this type transported their water supply in wooden tanks, a system the Portuguese were soon to adapt.[191]

To find out more, Vasco sent ashore one Fernão Martins, who spoke Arabic. After a short excursion he reported back that the port was in possession of many rich items, including spices that he had been told were imported from other Muslims to the north. This was welcome information, as it meant the city was in regular contact by trade with the Portuguese objective. He had been told tales, of course, about the origin of what he saw, that at the source 'the precious stones, pearls, and spices were in such great quantity that it was not necessary to buy them, but to gather them in baskets'.[192] The Portuguese were accustomed to such exaggerations and, if anything, found them reassuring.

Martins also reported that the people occupying the mainland near the island were quite different from those in this village. He had been told they were 'heathen who are like beasts, savages, naked except for a strip of cotton cloth around their loins, and with bodies smeared with red clay'. Their ornaments were bones, shells and small stones. The Portuguese had seen the indigenous locals in dug-outs in the harbour moving between the island and the mainland and were not surprised by his report.

Here at Mozambique Island the Portuguese saw their first coconut palms, with which they were much taken. 'The palms of this land produce a fruit as large as melons,' the *Roteiro* records, 'and they eat the kernel, which has the flavour of hazel-nuts; they also have cucumbers and melons in great quantities, which they brought to barter with us.'

Later on the day they arrived the local ruler came out and boarded Coelho's ship. A subsequent chronicler wrote of this first visit:

> He arrived in two canoes lashed together, and upon them poles and planks, covered over with mats which gave shade. Ten Moors came thus seated [on the canoes], and the sheik sitting on a low round stool covered with a silk cloth and a cushion. He was dark, well built, and of goodly appearance, and was attired in a pleated Arab jacket of velvet. He was wrapped in a knee-length blue cloak, ornamented with braid and gold thread. His trousers were of white cloth reaching to his ankles. His body was otherwise naked. Around his waist, over his cloak, he wore a silk sash, into which was thrust a silver-mounted dagger, and in his hand he carried a silver-mounted sword. On his head was a dark, tight-fitting cap of Mecca velvet, over which he wore a many-coloured silk turban, embroidered with braid and fringes of gold thread.

It was now that one of the most self-defeating aspects of this voyage presented itself. The three ships were new to this port, and the ruler, identified also as a sultan, was not a casual visitor. It was customary for those seeking to establish a trading relationship to give lavish gifts to the sultan since he controlled access. He had come, bluntly, with his hand extended, no doubt wondering what wonderful gifts these strangers in their immense, unfamiliar ships would make.

Instead of marvels, Coelho gave him what he had: a red hood. The sultan was under the impression these newcomers were Muslims and so accepted the pittance with grace, offering in exchange a black rosary for Coelho's use during Muslim prayers. Coelho, maintaining the illusion they were Muslims, accepted the rosary with pleasure. The sultan then invited the young captain and his officers to go ashore to his home for refreshments. Coelho, it is reported, was 'a well-conditioned man courteous in bearing and discreet'.[193] The meeting there was amicable and when Coelho prepared to leave he was presented with a jar of dates, preserved with cloves and cumin.

The sultan next met Vasco and went to his ship on several occasions to dine. During these visits Vasco raised the subject of acquiring local pilots who knew the waters. They were essential to the eventual success of his mission, but he received no firm commitment. The sultan knew how valuable were such men.

Unfortunately, the gifts the sultan received from the Captain-Major were no better than those he had been given the first day. They consisted of hats, silk clothing from Persia or India and coral. The sultan's initial graciousness began to turn. Now he treated everything offered him with contempt. At one point he asked for a gift of scarlet cloth but Vasco had none to give and this failure was greeted with scorn.

During this time the Portuguese were gathering all the information they could, most of which proved to be untrue or grossly misleading. The locals were apparently engaging in the time-honoured practice of telling strangers what they wanted to hear and fooling them whenever possible. Vasco was accordingly told that Prester John's kingdom was some distance away, 'that he owned many cities on the sea coast, and that their inhabitants were great merchants and possessed large ships'. His kingdom, however, could only be reached 'on the back of camels'.

Those first hearing this news 'cried with joy, and prayed God to grant us health, so that we might behold what we so much desired'.[194] They were told there was a great island to the east (Madagascar), where an equal number of Christians and Muslims lived who warred with one another, and that there were other, smaller islands with Christian communities.

Until now the Portuguese had successfully masked their faith. The Muslims of the east coast of Africa were commonly held to have converted in order to facilitate commerce with the Muslim Arabs who dominated the regional trade routes and ports. No one from Europe had ever sailed these waters before, so there was no reason for the local Muslims to be unduly suspicious. Strangers occasionally arrived and, if Vasco's men were even stranger than usual, the Muslims could not have been expected to guess they were Christians. But then the Portuguese luck turned bad.

One day crewmen in the village came across two native Christians who had been brought from India. They were taken aboard to the *São Gabriel* for Vasco to see personally. Aboard the ship the pair spotted the painted figure of the face of the angel Gabriel and fell to their knees in homage and prayer. When the Muslims accompanying them observed the pleasure Vasco took at this display of Christian faith and his expression of concern for the well-being of these captives, they suddenly realized these strangers were also Christian. With great haste they dragged their captives off and hurried ashore with word.

A week had now passed since Vasco had first arrived and he was eager to move on. Their twin objectives of Prester John and a route to India were within reach. His desire was given fresh impetus by a new development in events ashore. As seamen continued to acquire provisions, collect firewood and fill casks with water, the situation was becoming increasingly hostile. Word spread that these ships and crews were Christian and soon there were violent clashes between the Portuguese and the Muslims. Still, the ships were being supplied with vegetables, fowl, goats and pigeons, all for the modest cost of yellow glass beads.[195] Loading water by cask was slow work, however, especially as the only source was on the mainland, and the supply on board the ships remained marginal.

The question of the religion of these visitors was apparently not resolved in the mind of the sultan. He again invited Coelho ashore to dine with him in his home. Following an exchange of gifts and a meal he asked directly if the Portuguese were Turks or Moors from a distant land. The reply was apparently ambiguous, so he next asked Coelho to show him on a map where they came from and also allow him to see their books of prayer.[196] Coelho's reply is not recorded, but it did not put the sultan's suspicions to rest.

As word spread of their true identity, it may be that the anger of the Muslims was greater than it might otherwise have been because they had been temporarily deceived by the Portuguese, but given the level of hostility against all things Christian such a deception probably counted for little. Vasco expressed his concerns for their safety now that their faith had been disclosed, especially as crew members had already been lost to scurvy while others were not yet fully recovered. The greatest fear was that the Moors might mount a surprise attack and overwhelm them while the ships were at anchor and within easy reach. Clearly something was going to have to be done before matters got out of hand.

Vasco's men reported that they had been told there were many cities along the coast to the north but that the waters were treacherous, with numerous shoals. During one of his midday meals with the sultan Vasco asked again for pilots. Without them his ships could proceed only with peril and at a very slow pace. He had until now received no direct reply to his requests.

The sultan, who gave no indication he knew these men to be hated Christians (although there can be no question that he now knew), agreed to provide pilots, assuming that the men accepted the terms of employment – he would not force anyone to join them. When two pilots were presented, Vasco gave each of them 30 *mitkals* in gold (about 1,320 grams) and two *marlotas*, short silk or wool garments from India.[197] The men insisted on advance payment, which was given, but only on condition that one of the pilots always remained aboard Vasco's ship.

Violence ashore by now had reached an unacceptable level. The author of the *Roteiro* had no doubt what was afoot. 'When they learned that we were Christians they arranged to seize and kill us by treachery.' On 10 March the three ships retreated a short distance from the harbour and ready access by small boat. They dropped anchor at a smaller island, where it was deemed the Portuguese would be safer from surprise attack. The following day was the sabbath, and Vasco gave orders that Mass should be celebrated and confession taken. It may be that in relocating the Portuguese were also looking to celebrate a Christian service out of sight.

During the movement of the ships an altercation had broken out between the sultan's men and the Portuguese. Since the ships were leaving the harbour without having informed the sultan, there may well have been some question about port duties, one of the principal sources of income for the rulers of all trading ports in this region, as they were in Portugal. In the meantime one of the pilots slipped ashore in the confusion, but Vasco was intent on proceeding with his voyage and set out to locate and retrieve the man.

Vasco ordered the remaining pilot to join him, then took one longboat while Coelho led the other. As the two boats rowed rapidly towards the town, six Arab craft darted out from shore on course to intercept them, each crowded with men bearing shields and armed with arrows and longbows. Vasco seized the pilot with him and placed him at the front, where he would be the first to be struck if the Arabs fired at them, then ordered his men to discharge their bombards at the approaching boats.

Paulo was on board the *São Miguel*, the caravel commanded by Coelho, watching events. At the sound of gunfire he ordered the sails to be raised and the men to take arms.[198] Drums beat in a martial tempo and trumpets sounded. The wind filled the ship's sails and very quickly it was bearing down on the Muslims. The Arabs were already beginning to break off their attack under Vasco's strong response. As the much larger vessel approached they fled in panic, beached their boats, then took flight on foot.

Vasco could see he would not retrieve his missing pilot like this and gave orders for the boats to return to their ships. Once aboard, the small fleet immediately set sail north, intent on following the coastline. Any sense of relief was short-lived for on Tuesday the ships were becalmed. Two days later a gale forced them back down the coast and by 14 March they were forced to drop anchor near their former anchorage off Mozambique Island.

There is no account of these events from the Muslim side, but they must have raised some interesting questions. First, large and foreign ships had appeared in their port. The men were fair-skinned and ignorant of the usual trade routes and customs. They

213

were eager to acquire pilots, a strong indication that they did not know the waters. In general, the newcomers remained apart from the village, even drawing away unannounced and anchoring at a nearby island. They had expressed concern for the well-being of Christian captives, when it was learned the newcomers were Christians. When two of their boats approached shore, they fired on the sultan's men. They employed bombards, weapons not in use here but known to be used by the Turks – hence the question put to Coelho. Finally, the vessels had left without the customary formalities. Now they had arrived again, this time driven back by the forces of nature.

When the ships were observed at anchor the sultan dispatched an emissary, reportedly a drunken *sharif*,★ to assure the Portuguese that he wished to put aside any unpleasantness and be nothing but a good friend. A day or two later another Moor came aboard, accompanied by his small son. He said he had come to this place from Mecca as a pilot and wished to return with them.[199] The Portuguese suspected treachery, however, and declined to let him join them.

As the days passed, the winds remained unfavourable and their water supply dipped dangerously low. No offer of assistance or word of any kind came from shore. The only source of water known to Vasco and his men was on the mainland, near the village, but he feared he would have to fill the kegs under threat of attack or by force. The remaining Muslim pilot promised to guide his men to a water supply safe from danger.

Again Vasco and Coelho manned longboats and, as night gathered, rowed towards shore. The pilot directed them to a number of places but by morning they had still not found a water source. They were certain by now that the pilot was only looking for a chance to make his escape. The next night Vasco returned, and this time the pilot was persuaded to lead them to water.

The course of the Portuguese had been noted, however, and when they landed with their empty kegs twenty of the sultan's

---

★ A *sharif* is a descendant of the Prophet.

men, armed with assegais, ran to the beach and ordered them off. Vasco responded by having three of his men fire their bombards to drive them away, after which the casks were filled without further incident. When they returned to the ships, the Portuguese pilot of the *São Rafael* reported that the African slave he had brought with him on the voyage had escaped to shore.

Early on Sunday morning an Arab sailed out to the anchored Portuguese. With a sneer he told them they were welcome to attempt to take water again, but that they would be forced back if they did. Vasco did not take the threat kindly. 'He resolved to go, in order to show that we were able to do them harm if we desired it.'[200] Again Vasco was faced with the reality of being so far from home or any safe harbour. He might be forced to return here on his return leg, and he could not leave behind enemies prepared to fight him on sight. He had no idea what condition his vessels would be in or the state of his crew. These Muslims must fear the Portuguese. He ordered all the boats to be loaded with heavily armed men and led them on a punitive raid into the harbour.

The Arabs had constructed a barrier of lashed planks to prevent entry. It was occupied by men armed with swords, bows, slings and assegais, who were protected by the improvised structure. As the boats approached, soldiers on the nearby beach unleashed a fusillade of stones which rained down on the Portuguese. The bombards were fired for effect, causing these men to seek protection inside the palisades. For the next three hours the Portuguese fired their weapons at the men behind the barrier and into the village. They saw two defenders killed. Vasco finally grew tired of the one-sided match and ordered his men back to their ships for the midday meal.

The two Christian captives had not been forgotten and, as hostilities were in progress, it was decided that the Portuguese would attempt to rescue them and in the process to seize prisoners who could be traded for their missing pilot and the escaped slave. After the meal the boats were again rowed to the village. This time the inhabitants of the island were observed fleeing by dug-out towards the mainland. They had already been

fired on, seen the cannon on the large vessels and feared a determined assault on their village.

Paulo closed on some dug-outs and seized three of them,
along with four black oarsmen. One of the boats was found
to bear luxurious goods as well as 'books of the Law'.
Disappointingly, the Christians were not found. Vasco ordered
the fine cloth, perfume and baskets that had been seized to be
distributed among his officers, although he retained a Koran to
present to Manuel on his return.[201]

The next day casks were filled with water without difficulty
as those remaining in the village hid in their houses. Vasco
ordered bombards to be fired at random into the town as his
boats headed back to their ships. On Tuesday, with the wind
moderately favourable, the ships once again weighed anchor and
made their way north.

A conversation Vasco had with a Muslim pilot was to prove
prophetic. Vasco repeatedly assured the man that he had come
in peace. The pilot slowly shook his head. 'You will have to conquer', he said.

14

'Here is the land'

The wind was uncertain and by 31 March the ships had moved up the coast only some 28 leagues. Relations with the one Muslim pilot were not good, and both sides had come to consider him to be a captive. In the Portuguese view he had made it clear enough that he intended to jump ship at the first opportunity. Accounts are not clear, but somehow in all the commotion Vasco had managed to get the other pilot back aboard.

It is unlikely the sultan at Mozambique Island would have allowed Christians to acquire local pilots who would actually perform their duties. It is all but certain these men intended to escape at the earliest opportunity or, failing that, to thwart the Christian interlopers whenever possible. The pilots had been given as a means to acquire payment and to get the Portuguese out of their harbour. Vasco understood what was afoot.

Soon the ships came upon islands which one pilot incorrectly identified as being the mainland. There were many such islands in the area and the waters about them were clearly treacherous. When Vasco discovered the island was not the mainland, he ordered the pilot to be flogged for placing them in such peril, and even named the largest nearby isle the Island of the Flogged One.

It was probably at this point that the pilot was persuaded to reveal the Arabs' true intentions when the ships had been anchored near the village. He told them that once 'they learned that we were Christians they arranged to seize and kill us by treachery. The pilot . . . revealed to us all they intended to do, if they were able.'[202] The Portuguese had escaped a trap, but their education was proceeding at a rapid pace.

The powerful contrary current of the Mozambique Channel was proving very difficult for the ships to overcome. It required a strong, favourable wind, which came only infrequently and so far had not been of sufficient duration to allow them to escape the current. Every time the ships weighed anchor they were as likely to be pushed south as to make any headway north. Finally the wind changed.

On 4 April, Vasco spotted a large land mass with two islands close by, surrounded by shoals. Claiming to recognize this place, the two pilots assured the Portuguese that a short distance back the way they had just come was an island inhabited by Christians. Following their experience at Mozambique Island this was welcome news, if true. It is quite likely, of course, that the pilots simply wished not to be carried any farther away from their native port.

Throughout the day the three ships attempted to reach this island without success 'for the wind was too strong for us'. Vasco finally ordered the ships to resume their voyage north to the port of Mombasa, which had also been reported as being occupied by Christians. By the time the ships gave way and set their new course it was already late in the day and the wind was high. Just as the sun set the large island of Zanzibar was spotted to their immediate north. The pilots told Vasco that there were two towns on it, one Muslim, the other Christian.

Conditions forced the ships to remain out to sea for the night and they were carried past Zanzibar as well as the port of Kilwa on the mainland. Then, two hours before daylight, the *São Rafael* ran aground on a shoal. The crew shouted a warning to the other vessels, which immediately dropped anchor. Daylight and low tide revealed the *São Rafael* to be stranded 'high and dry'. Boats were lowered, anchors laid out, and the men made preparations for the rising tide and the opportunity to float the ship free.

While they were busy with this, two small coastal ships came into sight and the Portugese were able to trade for oranges 'better than those of Portugal'. Two of the Muslims aboard these ships agreed to remain with them for the voyage to Mombasa, almost certainly to serve as local pilots, given that Vasco had every reason not to trust either of the pair he had. With high tide the *São Rafael* floated clear amid triumphant shouts from the crews.[203]

The ships sailed along the coastline, spotting more islands, and on Saturday 7 April arrived with high expectations at Mombasa, the finest port on the east Africa coast. They had been told more on their way here by the pilots and been led to believe that Mombasa possessed a large Christian community that lived independently amid the Muslims in peace and prosperity. The pilots assured the Portuguese that they would be greeted with great honour upon their arrival and taken to reside within the homes of the Christians. Initially Vasco and his men were delighted to receive the news, especially as so many of his crew remained stricken with scurvy.

They were nearly at the equator and the air was thick with humidity. The view of the well-established, bustling port and in particular of the city must have proved nostalgic for the Portuguese, weary and so far from home.

> Its whitewashed stone houses had windows and terraces like those of the [Iberian] Peninsula – and it was so beautiful that our men felt as though they were entering some part of this kingdom [Portugal]. And although everyone was enamoured of the vista, Vasco da Gama would not permit the pilot to take the vessels inside as he desired, for he was already suspicious of him and anchored outside.[204]

Word of events on Mozambique Island had arrived ahead of the newcomers, for no sooner did they appear outside the port than a dhow with several Arabs sailed to them. The ships within the port itself were quickly decked out with flags and the Arabs bearing down on them could be seen to be well dressed.

Not to be outdone, and to make a point, Vasco ordered all of the sick to be taken below and the healthy to don their armour and be fully armed and visible. The officers dressed in their very best while colourful flags were unfurled from the ships, snapping in the breeze. The smiling Arabs climbed up the ladder to the deck of the *São Gabriel*, where they were greeted by the Captain-Major and his well-dressed but heavily armed men. Using one of Vasco's Arab speakers as interpreter, the Arabs asked from where these ships had come, who Vasco was and what he wanted. Vasco replied that he desired to obtain fresh provisions.

The Portuguese had a long history of regular dealings with the Moors, both within their own country and in north Africa, and this situation was one very familiar to them. Their Arab visitors took in the scene, then allowed that obtaining supplies would not be a problem and made their departure amid extravagant assurances of friendship and the promise to fulfil their every need. Vasco, however, ordered a well-armed, night-long guard on each ship and remained on alert himself.

Towards midnight a vessel carrying 100 men armed with cutlasses and bucklers drifted silently up to the *São Gabriel*. Without warning the men attempted to swarm over the side of the ship, but only a handful were able to get past the guard. These were the leaders, whom Vasco ordered to be allowed through and on to the deck as the attack broke off. They remained on board a time as temporary hostages before being permitted to leave in peace.[205] The Portuguese concluded the Arabs had been attempting a quick capture of one of the ships as well as a test of their defences. Although there had been much manhandling and shouting, Vasco had managed the affair without the shedding of blood. The last thing he wanted was a pitched battle.

The next day was Palm Sunday and the local sultan sent out eight men, two of whom were 'almost white' and said they were Christians, though the Portuguese doubted their claim. They brought with them a sheep and a large supply of oranges, lemons and sugar-cane, along with a ring that they presented as the sultan's pledge of safety. Vasco was assured that if he would only enter the port with his ships everything he required would be supplied. Vasco gave the emissaries a string of coral as a gift for the sultan and asked them to inform him that his ships would enter the harbour the next day.

Vasco sent two of the *delgradados* ashore with these 'Christians' to assure the sultan of his desire for peace and friendship. The pair were followed by a great curious crowd as they were led to the palace. There they passed through four doors, each of which was guarded by an imposing doorman with a drawn cutlass.

Inside, the men were well received by the sultan personally, who gave orders for them to be shown around the city. During the tour the Portuguese stopped at the house of two Christian merchants who showed them a sketch of the Holy Ghost, which they claimed to worship. As they left to return to their ships the Portuguese were presented with samples of cloves, pepper and corn, with the message that they could trade for these.[206]

The account of the *delgradados* was negative in many regards. They reported seeing 'many prisoners walking about . . . in irons, and these, it seemed to us, must have been Christians, because the Christians in this land are at war with the Moors'. Even the Christian merchants they had seen were oppressed by the local king.[207] The *Roteiro* reports that they were only in residence temporarily and were not 'allowed to do anything except by the order of the Moorish King'.

This report and events cast serious doubts on any claim of friendship. Although it was customary to enter a port formally, strictly speaking there was no reason the Portuguese ships could not be resupplied where they now lay at anchor. Vasco himself had not gone ashore as he had done previously, and he had not risked his regular crew in making this first contact. He was doing nothing to aggravate the situation but was prepared for violence. Tension aboard the Portuguese ships was high and they stood at a high state of readiness.

The next morning Arab boats swarmed about the Portuguese ships as they prepared to enter the harbour. Certain Arabs were allowed to come aboard, probably to assist in piloting the crowded port waters. Vasco moved off but before long his ship collided with the vessel following it astern, so he quickly dropped anchor, as did the other ship. When the Muslims on board saw that the Portuguese were not sailing into the harbour they hurriedly scrambled aboard one of their boats which was tethered to the rear of the *São Gabriel*. The two pilots from Mozambique Island exchanged glances and in the confusion leaped into the water, where they were quickly picked up and taken away.

It is not clear whether Vasco was serious about entering the harbour or simply testing the Arabs' reactions, but the day's events had further roused his suspicions. That night he ordered two of the four blacks they had taken at Mozambique Island to be brought before him. The men spoke Arabic and had been in communication with the Arabs who had been allowed aboard the *São Gabriel*. As the men were bound, Vasco gave instructions for oil and resin to be slowly brought to the boil and through an interpreter explained that he wanted to know what the Muslims had in store for his ships. The men protested they knew nothing.

When the oil was ready it was slowly dripped on to the men's exposed skin. Before long they were eager to speak. They said that orders had been given to lure the Portuguese into the port, where they would be captured. This was in revenge for what had taken place at Mozambique Island.[208]

Not yet satisfied he knew the full story, Vasco ordered more boiling oil to be dripped on to the men, but they had nothing more to give. One of the pair was able to tear himself free and leaped into the water, his hands still bound. The other also jumped into the sea the next morning. What became of them is not known; it is just possible that they were recovered by Arabs in the small boats that shadowed the Portuguese ships.

Vasco was in a difficult situation. The only positive development was that, because of the fresh fruit his crew had received, most of the sick were on their way to recovery. Otherwise there was little from which to derive satisfaction. He was at anchor outside a major Muslim port and under threat of attack. He had not yet been able to take on an adequate supply of water, and in the heat the need was becoming acute.

Although the Portuguese had entered the area of Arab influence where trade with India was routine, Vasco's small fleet was still a long way from their objective. It had been some weeks since his ships had last been serviced. He knew that in the warm equatorial waters of the Indian Ocean his hulls were slowly disintegrating beneath his feet. He required a safe harbour and he needed friends. Finally, he had lost his local pilots and, if he was to succeed, he had to replace them with trustworthy ones.

That night, at about midnight, two small boats crept up on the Portuguese ships. Arabs slipped into the dark water and swam silently to Paulo's ship, the *São Rafael*. Others made their way stealthily to Coelho's smaller *São Miguel*. The watch heard splashing but thought at first it was a school of tuna. At the *São Miguel* the swimmers were quietly hacking away on the ship's anchor cables. Others crept up the sides of the ship and began cutting away the rigging of the mizen-mast.

At last the watch realized they were under attack and sounded the alarm. The Arabs on board dived into the water and swam to their boats, where they were joined by those working on the cables. Once aboard, they quickly made their way back to shore. The *Roteiro* records that 'these and other wicked tricks were practised upon us by these dogs, but our Lord did not allow them to succeed, because they were unbelievers.'[209]

Vasco remained just outside the port for another two days as his crew continued to recover its strength but it was clear there would be no satisfactory resolution of differences at Mombasa. The Portuguese were simply in hostile waters and were in no position to prevail by force of arms. There was nothing to do but set sail, so on the morning of 13 April they left on a light breeze which carried them north.

With an eye to the future Vasco had insinuated on to Mozambique Island one of the *delgradados* to serve as a sort of propagandist. His name was John Machado and he had been imprisoned in Lisbon for killing 'another gentleman' on the promenade in Lisbon in a fight over a woman. He spoke Arabic and was a man 'of good presence and well instructed'. In time he was to persuade the sultan there that it was in his best interest to be friends with the Portuguese, since it was a powerful nation with many great ships. Later Machado was sent north by the sultan to Mombasa, where he successfully conveyed the same message. Eventually Machado established himself in Gôa, where he became an honoured member of the Portuguese community.[210]

After sailing a short distance from Mombasa, presumably out of sight of the city and its boats, Vasco ordered the three ships to lay anchor. Without a pilot they could only proceed at their peril. If they could not hire the services of a reliable pilot, there were others ways. At dawn the following day two boats were spotted not far away, making their way south in the open sea. Vasco gave orders for the vessels to be captured. The ships weighed anchor and filled their masts with canvas. The chase lasted for most of the day until finally they succeeded in capturing one of the ships. The crew initially leaped overboard, but were all retrieved from the water.

The boat proved to be an impressive catch. It carried seventeen men, a quantity of gold and silver and 'an abundance of maize and other provisions'. There was a young woman who told them she was the wife of one of the aged Moors on board.[211]

This was nothing less than an act of piracy, one identical to that practised off the coast of north Africa by Christian against Moor, and Moor against Christian. It was also very common in these waters. Muslim preyed on Hindu as well as on other Muslims, and vice versa. From his captives Vasco learned that the next significant port was only a short distance away. Even better, it was in regular direct trade with ports in India, and it was probable that ships from India would be at anchor in its harbour.

Vasco set sail immediately and at sunset that same day, Saturday 14 April, his ships dropped anchor at the port of Malindi. Word of the Portuguese had again preceded their arrival, not just of what had transpired at Mombasa and Mozambique Island, but also that they had seized a Muslim ship with its crew and goods. This time no boats came out to greet them. The three ships sat at anchor facing the port.

The following description of the city was made just a few years later by a Portuguese observer:

Malindi . . . is a fair town on the mainland . . . [It] has many
fair stone and mortar houses of many storeys, with great
plenty of windows and flat roofs after our fashion. The
place is well laid out in streets. The folk are both black and
white; they go naked, covering only their private parts with
cotton and silk cloths. Others of them wear cloths folded
like cloaks and waistbands, and turbans of many rich stuffs
on their heads.

They are great barterers, and deal in cloth, gold, ivory
and divers other wares . . . and to their haven come every
year many ships and cargoes . . . of gold, ivory and wax . . .
There is great plenty of food in this city and . . . abundance
of fruit, gardens and orchards. Here are plenty of fat-tailed
[Ethiopian] sheep, cows and other cattle, and great store of
oranges, also of hens.[212]

The following day was Easter Sunday. Vasco took the elderly
Muslim he had seized to one side and asked him to convey a
message to the local ruler on his behalf. On Monday the man
was placed on a sandbar and a short time later a boat was seen
coming from the city to recover him. The king met with the
man and received the message that the Portuguese had come in
peace and that they desired to be friends. Later that day the messenger returned to Vasco's ship accompanied by a king's officer
and a *sharif*, along with three sheep as a gift and word that he
wished to receive him. Further, the ruler said he would provide
the Portuguese with the provisions they wanted and, most
importantly, the pilots they needed.[213]

Again Vasco's ability to deal on an equitable level with local
rulers was brought to bear. He sent his good wishes along with
gifts consisting of an ecclesiastic's cloak, two strings of coral,
three water basins, a hat, bells and two pieces of striped cloth. In
return, the following day Vasco was presented with 'six sheep
and much cloves, cumin, ginger, nutmegs, and pepper'. He also
received a message that the ageing king's son, who served as
regent, would meet with Vasco by small boat out in the water.
Each would remain in his own, if that was what Vasco wished.

On 18 April the regent* approached the anchored ships in an ornate boat and, as arranged, met with Vasco, who had ordered his boat to be well decorated in anticipation of the occasion. The regent wore a damask robe lined with green satin, and a rich head covering and sat on a cushioned chair made of bronze. Extended above him was an umbrella of crimson satin, shielding him from the bright sun. Beside him was an elderly man carrying the ruler's short sword within its silver scabbard as a sign of his office. There were also musicians with beautifully carved trumpets of wood and ivory who made continuous 'sweet harmony'.[214]

Once the two boats were side by side, without fanfare or negotiation, the regent entered Vasco's boat and it was there the conversation took place. Another account says that it was Vasco who showed his good faith by entering the regent's boat.

After some discussion the regent invited Vasco to come to the palace to rest, after which the regent would visit him on board his ship. Given the recent well wishes he had received at Mombasa, only to be followed by secret attack, Vasco was suspicious and declined, saying that his king prohibited him from setting foot on shore during his voyage. What, the regent asked, was he to say to his people when it was learned the captain of these ships refused his offer of hospitality and would not come ashore? Vasco had no direct reply but instead sent word to his ship that those captives seized were to be immediately released as a demonstration of good faith. The regent was delighted, telling Vasco there was nothing greater he could have done to please him.

Still in the boats the regent and Vasco made a slow circuit of the Portuguese vessels. They were massive, stoutly constructed and carried a large number of cannon, easily outclassing any ship in the region. Vasco gave orders for the cannon to be fired in the regent's honour, much to the latter's delight. The regent then directed his young son and a *sharif* to join Vasco while the

---

* He is believed to have been Sheikh Wagerage, who later communicated directly with King Manuel in Portugal.

Captain-Major sent two representatives with him to visit his palace and report back. The meeting was concluded amicably after some three hours, with the regent saying that the following day he would go to the beach, where his horsemen would put on a demonstration for the Portuguese, and he hoped the captain would join him. The two parted on the friendliest of terms.[215]

Events up to this point still indicated to Vasco the need for caution, so the following morning he, joined by Coelho, rowed slowly along the front of the town to watch the display of horsemanship. As a precaution smaller bombards had been placed in the poops of the longboats. A crowd gathered along the shore both to observe the strangers and to witness the show. The regent himself arrived, carried in a palanquin, and from the beach again urged Vasco to come ashore. His ageing father, the king, desired very much to meet personally with him. As a pledge, the regent and his sons were to go aboard Vasco's vessels as hostages, but again the Captain-Major declined and the entertainment began. The display of mock fighting by the horsemen was well received by everyone.[216]

While Vasco was deciding whether he could trust the king and regent, an event took place that was to have a significant impact on what the Portuguese believed they were learning. They had come expecting to make contact with Prester John and been disappointed to learn that the only kingdom matching the description – Ethiopia – was inland. They knew there were other colonies of corrupted Christians in the region, yet thus far they had been unable to establish contact with any of them. Those Christians they had seen were treated as slaves and held in contempt by the Muslims. The Portuguese believed an independent community, especially one possessing a port where they could find safety, fresh provisions and service for their ships, was essential to their success.

India existed largely as a mythical land to Europeans, and there was much debate as to the nature of its predominant religion. There were many who believed from what little they knew that Hinduism was actually a corrupted version of Christianity. What was to prove significant was the reality that the Portuguese knew only three religions: Christianity, Islam and Judaism. If a people were not Muslims and not Jews, they must be Christian.

Vasco visited with his brother Paulo not long after arriving at Malindi. The Portuguese had learned there were four ships in the harbour from India belonging to 'Christians'. On this day several of these Indians, by some accounts the owners of each of the four Indian ships, came aboard the *São Rafael*. They were dark-skinned men who wore little clothing and had 'long beards and long hair, which they braid'. The men were escorted about the ship and at one point were shown an altarpiece that represented Our Lady at the foot of the cross with the infant Jesus Christ in her arms, surrounded by the Apostles.

When the Indians saw the picture they threw themselves on the deck and uttered extended prayers, followed by offerings of cloves and pepper. This was what the Portuguese were expecting, and they took considerable comfort from this display of homage to the cross. Later, when Vasco rowed past one of the Indian ships, the Indians fired their modest bombards in his honour and, leaning over the railing of their vessels, shouted words the Portuguese heard as 'Christ! Christ!'[217]

The reality was very different from what Vasco and his men perceived. The image on the *São Rafael* bore a close resemblance to one that Hindus in their region worshipped and the Indians were apparently under the impression this was the Western representation of that scene. The words they shouted were actually 'Krishna! Krishna!' The Portuguese, however, took great comfort in having confirmed, in their mind, that Indians were in fact Christians and when they resumed their voyage it was with that expectation.

The Portuguese were fascinated by the Indians, and their belief that they were Christians was further reinforced by the amicable treatment they received from them. That same night Vasco was greeted with honour by the Indians, who held a celebration aboard their ships, again firing their bombards, sending up rockets and raising their voices in 'loud shouts'. The Indians spoke only a smattering of Arabic but during the evening cautioned the Portuguese about going ashore. The good wishes they were receiving from the Arabs, they said, 'neither came from their hearts nor from their good will'.[218]

The Indians were mistaken. The delicate negotiations and contacts here were to prove the most fortuitous encounter of the voyage, for Malindi was in fierce competition with nearby Mombasa and greeted these newcomers as potentially powerful allies. The regent was not about to allow their differences in religion to interfere with what could become a highly profitable alliance.

Two more days passed, during which the regent ordered celebrations and entertaining displays on shore. The details are not reported, but steady provisioning was apparently taking place. Most importantly, the supply of water was being replenished. Still, Vasco was not satisfied. The Indians had warned him to be cautious, and his experiences with Muslims before arriving here had served to deepen his suspicion. Time was passing, with no progress.

On Sunday 22 April the regent sent one of his servants to the *São Gabriel* on a casual errand. Vasco ordered the man to be seized. He sent word ashore that he was to be provided with the pilots he had been promised, at which time he would free the man. The regent immediately dispatched a pilot and the servant was released.[219]

Vasco was 'much pleased' with the quality of this pilot, who is reported to have been well versed in navigation and a Christian from Gujarat, though the Portuguese decided at once that he was a Moor. But here again is a dispute among historians. Many consider it well established that this man was none other than Ahmad ibn Majid, an Arab from Julfar, and the greatest Arab navigator of the time. It has been said this was a most fortuitous matching of Vasco, one of western Europe's greatest navigators, and his counterpart from the Indian Ocean. If this pilot was indeed Ahmad, he would have been well into his sixties when he entered Vasco's service.

The evidence, however, does not support such a conclusion, although it does make for a great romantic image.[220] What is certain is that the pilot was highly skilled and greatly respected by Vasco and his crew. They learned from him that there was indeed an island (Kilwa) occupied by a population that was half Muslim, half Christian, though it was under the authority of the Muslims. Many pearls could be found there. It was a major commercial centre in the region, more dominant even than Mombasa. The pilot suggested the Portuguese should go there, as they would find friends.[221]

In his first meeting with Vasco the pilot unrolled detailed charts of the region which answered many questions for the Portuguese. The maps included an accurate depiction of the west coast of India, and most importantly, bearings, parallels and meridians laid out in the understandable Arabic fashion. Vasco was viewing a map of the final leg of his quest, surely a momentous occasion.

When shown a Portuguese astrolabe, the pilot demonstrated a great familiarity with it and indicated that such devices were in common use in the region. He made a demonstration of how he and other pilots in the Indian Ocean made their readings of the sun and stars.[222] Any reservations Vasco may have had were now completely dispelled. They had their man, and the regent on shore had made him available.

They had been at Malindi for nine days and despite Vasco's misgivings his ships had been fully resupplied. Even better, their pilot informed them that the monsoon had begun early and, if the Portuguese wished to ignore his suggestion that they go to Kilwa, passage across the Indian Ocean was now not only possible but relatively easy.

It may be that Vasco's mind was still uncertain as to the reliability of the ruler of Malindi, but he possessed all he needed to proceed. Without setting foot in the city he gave orders and on Tuesday 24 April the ships weighed anchor and set sail, passing slowly out of the huge bay and into a strait. By Sunday they had gone so far north along the coast of Africa that the North Star was again reassuringly visible. The monsoon winds now filled the great white sails of the ships and they made steady passage eastward across the Indian Ocean.

Three uneventful weeks passed, during which time Vasco came to know his new pilot. Through an interpreter they discussed what the Portuguese should expect to find when they reached India. He told Vasco that in speaking to Indians their speech should always be gentle, and they should harm no one unless in retaliation for harm done them without provocation. Most importantly, Vasco should be very careful about whom he allowed to go ashore, and especially about doing so himself. When crewmen did leave the ship, Vasco should be certain he had matching hostages aboard. This was the custom for new traders and no offence would be taken. Finally, the pilot cautioned, he must exercise care in making his purchases so as not to upset current prices. The Portuguese, he said, should trust him, that he knew the weights and measures as well as the prices the Portuguese should expect to pay. Vasco was deeply impressed with the man and his advice and referred to him among his men as the 'Good Moor'.

On the twenty-third day of the passage, 18 May, through a thick haze that clung to the water, 'lofty mountains' – probably Mount Eli in northern Kerala – were observed on the horizon. The pilot altered course but squalls prevented him from accurately determining their position. They sailed on until finally the Good Moor caught a proper sight of land and made his way across the deck to Vasco. 'We have arrived', he said. 'We are north of Calicut! Here is the land where you desired to go.'[222]

The outward voyage was complete. For eleven long, weary months the Portuguese had survived storm and calm, hostile attacks and treachery. The full numbers are not recorded but approximately 30 of the 170 to 180 who had left with them that triumphant day in Portugal were now buried at sea or on hostile shores. There was a great deal yet to be accomplished and the most difficult leg of the voyage lay ahead of them, but here at last was India. The men lined the railing of their ships, climbed into the rigging to get a better view and gazed in wonder and anticipation at the promised land.

On Sunday 20 May, a short distance north of Calicut, off the Malabar coast, Vasco gave orders and the Portuguese ships dropped anchor as dusk gathered.

15

'The devil take you!'

The Good Moor had mistaken a smaller town named Capua for Calicut. Four small boats came out to the strange, towering ships and asked where the men had come from and why they were here. There was nothing to be gained from deception at this point, so Vasco replied directly. The men pointed to a spot a few miles further south and told them there was the port they were seeking.[224]

The Portuguese sailors came from the poorest country of western Europe. All their lives, and certainly over the many tedious months of this long voyage, they had heard about the wonders of India, of its great riches. Each man had within his personal belongings a cache of valuables with which to make personal trades. With what they would earn from this, and the largesse of the king after their successful return home, every man expected to make his fortune. And why not? India was the land of legendary riches. They had succeeded in the journey to its source and expected to reap the reward.

What happened next the gawking sailors crowded against the rails found shocking. As night fell, hundreds of small boats of every sort swarmed the three Portuguese ships. Some were offering wares to sell or exchange, but most were simply begging. They were gaunt and clearly profoundly impoverished. The seamen from Europe's poorest country could hardly believe their eyes. Could this really be the fabled India?

That evening Hindu fishermen came out into nearby waters and with torches and lanterns gathered in their catch. To the Portuguese, who had never seen anything like this, it looked as though the fish all but leaped into the boats. The rest of the night passed uneventfully as Vasco laid plans with his officers as to how they would proceed the following morning.

Outside his quarters the crew were already anticipating their long overdue shore leave and the sensual delights they anticipated here in the mysterious and exotic East. The words of one of the most popular songs went:

> *How winsome is my beloved!*
> *How lovely and how fair!*
> *Tell me, if thou canst, O sailor,*
> *Thou who hast roamed*
> *The oceans wide,*
> *If there be ship at sea*
> *Or sail, or star in heaven*
> *As lovely as is she!*[225]

Early the next morning, when the same four boats came out, hundreds of ships could be seen to the south. Vasco sent for one of the *delgradados*, a converted Jew named João Nunes, who possessed some knowledge of Arabic and Hebrew. He was given instructions to go ashore with the Indians and return with a report of all he could see and hear. Nunes climbed into one of the boats with the Indians and sailed to Calicut, where a great crowd pressed the shore, eager to see what sort of man came from such strange, alien ships.

Calicut was the richest and most prominent of the ports in this region and, although there was no harbour to speak of, as many as 700 ships at any time lay at anchor in its waters. A Florentine permitted by Vasco to take part in this voyage recorded what he observed of the city, naturally focusing on matters relating to trade. The leading merchants, he wrote, came from Cambay to the north, and Malmsey, a sweet wine usually made in Cyprus, was available in Calicut. Both Egyptian and Venetian gold coins were in common use.[226]

The most common anchorage was at the mouth of a river to the south of the city, although there were other places before the many streams and man-made canals that flowed into the ocean which were also used. The muddy banks were thick with small red crabs. Crocodiles lay in the waters about the streams, while vast flocks of egrets and kingfishers could be seen in the shallows.

The city itself was not especially imposing, although it and the surrounding region were heavily populated. The crowded houses were clustered along the shore for about one mile, then were spread further apart for another six, extending inland only a short distance. Few structures were of more than a single storey since the soil was inadequate to support heavy buildings. Most houses were of adobe or well-carved wood and there was no doubt that, despite the widespread poverty, many living here were quite prosperous. The city wall was no taller than a man on horseback.

Along the ocean front were spacious warehouses designed to withstand the pervasive dampness, and housed within were wares from throughout Asia. These included silk from China, spices of every sort including pepper, which was grown and processed locally, cinnamon, mace, nutmeg, cloves, camphor and large quantities of local cotton cloth, all bundled and ready for immediate sale and transport. There was also ivory, cassia, unknown medicinal plants, cardamon, copra, coir and piles of sandalwood.[227] It was a cornucopia of all that the Portuguese had come to find.

In the seventeenth century Pietro della Valle recorded what he saw in Calicut, observations that must have been very similar to those witnessed by the Portuguese when they first arrived:

> We went to see the Bazar which is near the shore; the Houses or rather Cottages are built of Earth and thatched with Palm-leaves, being very low; the streets also are very narrow, but sufficiently long; the Market was full of all sorts of Provisions and other things necessary to the livelihood of that people, conformably to their custom; for, as for clothing they need little, both men and women going quite naked, saving that they have a piece either of Cotton, or silk, hanging down from the girdle to the knees and covering their shame; the better sort are either wont to wear it

all blew [*sic*], or white striped with Azure, or Azure and some other colour; a dark blew being most esteemed amongst them. Moreover both Men and Women wear their hair long and ty'd about their head; the women with a lock hanging in one side under the ear becomingly enough as almost all Indian women do; the dressing of whose head is, in my opinion, the gallantest that I have seen in any other nation. The Men have a lock hanging down from the crown of the head, sometimes a little inclined on one side; some of them use a small coloured head-band, but the Women use none at all. Both sexes have their Arms adorned with bracelets, their ears with pendants, and their necks with jewels; the Men commonly go with their Swords and Bucklers, or other Arms, in their hands.[228]

When the Russian merchant Athanasius Nikitan first came ashore at Chaul, a port city some 30 miles from Bombay to the north, he recorded that:

People go about naked, with their heads uncovered and their breasts bare, the hair tressed into one tail, and thick bellies. They bring forth children every year and the children are many . . . When I go out many people follow me and stare at the white man. Women who know you willingly concede their favours for they like white men.[229]

The Malabar coast of southern India was one of the most beautiful places on Earth. Palm trees swayed in the ocean breeze. Pristine white beaches stretched endlessly, embraced by the surf of the Indian Ocean. The not distant mountains were shrouded in clouds set against an azure sky. Numerous small lakes were strung out like a necklace. Calicut and the nearby towns lay surrounded by fields of rice in their watery plots. When the monsoon came, the urban areas were islands in the flooded lands. The taking of life was forbidden, so the native animals thrived even about and within the towns, especially venomous snakes, which exacted a steady toll on the population.

Only with difficulty was Nunes, shielded by the men who had rowed him ashore, able to make his way slowly through the pressing throng that awaited him as he stepped on to land. Although this was a Hindu part of the Vijayanagar empire, trade was primarily under the control of Muslims, so he was taken directly to the house of two Arabs from Tunis 'who could speak Castilian and Genoese'.[230]

Word had surely reached these men by this time that unusual and large ships had arrived. They would have speculated between themselves as to who these newcomers might be. Ships of this sort were foreign to these waters and could only have come by passage around the tip of Africa. Still, there would have been doubts until the moment Nunes was shown into their presence. One of the Arabs all but shouted, 'May the Devil take thee! What brought you hither?'

Nunes then uttered what were to become the most quoted words of this epic voyage. 'We come in search of Christians and spices.' Realizing at once that he was Portuguese, the Arabs then asked, 'Why does not the King of Castile, the King of France or the Signoria of Venice send hither?' Nunes was ready with his reply. 'Because the King of Portugal will not permit it.'

Arab hospitality now asserted itself and Nunes was taken back to their lodgings and given wheaten bread and honey. After eating and some discussion he returned to the *São Gabriel* accompanied by one of the Arabs whom the Portuguese called Monçaide, probably a corruption of the Arabic words for 'the happy one'. He was clearly not concerned about the implications of the Portuguese arrival or its threat to his position. No sooner was he aboard the ship than he said to Vasco, 'A lucky venture, a lucky venture! Plenty of rubies, plenty of emeralds! You owe great thanks to God, for having brought you to a country holding such riches!' Most astonishingly, the words were spoken in Portuguese, something none of them aboard ship had anticipated 'so far away from Portugal'.[231] Although the Christians and Moors were great enemies, here was someone Vasco could understand; in a strange way so distant from home this was a familiar face.

Following the usual formalities of hospitality Vasco inquired after the local ruler. Monçaide, who proved to be unusually forthcoming, answered that the Zamorin was at Panane, a coastal town 28 miles south of Calicut. Vasco immediately dispatched two men: one of them presumably Nunes, who had acquitted himself so well thus far; the other Fernão Martins, in whom he had great confidence. Monçaide agreed to accompany the pair. They bore the message that Vasco da Gama was an ambassador who had arrived from the King of Portugal with important letters and that he was prepared to travel to the ruler to present them.[232]

News had already reached the Zamorin of the arrival of such unusual ships manned by fair-skinned men. He consulted at once with his diviners to determine the implications. He learned of a 400-year-old prophecy which said that the day would come when India would be ruled by a distant king whose subjects were white and that he would harm those who were not his friend.

After some consideration the diviners told the Zamorin that the Portuguese had arrived in fulfilment of the prophecy, but that neither he nor his kingdom would suffer if the Zamorin behaved towards them in a friendly manner. 'The people on land would have to obey those who were masters of the sea', he was told. One diviner went on to say that if his words had not come true within a period of five years, he would forfeit his life.

This was sobering news. The Zamorin next consulted with his advisers, who made light of the prophecy and the likelihood that it was now being fulfilled. Thousands of ships had come to the Malabar coast, yet not one had so much as attempted to conquer India by sea.

The Zamorin was still in a quandary about how to proceed when the two Portuguese arrived with Monçaide. The message he received from them through an intermediary was that these strangers were servants of a powerful Christian king, and that these three ships had become separated from a great fleet of fifty such ships which they expected to soon join them off Calicut. These newcomers sought to trade for pepper and other spices and were prepared to exchange gold and other merchandise.[233]

Hearing this, the Zamorin decided that he would engage the Portuguese in a friendly manner and await the unfolding of events. The source of his wealth and power was, after all, trade and a new outlet was not to be scorned. He presented the Portuguese emissaries with 'much fine cloth' and asked them to convey word to their captain bidding him welcome on his behalf and announcing that he would immediately return to Calicut. In fact, he set out almost that moment with his vast retinue.[234]

When Martins and Nuñes rejoined Vasco aboard the *São Gabriel* and reported the ruler's words, they were accompanied by a pilot sent by the Zamorin to direct the relocation of the three ships to a safer anchorage. The ships moved slowly south through the anchored fleet of trading ships and assumed station directly off Pandarani, a small town near by and closer to Calicut, inside a protective barrier of banks and reefs. This place was better, the pilot said, commenting that there was a stony bottom where they had been. The anchorage was much closer to the city of Calicut and here they would have readier access to trade. Vasco co-operated but still exercised caution, declining to anchor his ships as close to shore as the pilot urged.

By the time all this was accomplished the Zamorin had already arrived at his palace within Calicut and summoned Vasco through a *wali*, a chief of police, attended by some 200 armed men. It was late in the day, so Vasco replied he would come ashore the next morning.[235]

This was an auspicious beginning, which was not to last. Ships were arriving from east Africa with word of events there. While this would have been of little interest to the Zamorin, who was Hindu, the Arab traders would have received the news with keen interest. Vasco was now claiming to be part of a great fleet, but no one reported having seen one. Some historians have speculated that this attempt at deception branded the Portuguese as liars and, in the minds of Arabs, little more than pirates.

Logic suggests there is some truth in this, but it ignores the basic reality. Despite the assistance of one Arab, whose motives could as easily have been espionage as beneficence, the fact was that Muslims controlled a substantial majority of the local trade and any interloper, especially the hated Christians, was going to be opposed by every means. What had occurred in Africa meant nothing. These Portuguese were a clear threat to the Muslims and had to be destroyed.

The king of the Vijayanagar empire expected the regular payment of taxes and port duties from the Zamorin. In Calicut his representatives carefully scrutinized all events and dispatched independent reports to the capital. It was important that the Zamorin should maintain good relations with the source of this income, that is, with the Arabs already in place. While newcomers were welcome, since the Muslim monopoly on movement of trade into Europe worked to keep prices lower than they might otherwise have been, the Zamorin must not upset the relationships that already existed. The representatives of the local Arabs had the ear of the Zamorin, and most especially that of his advisers, and the message he was receiving about the Portuguese was very different from the one Vasco was seeking to convey.

Time and the pace of life moved slowly in the heat of southwestern India. Events consumed just over a week since they had arrived, so it was on Monday 28 May 1498 that Vasco da Gama ordered his ships to be decked out in full pageantry. His officers and men were directed to wear their finest clothing. He and those who were to go ashore with him were splendidly attired. He ordered 'many flags' and gave instructions for bombards to be placed in the longboats and carried in them, as well as trumpeters to sound fanfares.

Vasco was turned out in his best apparel, probably selected before he departed from Lisbon. He wore a long brocaded satin cloak over a tunic of blue satin, and fine white calf-high boots. On his shoulders rested a lace collar, and placed in his sash was a decorative dagger. On his head he wore a cap with lappets of blue velvet, crowned with a white feather fastened by an exquisite hasp.[236]

The Portuguese had little doubt they were among corrupted Christians, and it was through this lens of belief that they saw Calicut. Indeed the *Roteiro*, written contemporaneously, records that Calicut was 'inhabited by Christians'. It notes that they were of tawny complexion, many of them with beards and long hair, others with their hair clipped short or a shaved head. It observes how common were moustaches. While the well-to-do wore skimpy clothing, 'the others manage as best they are able'. It goes on to say:

> The women of this country, as a rule, are ugly and of small stature. They wear many jewels of gold round the neck, numerous bracelets on their arms, and rings set with precious stones on their toes. All these people are well-disposed and apparently of mild temper. At first sight they seem covetous and ignorant.[237]

Vasco selected thirteen men to accompany him ashore, one of them fortunately the author of the *Roteiro*, so this source constitutes a firsthand description of events. Left behind were his brother, Paulo, who commanded the ships, and Nicolau Coelho, who remained with the longboats and a guard of men on shore to await Vasco's return. Both Paulo and Coelho were given direct orders to retreat should disaster fall and sail at once to Portugal with the vital information they had gained of how to make the successful passage to India. No attempt was to be made to rescue their captain or his men.[238]

As the longboats set off, the ships' cannon fired in salute. The *wali* and his men greeted the Portuguese ashore with naked swords, as was customary, although their manner was quite friendly. They had brought with them a palanquin carried by six men for the Captain-Major, as the custom called for men of distinction to travel in such a fashion. In fact, local merchants paid the Zamorin for the right to be carried about in this manner.

A vast, curious throng crowded the streets to witness the procession. The Portuguese were taken some 7 miles to the house of a man of rank, where they were provided with food 'consisting of rice, with much butter, and excellent boiled fish'. Too nervous, or perhaps fearing poison, Vasco elected not to eat. The men were then taken to the nearby Elatur river, where they boarded two boats that had been lashed together. Numerous other small boats, crowded with onlookers, joined them, while those watching from shore were 'infinite' in number. As the procession made its way upriver, they observed many large ships drawn up on the banks for servicing.[239]

After being rowed about 2 miles Vasco and his men were taken ashore, where once again the Captain-Major entered a palanquin. The road here was also crowded with a great multitude anxious to see the newcomers. The Portuguese found it reassuring that smiling women came out from their huts bearing small children in their arms, then eagerly followed along.

The procession arrived at a Hindu temple or pagoda, which they immediately took to be a church of the corrupted Christian faith of the Hindus. It was constructed of carved stone and covered with tiles. At the entrance was a pillar of bronze 'as high as a mast', on top of which was perched a bird, 'apparently a cock'. (By coincidence, the cock is the national symbol of Portugal.) Within the building 'rose a chapel' built of stone, with a heavy bronze door and stone steps leading up to it. 'Within this sanctuary stood a small image which they said represented Our Lady. Along the walls, by the main entrance, hung seven small bells.'[240]

Here Vasco stopped what had become a tour and in the outer portion of the structure, as only certain Hindus were permitted within the inner sanctum, led his men in prayer of gratitude. One version has the Hindu priests joining them, chanting over and over the words 'Maria, Maria, Maria'. If true, what they were actually saying was probably 'Maha Maja', one of the many Hindu gods. Another source suggests the words may have been 'Mari' or 'Mariamma', a local deity, goddess of the much-dreaded smallpox.

It was a time of festivity for the Hindus. The tall pillar was actually of wood covered with copper, and the cock was the symbol of the war god, Subraumainar. The bells were there to be struck when the priests entered the most holy portion of the temple. About the interior were many representations and images of various Hindu gods, a number of whom were depicted wearing crowns, which the Portuguese took to be the Indian version of Christian saints, though some possessed 'four or five arms'.

The similarities must have been striking, since weeks earlier Hindus aboard Vasco's ship had taken a Christian carving to be Hindu. Also, as Muslims forbade the use of depictions, the Portuguese were inclined to accept any religion that worshipped before carvings and drawings as being Christian in origin, if not immediately identifiable as such. The situation was further compounded by the interpreters, who tended to use a Christian word in place of the Hindu one originally spoken. Still, not everyone was convinced. One of the men kneeling in prayer before the statues muttered to Vasco, 'If these be devils I worship the true God.' Hearing these words, Vasco allowed one of his infrequent smiles.[241]

Following the prayers the priests presented the Portuguese with 'some white earth', then threw holy water over them. The 'earth' was a concoction of cow dung, ashes, dust, sandalwood and other materials mixed with rice water. It was to be placed on their foreheads and breasts, about their necks and on their forearms. Vasco graciously allowed he would put the earth on later.[242]

After leaving the temple the colourful procession advanced slowly into Calicut, where the Portuguese observed another Hindu temple as they passed. Word of the strangers had spread and the crowd grew in size until it 'became next to impossible' for them to make progress. These strangers had generated tremendous interest and excitement. The *wali* put Vasco and his men into a nearby house while he sent word ahead of the difficulty.

A short time later the *wali*'s brother, identified as a lord, arrived to accompany the Portuguese. With him was a body of men who beat drums, blew *anafils* and bagpipes, and fired matchlocks in the air to clear the way. Vasco himself was treated with the greatest of courtesy, being given more respect 'than is shown in Spain to a king'. The procession and mob had grown immensely. 'The number of people was countless, for in addition to those who surrounded us, and among whom there were two thousand armed men, they crowded the roofs and houses.'[243]

The number of onlookers continued to grow as they

approached the palace of the Zamorin. As they drew near, 'men of much distinction and great lords came out to meet the captain' and joined the procession. It had taken the entire day to come this distance, and nightfall was just an hour away as they reached the courtyard of the palace. The procession was directed through four gateways before, at last, reaching the door where the Zamorin waited. Then 'a little old man', taken to be a royal adviser, stepped forward and embraced Vasco in welcome.[244] So great was the throng it had streamed into the courtyard with them and formed a barrier through which the procession could not advance those last steps. Upon command the Hindu escort drew daggers and several Indians were stabbed in order to clear a path and gain entrance.

The Zamorin was waiting within a small court, reclining on a couch covered with green velvet. To his left, held by a slave, was an immense golden cup which served as his spittoon, already overflowing with the husks of the betel nuts he chewed. The nut was popular throughout this region for its reputed medicinal benefits and, although it discoloured the teeth, it was said to make the 'breath sweet'. To the right of the Zamorin was held a gold basin, so large that it would be difficult for a man to encircle with his arms, filled to capacity with the nuts. Placed about were a number of silver jugs and an impressive display of precious gems, while spread above was a gilded canopy.[245]

The Zamorin wore only a white cloth from his waist down, this garment ending in points on which were fastened gold rings, set with rubies. On one of his arms he wore a gold bracelet of three strands, beset with a diamond 'the thickness of a thumb'. About his neck was a strand of pearls, each the size of a hazelnut, twisted in triplicate, falling to his waist. One emerald amid the pearls was the size of a bean. The Zamorin's hair was arranged in a knot, which was wrapped by another string of pearls and a pendant with a single pearl shaped like a pear. In his ears were studs of gold.[246]

Vasco stepped gravely forward and saluted the ruler with his joined hands raised. He opened them and then quickly shut them, in the manner he had observed among the Indians. The

Zamorin bid the rest of the Portuguese be seated near by on a stone bench where he could see them more clearly. He gave instructions for water to be poured over their hands and for them to be served with jack fruit and bananas, food unknown to the Portuguese. They dived into it with unseemly gusto. The Zamorin watched the men with a smile at their behaviour and instructed servants to provide the men with a supply of betel nuts since they had enjoyed the fruit so much. Through the two interpreters – one translated his words into Arabic, which Vasco's interpreter then translated into Portuguese – he said that he could discern the Portuguese were 'men of much distinction'. He bade Vasco to tell him of his voyage and his purpose in coming.

Vasco replied that such information could only be delivered personally and not before such a large gathering, probably a reference to the Muslim traders present. The Zamorin consented and withdrew with a few of his advisers into a nearby chamber, where he met alone with the Portuguese Captain-Major. Here the ruler reclined on another seat 'embroidered in gold'.[247]

Darkness had fallen as Vasco now related the story of the Portuguese discoveries, of their decades-long probing for the passage to India, and of how he and his ships had finally succeeded. The King of Portugal already possessed great wealth and had no need of more. They had come in peace to find fellow Christians and to trade for spices. His king had personally charged him with success and ordered that he was 'not to return to Portugal until he should have discovered this King of the Christians, on pain of having his head cut off'. Vasco concluded with these words:

> Manuel, a prince of vast dignity and aspiring soul and great curiosity, having heard much of India, particularly of the empire of Calicut, was struck with admiration at the ingenuity of the people as well as the dignity and grandeur of their sovereign, and was extremely solicitous to enter into a league of friendship with so renowned a monarch. For this purpose he, Gama, had been sent into these parts, nor

did he doubt but such a league would greatly tend to the mutual advantage of both princes.[248]

Vasco told the Zamorin he had letters for him from the King of Portugal, which he would deliver the next day. He had also been instructed 'by word of mouth' to tell the ruler that his king 'desired to be his friend and brother'.[249] The Zamorin was deeply touched by the presentation and was very gracious in his reply. He welcomed Vasco to his court, saying 'he held him as a friend and brother, and would send ambassadors with him to Portugal'.

It was now quite late and the Zamorin asked if Vasco and his men wished to spend the night with Christians or Muslims, as it was the custom for traders to reside within their own community when in port. Vasco said neither, that they desired to lodge by themselves. The Zamorin agreed and then returned to the court, which was lit by a huge candlestick, where he graciously bid the other Portuguese goodnight.

Vasco and his men returned to the procession, where he again entered the palanquin. The Portuguese noted that the immense crowd that had followed them throughout the day was not visibly reduced in size. They were now led by the Zamorin's factor, a Moor. As they made their slow way back along the course they had earlier taken, a violent thunderstorm struck and the streets ran with water, quickly turning to mud. The going was difficult and the procession had lasted so long that Vasco was visibly tired. The Portuguese were given shelter on the factor's veranda until the storm abated. Carpets were spread about and heavy candlesticks mounted with lamps gave them light. At last they were able to leave and reached the house arranged for them, only to find to their pleasure some of their shipmates, along with Vasco's own bed from the *São Gabriel*, already prepared; also placed in his sleeping chamber were the gifts to present the next day to the Zamorin.[250]

The momentous day had gone exceptionally well and had met Vasco's very best hopes. More was to come, not the least of which was establishing a permanent trade mission in Calicut, but this was an auspicious beginning. He surely knew he was hampered by the short-sightedness of the royal planners in Lisbon. Although there was much poverty in Calicut, there was also incredible wealth. He had seen the degree of ostentation and affluence to which the Zamorin was accustomed and the meagre gifts he was preparing to offer would surely have been troubling.

Such gifts were an honorific which was more than simply a bribe. They also signified at least temporary subordination or, as the Portuguese elected to see it, 'rendering service', to local authority, and those Vasco had were scant for such a purpose. The gifts to be presented were twelve pieces of striped cloth, four scarlet hoods, six hats, four strings of coral, a supply of hand basins, a case of sugar, two casks of oil and two of honey.

It was the custom for such gifts to be observed first by the royal factor before being formally presented to the ruler. The next morning the factor arrived, accompanied by Arab merchants who ostensibly represented the Zamorin. When shown the gifts, the factor laughed aloud, saying that none of this was appropriate to give to the ruler. Such gifts, he said, would not be offered by the poorest merchant from Mecca or any part of India. The only gift suitable to the occasion was gold.[251]

Much has been made of the Portuguese failure to observe the customary courtesies for such an occasion, and that failure has been used to explain the difficulties they were soon to encounter. While it was true that Vasco's gifts were of such inferior quality that his mission might have been better served had he not even offered them, it is highly unlikely they had anything to do with the events that followed. The three Portuguese ships were far superior to, and larger than, any vessel in regular use in the Indian ocean. The Portuguese possessed more advanced weaponry and armour, and they had the means to sail the extraordinary distance around the flank of the Muslim-controlled Middle East, which blocked direct trade with Christian Europe. They were certainly men of substance and there was no question they were men of great power. In the face of such sobering realities their failure to observe certain trading niceties, while a modest affront, was not especially significant in the greater course of events.

Vasco expressed his dismay to the factor and explained that he brought no gold; but then, he was not a merchant but rather an ambassador. He claimed that these modest gifts were his own and not from the King of Portugal. They were such as they were because he was not a man of independent wealth. Should he be fortunate enough to be sent again to India, he would surely return with rich gifts of gold from his king.

Nevertheless, the factor declined to allow such gifts as he now had to be presented to the Zamorin. The other Arab merchants in turn disparaged the items he had brought, as was to be expected. These meagre offerings were nothing less than an insult, they snorted. Vasco relented and said in that case he would forego the gifts, but he still needed to speak with the ruler as he had letters from his king to present. The men promised to return later that day and take him to the Zamorin but, although Vasco waited patiently throughout the afternoon, they did not come back or send word.

Vasco was 'very wroth' at being treated in such a way by 'unreliable' people. When it became apparent the Arabs would not return, he resolved to go to the palace on his own but quickly reconsidered and decided it was best to wait until the next day.

The general mood at their new quarters was very different, however. Those of his crew with him were taking the opportunity to explore Calicut and, though there is no direct record of it, to enjoy the pleasures of the prostitutes and women of easy virtue who frequented all such ports throughout the world. There had been little opportunity for such diversions along the coast of Africa. In addition, the sights of this exotic city could have been nothing less than fascinating to the Portuguese, raised on the fables and legends of the mythical East. They observed three elephants arrive by sea and noted that the creatures served in many ways. Working along the shore were other massive elephants employed in the dragging and handling of logs and to haul heavy loads. Ships were beached sideways, rollers were placed beneath the keel, and then mounted elephants used their heads to push the vessels on to dry land for servicing and repair. These were men accustomed to constructing scaffolding and using pulleys and ropes to manage the same feat.

The wonders of Calicut were an amazement, but the Portuguese were most deeply moved by the plight of the poor. Never before had they witnessed such poverty. Everywhere they went both adults and children pressed against them begging for money or food.[252]

The greater part of the day was probably occupied with pleasures and enjoyable sightseeing, for despite the indignity their Captain-Major was suffering, they arrived back at their quarters in a festive mood. The author of the *Roteiro* records of that evening, 'we diverted ourselves, singing and dancing to the sound of trumpets, and enjoyed ourselves much.' He does not record how Vasco in his black mood took such behaviour.

The following morning the Muslim advisers returned and without explanation escorted Vasco and his men to the palace, where they found the environs 'crowded with armed men'. Once there, Vasco was forced to waited 'four long hours outside a door'. No inquiry he made produced any progress, and he was left fretting at the delay and what he came to understand was a deliberate affront. New merchants always presented lavish gifts to the Zamorin and by now he had been informed of the paltry gifts brought by the Portuguese. More significantly, there had also been ample time for the Arab traders to make their own version of events.

A number of these came to this region from the Mediterranean and understood the profound significance of Portuguese ships in this port having arrived by sailing around the tip of Africa. No greater threat to their prosperity existed than the one represented by the holds of the three ships at anchor. We know the gist of the arguments they put forward while Vasco was cooling his heels at his quarters and just outside the door.

According to one unattributable source, the Muslims told the Zamorin that this Portuguese captain was a 'cruel, bloody-

minded pirate'. The Arab merchants pointed out their long asso-
ciation and claim to friendship with the Zamorin. 'The increase
of your revenues from our trade is apparently so considerable that
we shall but just mention it.' They suggested he consult his
bookkeepers for the sums. They reminded him of their long
'attachment to this country' and how they and their predecessors had been 'ever dutiful and loyal to the kings of Calicut'.
They urged him not to 'allow this agreeable harmony, this
ancient friendship to be dissolved by a set of abandoned wretches
lately arrived in these parts'.

The Arabs went on to acknowledge that they understood that
the Zamorin had no prior experience with men of this sort,
with Franks,

> but we have known numberless instances of their perfidy
> and villainy. They have destroyed nations; they have ravaged
> countries – and all this without provocation, merely to
> soothe their ambition and gratify their lust of power. Can
> you then suppose that men of such a stamp would come
> from regions so remote and encounter such horrid dangers
> only to engage in commerce with your people? No, it is
> incredible. . . . They have fallen upon Mozambique with
> their hostile arms; they have made great slaughter at
> Mombasa.

If the Zamorin had 'any regard for the welfare' of his kingdom,
he must 'destroy these pernicious wretches' and 'put an end to
this dangerous navigation and prevent the rest of the Portuguese
from coming into these parts'.

The Arabs acknowledged they possessed 'an utter aversion' to
all things Christian but that for their friend the Zamorin 'your
all is at stake'. If he elected to do business with these men, the
Arabs could move on to new opportunities 'and settle more
advantageously . . . Wherever we go we shall be enabled to carry
on our trade with equal gain and advantage.' The same could not
be said of the Zamorin. '[I]f you do not immediately exert your-
self with spirit . . . in a few years not only your crown but your

life will be in the greatest jeopardy from a people so covetous, so ambitious, so warlike.'[253]

These were surely sober words from men the Zamorin had come to know and from whom came the greatest measure of his prosperity. He owed allegiance to the king in Vijayanagar and if there was a serious disruption in the flow of revenue from the Zamorin to him, the Calicut ruler knew his own throne, and life, would indeed be in jeopardy. His court was riddled with spies and no one knew better than he that his every action was under close scrutiny. This was a situation to be handled with the greatest care.

Despite the serious implications, there was no simple answer. The Hindus definitely chafed at the Muslim wall that controlled the trade to Europe, viewing it much as the Christians there did. They knew the Arabs restricted the price paid for spices in India and that they in turn made great profits from their resale. The Portuguese presented the Zamorin with a highly desirable development as they represented another outlet for spices and placed the Hindus, and in particular the Zamorin, in a much improved position. Another trading source would probably mean better prices. Even if no meaningful commercial relationship was established with these newcomers, their presence was a powerful card that could be played to the Zamorin's advantage. While local relations with the Muslims were congenial, this does not necessarily mean that he trusted them. The history between Hindus and Muslims had been long and bloody, and the ruler owed the Arabs no undue loyalty.

The ships the Portuguese possessed were formidable, and recent events in east Africa had demonstrated that these newcomers were prepared to use violence if they judged it to be in their interest. Moreover, while these three ships might present no great threat to the Zamorin, the Portuguese had demonstrated their ability to reach his shore from Europe, and who was to say how great a fleet might next arrive? He potentially stood to lose as much by making Vasco his enemy as by embracing him as a friend.

But reality was reality, and there was probably some truth in what the Arab advisers told him. Better the situation he knew than the risk of the unknown. The ruler decided to throw in his lot and that of his kingdom with the Arabs.★ Such was the situation when Vasco and his men were finally readmitted to the presence of the Zamorin.

★ The Zamorin lost his gamble. From this time on Calicut diminished in wealth and prosperity. The Portuguese were here to stay and, because of the ever more hostile response at Calicut, established alliances with other cities and located their permanent presence north at Gôa.

16

Treachery

The Zamorin's intermediaries informed Vasco that only two of his men could accompany him for the audience. He selected Fernão Martins, who would interpret, and his secretary, Diogo Dias, who also served as comptroller of the voyage. Those who remained outside waited apprehensively, fearing after such a long delay that this separation would end badly. There had not been a moment since they reached the coast of east Africa when the Portuguese had not understood that they could be overwhelmed in moments.

Among those present for the meeting were four Arab advisers to the Zamorin whom Vasco now viewed with deep suspicion, as well he might. The favourable climate in which the Captain-Major and the ruler had previously parted had clearly dissipated. The Zamorin began by saying he had expected to see Vasco on Tuesday. Rather than point out that these very Muslim advisers had not returned to escort him as promised, words that would almost certainly degenerate into mutual accusations, Vasco responded that his long journey had tired him and that was the reason he had not come.

The Zamorin said that, though Vasco had told him earlier he came from a 'very rich kingdom', he had brought no gifts for him. He had also said he bore letters from his king but the Zamorin had yet to see them. Vasco replied that he had not brought suitable gifts because the object of his voyage was to make discoveries and establish contact, but that when other ships came he would see to it they brought with them lavish gifts. As for the letters, it was true he had them and would deliver them now, if that was desired.

But the subject of gifts was not so easily dismissed. Had Vasco come to discover stones or men, the Zamorin wanted to know. If he had come to discover men, why had he not brought anything suitable to give? The ruler had been told that Vasco carried with him the golden image of the Santa Maria. Why not give that, if he had nothing else? Vasco explained that the Santa Maria was not made of gold but that, even if she were, he could not part with her as she had guided him across the seas and would guide him back safely home. With that the Zamorin asked to see the letters.

One of the messages was written in Portuguese; the other was a copy in Arabic. Vasco begged a favour of the ruler and explained that the Moors now present wished him ill and could very well misrepresent the contents of the letter. He asked for a local 'Christian' who spoke Arabic to be summoned to read it. This was done, but it transpired that while the Hindu could speak Arabic he could not read it. The impasse was resolved by having the four Muslims read the letter written in Arabic, then translating its contents for the Zamorin aloud in Malayalam, the local language. The Zamorin's interpreter translated this back into Arabic for Martins, who repeated what was said to Vasco, who matched the words to the letter written in Portuguese.[254]

In fact, the content of the letter was of such a general and harmless nature there was no difficulty in its translation. The King of Portugal had written of trade, so the Zamorin wanted to know what kind of merchandise was to be found in his country that could be traded. Vasco answered they had much 'corn, cloth, iron, bronze and many other things'.

The Zamorin asked if any of these were within his ships now. As there had been no room in the original four ships to carry a sufficient quantity of such trade items, Vasco replied that he had little of each, only enough to use as samples, and that if he were permitted to return to his ships he would see that what he had was landed. In the meantime he would leave four or five of his men behind at the lodgings provided to him. To this the Zamorin strongly objected. Vasco was to take all of his men with him. He should offload his merchandise and sell it to the city merchants as best he could. He was to leave no one behind in the city.

On this not especially friendly note Vasco was given summary leave and the audience came to an abrupt end. This was the last meeting the Portuguese had with the Zamorin. When Pedro Alvares Cabral returned in 1500, another ruler sat on the throne, one certainly more to the liking of the local Arab traders, who aggressively opposed him. Vasco and his men went to their quarters and, as it was already late in the day, decided to return to their ships in the morning.

The next day Vasco was brought a horse without a saddle, which he refused as being beneath his station. The point of the offer was probably to humiliate the Portuguese leader, as he clearly appreciated. After a short time a palanquin was brought, which Vasco entered. He and his retinue set off for the long walk to Pantalayini, where their ships were anchored. The six bearers, however, soon outstripped Vasco's men, who were left behind, surrounded by the mass of Hindu humanity. This was not necessarily a problem, for the Hindus were consistently well disposed towards the Portuguese, usually attempting to engage them in trade whenever possible or, when not, begging from them.

The men tried to find their way in the crowded and twisting streets but only ended up becoming lost. Finally, with local help, they found the right route and caught up with the *wali*, who was himself hurrying to catch Vasco. The Portuguese joined him and soon reached the Captain-Major, who was resting, and probably waiting for his men, at one of the many wayside rest houses established 'so that travellers and wayfarers might find protection against the rain'.[255]

Vasco had grown melancholy at events, although the situation was not entirely bad. While the Zamorin was not as favourably disposed towards him as he had seemed during their first audience, he clearly was interested in trade and not overtly hostile. The Arabs were another matter altogether and that was cause for serious concern. Vasco didn't know it, but the Zamorin had his own difficulties with his Muslim factors and as a result did not necessarily trust their advice or actions. The previous factor had been executed for extorting personal bribes from traders.

Vasco asked the *wali*, a Muslim, to be certain that he and his men were provided with a boat once they reached the shore opposite their ships. The *wali* answered that it was already too late in the day for that as the sun had set, and anyway, as the wind had come up, it was not practical to row out to the Portuguese ships. He would see to it the next day.

This struck Vasco as a deception, designed to keep him and his men ashore overnight. With 'dark looks' he told the *wali* that if they were not taken to their ships, he would return at once to the Zamorin to report this lack of co-operation, which was contrary to the orders he had given. If the *wali* tried to detain him, that would be ill advised because the ruler was a 'Christian' like himself and would be angry.

With extravagant protestations, the *wali* assured Vasco this would not be necessary. He was, of course, free to depart for his ships at once. If he needed thirty boats, the *wali* would see to it. There was absolutely no difficulty. In the gathering darkness the Portuguese were led away by the seemingly deferential *wali*. Vasco was extremely suspicious, believing the Moor harboured some 'evil design' against them, and quietly dispatched three of his men by a different route to warn his brother Paulo to protect himself well, as Vasco suspected treachery.

On the shore at Pantalayini there was not a single boat to be had, let alone thirty of them. The *wali* expressed surprise, then suggested that the Portuguese would after all be compelled to spend the night ashore. Vasco saw he had no choice and relented, so the *wali* arranged their quarters at the home of another Muslim. Vasco sent men to buy chickens and rice, which was prepared, and instructed that the three men he had sent earlier should be located, if possible, as he was eager to learn if word had reached Paulo. The men, in fact, had been unable to find Vasco's brother and had turned back but followed another route and missed the Captain-Major.

By this time the Portuguese had been on their feet all day and were weary. The dinner was well received and Vasco's mood lightened. Perhaps, he allowed, he should not have been so suspicious of the *wali*, even though he was a Moor. It might very well have been imprudent to have rowed out to the ships in the dark during a wind. His suspicions, he told his men, had been based on what had already transpired in Calicut, which had persuaded him the Arabs were 'ill-disposed' towards them.[256]

The good humour was short-lived for Vasco had in fact assessed the situation accurately. Early the next morning he again asked for boats so that he could return to his ships as the Zamorin had promised. The Muslims who had come to their lodgings whispered among themselves in a furtive way. At last one stepped forward and with an indulgent smile said that would only be possible if Vasco gave the order to have his ships move and anchor close to shore.[257]

This was an obvious ploy and Vasco refused, adding that his brother Paulo, upon receiving such an order, would assume Vasco and his men were being held prisoner and had given the instruction under duress. In such an event Paulo would obey his standing orders and immediately weigh anchor, then sail directly to Portugal. A lengthy argument ensued but the Arabs made no headway with Vasco, who was utterly – and rightly – convinced that treachery was afoot.

Vasco pointed out that it was the Zamorin himself who had given the order for him and all his men to return to their ships so that trading could be commenced. He had made it clear he did not desire any of the Portuguese to remain ashore. But if these Arabs wanted to go against the orders of the ruler, that was their business. As for himself, Vasco was content to remain here among the friendly local 'Christians'. Still, he was obliged to report this state of affairs directly to the Zamorin, who no doubt would have a response. The Arabs consulted in whispers, then one told Vasco that he was free to go, if that was what he wanted.

But at this point the doors and shutters to the house were banged shut on the Portuguese. Within moments the Captain-Major was informed that they were surrounded by at least 100 men, 'all armed with swords, two-edged battle axes, shields and bows and arrows'.[258] When Vasco asked what this was all about, the Arabs said he was not free to go to his ships until he had ordered their 'sails and rudders' to be surrendered. This would make it impossible for the ships to leave.[259]

The kindest explanation of this development is that the Muslims were afraid Vasco might leave without paying the accumulating port duties, though their actions were out of proportion to such a minor dispute. It is more likely that they were deeply troubled by the threat of the ships leaving at once for Portugal with the charts and pilots filled with knowledge of the passage to India.

Vasco answered that giving up the rudders and sails was out of the question. The Zamorin had instructed him to return to his ships without conditions. They could try and do whatever they liked to him, but he would give no such order. As the Arabs talked among themselves, Vasco pointed out that his men were hungry and he asked leave for some to pass through the armed men to acquire food. His request was flatly denied.

The Portuguese were very distressed at the unfolding events, though they made every effort not to show it. Vasco said, as matters were, why not simply let his men go? He would remain there. Since their request for food was being refused, and there was none within the house, his men 'would die of hunger' if compelled to remain indefinitely. 'Remain where you are', an Arab said haughtily, 'if you die of hunger, you must bear it. We care nothing about that.'

At this moment one of the three men Vasco had sent with word to Paulo the previous night arrived and was able to gain entry to the house. He met in private with Vasco and reported that Coelho had waited with longboats for the Captain-Major and his men throughout the previous night. Vasco instructed the messenger to find some secret way out and get word to Coelho that before he too became trapped he was to return to the ships and be certain they were anchored in a secure location.

The messenger managed to make his exit and soon reached Coelho, who immediately ordered his waiting longboats back to the three Portuguese ships. Some of the armed guards, on hearing this, rushed to shore and in several *almadias* (a type of long narrow boat) pursued Coelho a short distance. Seeing the futility of it, they abandoned the chase.

Again the Arabs demanded that Vasco send word for the ships to be moved more deeply within the port. He was not to trifle with them, for they knew his brother was compelled to obey his every order. Vasco responded that he did not want the ships to move in closer, because 'once inside they could easily be captured', after which he would be killed, as would all the others.[260] He would give no such order.

The remainder of the day passed 'most anxiously' for the Portuguese. As night fell the Muslim guard was increased in number. During the events the Portuguese found themselves standing in the 'small tiled court' where they were surrounded at close hand by the armed men. Throughout the long night they remained on alert, ready at any moment for an attack that did not come.

The next morning, 2 June, the devious *wali* and other Arabs wearing 'better faces' reappeared, this time insisting that Vasco give the order for his merchandise to be landed. No mention was made of moving the ships deeper within the port, but also to come ashore was the entire crew of all three ships, who would not be permitted back on board until the goods had been sold, for such, they claimed, was the local custom. Vasco assumed a friendly manner, assured them he wished to honour the local practice and appeared to consent. He immediately wrote a message to Paulo, instructing him to begin the process of landing their modest supply of trade goods.

The Arabs were pleased and soon the first of the goods reached shore. So convincing was Vasco in appearing to be duped that they lifted the siege and allowed him to return to his ships. He left behind in charge of the goods Diogo Dias as factor, joined by an assistant. The moment Vasco was aboard the *São Gabriel* he countermanded his written order and no more merchandise was taken ashore.[261] With their heavy cannon pointed at the port, the Portuguese were reasonably satisfied that no harm would come to Dias or his assistant.

Over the next several days Arab traders examined the supply of trade goods ashore but made not a single offer to buy any. Instead, they manhandled and disparaged the items. On the fifth

day Vasco dispatched a letter to the Zamorin informing him that
he and his men had been detained on the way back to their ships,
contrary to the ruler's orders. He had landed his goods as
instructed, but the Moors only mocked them and refused to give
them a value. He awaited the Zamorin's instructions and placed
himself, his men and his ships 'at his service'.

The Zamorin immediately replied, saying that those who had
acted against his orders would be punished at once. He himself
would send several traders to deal honestly with the Portuguese.
In addition, with them would be 'a man of quality', who would
remain with the Portuguese factor and who would be authorized summarily to 'kill any Moor' who offered further interfer-
ence.[262]

Although Vasco was initially pleased with this response, the
situation did not improve with the arrival of the Zamorin's special envoys. They remained for eight days examining the trade
goods but, like the other Arabs before them, refused to assign a
value and constantly disparaged them. Finally they declined even
to go to the house where the goods were located and, when sailors landed ashore with more, the Arabs spat on the ground
before them, uttering 'Portugal! Portugal!' as if cursing. The
Portuguese were more convinced than ever that the Moors had
'from the very first . . . sought means to take and kill us'.

Throughout these unfolding events Vasco had taken counsel
from his Good Moor, the pilot who had been provided him in
Malindi and who had consistently demonstrated his integrity.
Aboard the *São Gabriel* the Captain-Major and the pilot often
spoke at length, with the Moor repeatedly urging caution.
Through his own contacts he had learned that the Arabs had
proffered enormous bribes to the Zamorin to destroy the three
ships as well as the Portuguese. The Arabs had told the Zamorin
that the Portuguese were thieves and paupers, that Portugal had
nothing to give and would only take. Once the Portuguese
established a regular route to Calicut, no ships from the Arabian
peninsula would ever come to this port again. If he failed to act
against them, he would be ruined and his kingdom destroyed.

The Good Moor also warned that neither Vasco nor any of

his officers should again go ashore. They would certainly meet a violent death if they did. His words of warning were reinforced by reports from the friendly Hindus that if any of the officers went ashore, 'their heads would be cut off, as this was the way the Zamorin dealt with those who came to his country without giving him gold'.[263]

The situation could not continue indefinitely for many reasons, not the least of which was that the annual great Arab trading fleet from the north was due to arrive in a month or two. They would see the Portuguese as enemies to be destroyed at once, and no intercession by the Zamorin would prevent their falling on them. The ships' hulls had deteriorated as well and some means had to be found to service them.

Amid increasing tension and constant distrust the situation remained unchanged until 23 June, when Vasco asked permission of the Zamorin to convey his goods from Pandarani to Calicut itself. The ruler immediately agreed, going so far in demonstrating his good will as to order the *wali* to gather 'a sufficient number of men who were to carry the whole on their backs to Calecut [*sic*], this to be done at [the Zamorin's] expense, as nothing belonging to the King of Portugal was to be burthened with expenses whilst in his country'. But by this time the suspicions of the Portuguese were so aroused that even this kind act was received with misgivings. The Zamorin had been told that they 'were thieves and went about to steal', so his motives in making this gesture could not be trusted.[264]

However, the goods were moved as ordered and Vasco gave initial instructions for one man from each ship to go to Calicut in turn, to enjoy shore leave and to trade as they wished. The Portuguese continued to be well received by the Hindus in the city and were freely provided with shelter and food wherever they went. The Hindus had no love of the local Muslims, and seeing how they treated the Portuguese could only have increased their regard for these newcomers.

Sailors were soon going ashore in pairs or small groups, bearing bracelets, shirts, clothes and other articles for sale. The prices were lower than the sums they had received in similar trading in east Africa, so the men were disappointed, yet they sold everything they could spare 'in order to take some things away from this country'. It was not in vain, nor perhaps as one-sided as the *Roteiro* states, for its author also adds that 'those who visited the city brought there cloves, cinnamon, and precious stones', all for very low prices. Besides barter, there was much to enjoy ashore for these Europeans. The Hindu women found men with fair skin highly desirable and offered themselves for little more than a few glass beads or no gift at all. Left in the wake of the Portuguese mariners was the new disease syphilis.

Hindus, in turn, were allowed aboard the ships to trade fish for bread, and in many cases to receive a substantial meal gratis. 'All this was done for the sake of establishing relations of peace and amity, and to induce them to speak well of us and not evil.'[265] Nevertheless, some of the locals reportedly snatched food from the hands of sailors engaged in mending sails, leaving them with nothing. So many locals came to the ships that it was difficult to get them all to leave when night came. During the month of July and through the first week of August, Vasco continued to extend the hand of friendship to the Hindu population while an intermittent trade took place in Calicut, both on behalf of the King of Portugal and by the crew members personally.

From these contacts and by a concerted effort the Portuguese gained a full understanding of the spice trade. In so doing they stripped it of the mystery with which distance, time and design had imbued it. They learned the original source of spices, how many days' journey it took for them to reach Calicut and how they were trans-shipped to the Middle East, and they understood the elaborate price structure built into the trade. It was an encyclopaedia of invaluable information which, when joined with their fresh knowledge of the sea passage to India, was of far greater value than whatever spices they could acquire ashore. They were not the only ones who understood that this information was the true loss to the Arab monopoly.

After two months on the coast of India it was apparent there was nothing of significance to be gained by remaining as they were. For all the dangers and difficulties Vasco could not have been completely unhappy with events. The Zamorin had dealt with him honestly and was clearly interested in further trade, provided the Portuguese returned with the proper goods, and gold. The Good Moor had cautioned that Vasco and his men were paying too much for the spices they were gathering, but the prices were so low it had no impact on them. Also it was essential that the expedition return to Lisbon with at least some spices.

In addition the Portuguese had been consistently well treated by the Hindus, the so-called 'Christians', and these made up the overwhelming majority of the population. While it was true the Portuguese supply of trade goods was not well received, this was primarily because they were the wrong kind and because the Arab merchants were exerting all of their considerable influence to stop trade with the Portuguese.

One important task still remained. If at all possible, Vasco was to establish a permanent trade mission in Calicut. Diogo Dias and those assisting him had been adequately received and Vasco was satisfied that he could leave him behind, along with a scribe, Fernão Martins and four other men in comparative safety. What he required was the Zamorin's consent.

On 9 August he sent Dias to the Zamorin bearing a personal present of amber and coral along with other unspecified gifts. For four frustrating days Dias waited for his audience. He was finally ushered unceremoniously into the presence of the Zamorin, where he was greeted with a 'bad face'. He conveyed the message that the Portuguese wished to return home. Such news surely caught the ruler by surprise as the winter monsoon, which winds blew steadily from India to the coast of east Africa, would not begin until October, and that was when the Portuguese would be expected to leave.

Dias asked the ruler to send with him emissaries to King Manuel, and in exchange Vasco would leave behind a balancing number of men who would be in charge of their remaining trade goods. In point of fact, what Vasco sought were hostages as further security for the lives of his own men. He also requested some 200 kilograms each of cloves, cinnamon and other spices, which he required as samples to show his king, and for which, of course if it was so desired, he would pay.[266]

The Zamorin dismissed the Portuguese gifts as inconsequential, declining so much as to look at them. He disregarded Vasco's request for samples of spices and instead stated that the Captain-Major should be informed that if he wished to leave the port, he must first pay the customs duty on his goods and the departure fee, which came to the equivalent of about $1,000. With this the meeting was concluded.

As he returned, Dias was followed by officers of the Zamorin, who then entered the house where the remaining goods were stored in order to prevent their removal. Dias and the others were now held essentially as prisoners. That same day a proclamation was issued preventing any boat from going out to the Portuguese ships. After dark, and with great secrecy, Dias was able to send a trusted Hindu in a fishing boat bearing his sobering report to his captain.[267]

This was depressing news. Some of Vasco's crew were now held on shore as prisoners, his ships were cut off from contact with the local population and it appeared their departure was not to be an easy one. The next day none of the usual boats came out to barter, and the rest of the day passed in a sombre mood. Vasco and his men found it difficult to accept that they could be first spurned, then treated in such a fashion. The had conducted themselves as men of honour and as honest brokers, and had done nothing to deserve this. They bore little ill will towards the Zamorin himself, as they understood the lies he had been told by those 'merchants from Mecca', but the situation was potentially critical.

The following day an *almadia* with four young men selling gems came out to the *São Gabriel*. This was apparently a test of some kind, as the stand-off was not one-sided. Pointed at the city were the ships' heavy cannon, the potential of which was not lost on the Arabs and Zamorin. Vasco's response was to invite the men aboard, where they were well received and then given an enormous meal. Vasco penned a letter to his people on shore, which the young men took with them. On subsequent days matters slowly returned to the state of affairs that had existed the past two months. Many small boats came out to barter and Vasco ordered the free meals to be resumed, although Dias and his men remained ashore as *de facto* prisoners.

On 19 August a number of *almadias* approached the Portuguese. Within were some twenty-five men, including six 'persons of quality' who had come to parlay. Vasco greeted them warmly but then, once they were within his power, ordered the six and twelve others to be seized and held. The remainder were sent back with word that he would exchange his hostages for his men being held ashore. When word spread of this, a large crowd gathered at the house where Dias and the others were detained and forced them to go to the residence of the *wali*.

Four days passed in vain. Vasco finally sent word that he was leaving for Portugal. On 23 August he ordered the anchors to be weighed and the sails raised, but after sailing only a short distance a strong wind forced them back and the next day they anchored once again within sight of Calicut, waiting for the wind. Given subsequent events, it is unlikely the Portuguese actually intended to leave, but the unfavourable wind had made their bluff all the more convincing.

On Sunday 26 August a boat approached from shore bearing the news that Diogo Dias was with the Zamorin and that, if Vasco released his hostages, Dias would be immediately brought on board. Vasco's suspicions were aroused and he expressed the opinion to his officers that Dias was surely dead by this time, and this was a ruse meant to delay their departure until 'ships of Mecca able to capture' them had arrived. He ordered the boat to return to shore, and when this did not happen he threatened to fire on it. The boat was not to come back under threat of destruction unless it carried Dias in it, or at the least a letter from him, and returned to the Portuguese their remaining goods on shore. This must be quickly done, or Vasco would give orders for his captives to be beheaded.[268]

When the Zamorin learned what had transpired, he hastily summoned Dias, who in fact was alive, for an audience. He received the Portuguese representative with 'marked kindness' and politely requested an explanation of Vasco's behavior. Dias replied that he was holding hostages because Dias and his assistant were being detained ashore against their will. There was some discussion of the duty payment, which the Portuguese viewed as a form of extortion. The ruler attempted to place the blame for any misunderstanding on his factor, telling Dias he had only recently executed the previous factor for misconduct with traders.

The Zamorin said, 'Go you back to the ships, you and the others [*sic*] who are with you; tell the captain to send me back the men he took; that the pillar,* which I understood him to say he desires to be erected on the land, shall be taken away by those who bring you back, and put up; and, moreover, that you will remain here with the merchandise.' He then produced a palm leaf and with an iron pen wrote the following message for Vasco to convey to his king:

> Vasco da Gama, a gentleman of your household, came to my country, whereat I was pleased. My country is rich in cinnamon, cloves, ginger, pepper, and precious stones. That which I ask of you in exchange is gold, silver, corals and scarlet cloth.

On Monday morning seven *almadias* slowly approached the *São Gabriel*. Fearful of being fired on, four of the boats held back while three eased their way gingerly to the longboat tied to the stern of the ship.** Dias and his assistant were transferred to the Portuguese boat, then climbed up to meet Vasco. The seven boats stood off a distance as they waited. Since the Zamorin had

---

* The matter of the *padrõe* had obviously been raised at some point, though there is no record of when or in what context.
** For all the insecurity and vulnerability the Portuguese felt so far from home, it should not be forgotten that their three vessels, massive by local standards and armed with heavy cannon, were a source of intimidation to both the Hindus and Muslims.

agreed that Dias could remain in peace, they expected to take him back ashore and had not brought with them the remaining trade goods.

Dias reported his meeting with the Zamorin to the Captain-Major and presented to him the ruler's handwritten letter. This was a favourable development, but matters were becoming so convoluted that Vasco's suspicions remained. He transferred the six most distinguished of his hostages to the waiting boats along with the *padrõe* that had been loaded aboard in Lisbon to be planted on the shore of India. Those waiting were informed that Dias and his assistant would be remaining aboard ship and would not go back ashore. The remaining hostages would be released when the trade goods were returned.

Given all that had happened, it is unlikely the remaining merchandise was of any value to Vasco other than as a bargaining tool. The last thing he would have wanted was to take up space to return them to Portugal. He was, it can be assumed, looking for an excuse to keep the remaining six hostages.

The next day Monçaide, the happy Moor who had proved so helpful those first days following their arrival, came out to the Portuguese ships seeking asylum. He reported that all his possessions had been taken from him by the other Muslims, who disapproved of his co-operation. This, he told them, was the kind of luck he usually had. They were accusing him of being a secret Christian sent here by the king of Portugal. If he remained, Monçaide was certain he would be murdered. Vasco agreed and took the man on board.

On Tuesday at mid-morning seven *almadias* again approached the Portuguese ships. Three boats drew within easy view. Spread on their benches was some striped cloth, which they claimed was all that remained of the trade goods ashore. This would be returned as soon as the remaining hostages were released to them.

The Portuguese were not fooled, however. This was but a pittance of their goods and Vasco replied that 'he cared naught for the merchandise' but would instead take these men he had safely to Portugal. When he returned to Calicut, they would see for themselves whether or not the Portuguese were thieves, as the Moors claimed.

It is unlikely the return of the trade goods had anything to do with the decision to take hostages back to Portugal. It had long been the practice of the Portuguese to carry natives of new regions back with them. In Lisbon they could be debriefed at length and their loyalty won in many cases, and they had often proved invaluable on subsequent expeditions. It is possible Vasco would have returned these six if all his merchandise had been returned and he would then have bargained with the Zamorin for others of the ruler's choosing to take with him, leaving Dias and companions to establish the trade mission, but given the deterioration of contact this seems unlikely. In any event, the goods were not returned and Vasco had his excuse.

On Wednesday 29 August the Captain-Major gathered the other captains aboard the *São Gabriel* for consultation. It was agreed that they had discovered the country for which they had come and that they had gathered as good a supply of spices and precious gems as could be expected under the circumstances, modest as it was. Given the hostility of the Moors who held sway over the Zamorin, it appeared impossible to establish the kind of cordial relations they would have liked. The time for departure had arrived. Not mentioned, but no doubt in everyone's mind, was the imminent arrival of the massive annual Arab trading fleet.

So it was that with six prisoners and an insubstantial supply of spices, but with the coveted knowledge of the sea route to India in their logs and the minds of the pilots, the three remaining Portuguese ships weighed anchor on 29 August 1498 and set sail for home. 'We . . . left for Portugal,' the *Roteiro* records, 'greatly rejoicing at our good fortune in having made so great a discovery.'

What the Portuguese did not understand, or perhaps fully appreciate, was that the monsoon which provided a steady, gentle wind from India to the east coast of Africa would not arrive until October, and that attempted passage across the largely wind-barren Indian Ocean at this time of the season was to court near-certain death.

17

The murderous passage

The 23-day May crossing from the African east coast to south-western India had taken place at the start of the summer monsoon, which had fortuitously arrived a few weeks early. The voyage had passed uneventfully as the great sails of the ships bearing the immense crimson cross of the Order of Christ were filled with the steady humid monsoon winds, and the tired crew passed the time in routine chores and conversation filled with the prospect ahead of them.

Although there is no record of it, it is safe to assume that at the time of the return passage the Good Moor, who had been of such enormous service thus far, cautioned the Portuguese that the winter monsoon, which would produce the favourable winds to sail to Africa, would not arrive for two months, and that a crossing attempted at this time would be nearly impossible. In fact, the Portuguese would be trying to sail against the final weeks of the summer monsoon, or even worse could find themselves becalmed far out to sea beyond all hope of help. Clearly the decision to proceed was being made for reasons other than sound navigation. Vasco simply did not believe he had the luxury of waiting.

The winds now were weak and unpredictable, blowing erratically from the sea and from land, so the three ships had moved only a short distance north of Calicut by noon the following day, when they were becalmed. At this time some seventy ships of various sizes filled with heavily armed men were spotted descending on them. There could be little doubt of their intentions. Trumpets sounded amid the martial tattoo of drums, and the decks were made ready for combat. When the hostile ships drew within range, Vasco gave the order to fire on them. A running sea battle ensued which lasted for the next hour and a half, as all the ships attempted to manoeuvre in the modest breezes. A squall suddenly descended on the combatants, which allowed the Portuguese to sail out to sea more rapidly than the other, smaller ships could follow and they had no choice but to break off the attack.[269]

This assault is certainly understandable. The Portuguese had left the port of Calicut without paying the customary duties that were the Zamorin's primary source of income and for which he was held liable by the king of Vijayanagar. On board were six kidnapped subjects, leaving behind family and contacts of every sort. There were no matching hostages on shore because, it could be argued – and certainly was by the Muslims – the Zamorin had been tricked into releasing them. All in all, this visit by Christians was ending as a sorry affair for the Hindu ruler.

The thunderstorm was short-lived and, though there were no more immediate attacks, the three Portuguese ships were able to make only modest progress as they coasted northward. On 10 September they drew close to a small town and Vasco decided to attempt to repair his relations with the Zamorin as he was still no great distance from Calicut. He directed that a conciliatory letter should be written in Arabic, in which he said that he had taken his prisoners so that he would have proof to his king of the discoveries he had made, and that he had not left Dias behind as they had discussed out of fear the Moors would murder him. The men, he promised, would all be safely returned.

This letter was given to one of the six, who was missing an eye. He was set ashore and returned with it to Calicut. One chronicler of these events, who unfortunately is unreliable in much of his reporting, records from sources he does not identify that the Zamorin was very pleased with the letter and directed it be read to the wives and families of those men still with the Portuguese.*

---

* The prisoners were all returned unharmed the following year. Being of lower caste, they were largely ignored by the new Zamorin, which makes the account of the letter-reading suspect.

Five days later, still moving northward along the coastline, the Portuguese sighted the island of Santa Maria. Local fisherman came out to trade and reportedly claimed they were Christians. Here Vasco ordered erected the third *padrõe* and did so with the assistance of the locals, who said they wanted the marker as proof of their devotion.

The Portuguese resumed their slow way up the coast. They were probably conducting a survey of the area, searching for a safe location to service their ships and also awaiting the end of the summer monsoon. They encountered a number of local trading vessels, which the Good Moor urged Vasco to seize as they were sure to contain large quantities of spices, but he refused. 'We are not thieves', he answered.

On 20 September the ships reached the Angediva Islands, situated not far south of Gôa, a major port for the Vijayanagar empire, where the Portuguese were to establish their permanent presence in India for nearly 500 years. Here they took on drinking water and gathered firewood. That night, with a steady land breeze, they set sail and the following day came to hilly land 'very beautiful and salubrious', with six small islands near by.[270] A boat was launched with the purpose of taking on sufficient water and wood to last for the voyage to Africa, as the breeze had made them optimistic that the winds favoured passage. They had been fortunate with the summer monsoon and now hoped they would be blessed with a similar early return monsoon.

Two becalmed ships were spotted not far distant, then a short time later seven more were observed also becalmed off shore. Assuming the worst, Vasco gave orders to attack the ships at once. A slight breeze allowed some manoeuvring of all the vessels and when the strangers spotted the Portuguese ships bearing down, they attempted to make for the open sea. One ship damaged its rudder and was abandoned and then seized by the Portuguese, who boarded and found a quantity of arms. The other ships soon grounded and were fired on from a distance to make their point. The following morning several local men came to the Portuguese ships and reported that the other vessels were from Calicut and had been sent to find and destroy the Portuguese.

Vasco prudently decided to remain a moving target and the next day the Portuguese found and explored a larger island, apparently used as a base by pirates. Here the Captain-Major gave orders for the *Berrio* and *São Gabriel* to be careened in turn on the beach, their hulls serviced and prepared for the crossing to Africa. Significantly, the *São Rafael* was not beached 'on account of difficulties' that are not specified. More water was collected. While the *Berrio* was disabled two large boats (*fustas*) approached, filled with an imposing number of men. They rowed to the beat of drums and bagpipes, and on their masts were displayed flags. Five other ships remained a distance off but close enough for concern.

Locals with the Portuguese warned that on no account should these newcomers be permitted to board one of the ships. They were well-known pirates in these waters. It was their practice to appear friendly, to board ships armed and then, when they were on board in sufficient numbers, to seize the vessel. Vasco ordered his crew to fire on the first two boats as soon as they came within range. All the ships fled, shouting back to no avail that they were Christians, as Coelho gave pursuit for a short distance.[271]

For twelve days the Portuguese were occupied with preparing their ships and with gathering wood and filling their casks. During this time a well-dressed and well-mannered man of about forty years of age presented himself to Vasco with a warm embrace of friendship. He spoke the Venetian dialect fluently and said that he was a Christian who had come to India from the West in his youth and that, though he had converted to Islam of necessity, 'at heart' he remained a Christian. When he learned that Franks had reached Calicut he had asked permission of his powerful master at Gôa to visit them, and here he was. He was long-winded and during his protracted words of friendship and personal exclamation contradicted himself, arousing suspicion.

Paulo da Gama made quiet inquiry of the Hindus with him and learned that he was a pirate. Vasco accordingly ordered the man to be seized and taken ashore, where he was thrashed and questioned. He confessed that a number of ships lay in wait in various creeks and inlets, gathering forces waiting for an additional forty vessels before the attack. Under further torture to test the accuracy of this new information the man admitted he had come as a spy to gather information of the numbers of men and their weapons for his master. He was released but confined to the *São Gabriel*. Some days later, once the Portuguese were well under way, he changed his story. His master had told him the strangers were obviously lost and unable to find their way home. His mission had been to lure the ships to his master, who desired to employ them and the Portuguese against his enemies.[272] Despite this inauspicious beginning, relations between this man and Vasco became quite friendly on the homeward voyage.

During their stay here the Portuguese ate fish, pumpkins and cucumbers acquired by barter. Although the captain of the captured ship offered a generous sum for its return, Vasco ordered it to be burnt as an example. With preparations complete, on 5 October 1498 and with no sign of the winter monsoon, the three Portuguese ships turned west and began the long voyage home.

By and large, and especially given the distances sailed and the dangers overcome, Vasco had been extraordinarily lucky in the number of deaths suffered by his crew. No actual head count has survived but it is reasonable to estimate that 120 to 130 of the 170 to 180 souls who boarded the ships in Lisbon were alive at this time. But now the truly dangerous part of the journey was at hand.

The monsoons of the Indian Ocean varied greatly, not just in the times they began and ended but also in their magnitude and wind direction. The situation was further complicated for the Portuguese by ocean currents that stubbornly flowed in directions contrary to experience. As fortunate as they had been in reaching India, misfortune now plagued their return. A favourable wind refused to fill the sails and the ships were frequently becalmed. When a breeze did stir, it was often from the wrong direction and even with hard work and careful tacking the ships managed only modest progress. As the days marked the passage of time, the winter monsoon simply failed to materialize. The three weeks it had taken to reach India from Africa came and passed. The fresh fruit and other produce were consumed, the handful of fowls slaughtered and eaten.

Clearly the crew were not in as good a state of health as they had been at departure from Portugal. In the three-month *volta da Guiné* from Cape Verde to the tip of Africa signs of scurvy appeared only in the days after reaching land. But during their months off the coast of India, with only limited shore leave and relying primarily on ships' stores for food, the crew had simply not consumed sufficient fresh fruit of the right sort to immunize themselves. Cases of scurvy now appeared among the crew, growing worse with each passing day, until over the course of eleven terrible weeks every member was affected to some degree.

The disease was terrifying as it relentlessly spread from man to man. Although the affliction initially manifested itself in various forms, it progressed at a steady and, in time, predictable rate. Skin discoloration, putrid gums, swollen limbs and the whole-sale loss of teeth were all inevitable. In its final stages ulcers appeared which would not heal and fell open repeatedly, like fresh wounds. There was nothing aboard any of the ships that could offer a cure or even impede the progress of what the Portuguese saw as a plague.

The debilitating lassitude that early on gripped those afflicted was most disturbing. Every chore, however modest, brought on extreme exhaustion. Men pausing to catch their breath or recover they strength after the slightest task simply keeled over, dead. As the numbers of the sick grew and the interminable weeks passed, those available to man the ship effectively fell steadily, while even those still able to work were in a seriously weakened state. Healthy men were needed to climb aloft, to man the lines, to perform the countless skilful and arduous acts required to sail the ships. With each rising sun fewer of these were available.

The *Roteiro* records the terrible effects the disease took on the mariners.

> [A]ll our people again suffered from their gums, which drew over their teeth, so that they could not eat. Their legs also swelled, and other parts of the body, and these swellings spread until the sufferer died, without exhibiting symptoms of any other disease. Thirty of our men died in this manner . . . and those able to navigate each ship were only seven or eight, and even these were not as well as they ought to have been. I assure you that if this state of affairs had continued for another fortnight, there would have been no men at all to navigate the ships.

Not recorded is the emotional toll the disease took on the survivors. Those afflicted were cared for by brother seamen who hoped against hope for recovery, or the sight of land and salvation. Each sad death meant burial at sea, anathema to every Catholic aboard ship although sanctioned by the church. Those who survived were consumed with the conflicting emotions of elation and guilt. It is unlikely any man survived this passage unscarred.

If there was any single aspect of his performance as Captain-Major to which Vasco da Gama could point with pride, it was his unchallenged authority which had not only made possible the many difficult decisions but which had commanded the obedience of his crew. Even the highly respected and very able captain Bartholomeu Dias had faced a virtual mutiny on his voyage. On this epic expedition the Portuguese had gone farther and faced greater risks than ever before without any incident ultimately calling into question Vasco's authority. Now, under the effects of scurvy, discipline collapsed.

'We had come to such a pass that all bonds of discipline had gone', the *Roteiro* reports, putting in a few succinct words the most disturbing part of the voyage.

> Whilst suffering this affliction we addressed vows and petitions to the saints on behalf of our ships. The captains had

held council, and they had agreed that if a favourable wind enabled us we would return to India, whence we had come. But it pleased God in his mercy to send us a wind which, in the course of six days, carried us within sight of land, and at this we rejoiced as much as if the land we saw had been Portugal, for with the help of God we hoped to recover our health there, as we had done once before.

On 2 January 1499, 'three months less three days' after their departure, as night approached, the Portuguese spotted the east African coast and lay to. The next morning no one, not even the pilots, could say where on the coast they were. A short distance away they passed the large Moorish town of Mogadishu but did not even consider trying to make a landing, so weakened were they and so certain of a hostile reception. As they passed, they loosed a fusillade of bombards into the city. With a favourable breeze they made their way down the African coastline, laying up at night. All the while scurvy raged among the crew.

On 5 January they were becalmed, then in the middle of a thunderstorm pirates manning eight boats with 'many men' attacked but were successfully driven off. Two days later, a Monday, the beleaguered Portuguese ships, their hulls thick with barnacles and sea growth, riddled with worms, moving sluggishly in the warm water, cast anchor off Malindi. At once a longboat carrying many people was dispatched to the ships with word from the king and the regent, whose relations with Vasco had been so cordial those long months before. A sheep was presented to the Captain-Major, along with a message from the king that the Portuguese had been expected for some days and they were to consider themselves most welcome once again. The king and regent were resuming their efforts to establish a friendly relationship with them to gain the upper hand in their competition against their chief rival port, Mombasa.

Vasco sent a request for a large supply of oranges, as the sick were pleading for them. Moors came out in boats, ordered by the king, bringing eggs and fowls. The next day a generous supply of oranges was received on all the ships, as was a great quantity of other kinds of fruit 'but our sick did not much profit by this,' the *Roteiro* notes, 'for the climate affected them in such a way that many of them died here'.

Still, for all the additional deaths, Vasco found himself in a safe harbour. The nightmare of the long murderous passage was behind him. The known route to home, and honour, lay before him.

18

'Risen from the dead'

Vasco was also eager to establish friendly relations with a ruler situated at such a vital point on the sea route to India. In vain he had sought a Christian port; a friendly Muslim one would have to do. He sent word that he desired to carry an ivory tusk as a gift from the king in Malindi to his own sovereign. In exchange, he wished to present the local ruler with a *padrõe* which he would be very pleased to see erected in this land as a 'sign of friendship'.

Vasco received word in reply that the king would do as asked 'out of love for the King of Portugal, whom he desired to serve'. A tusk arrived and a pillar was sent ashore and erected as promised. Also received aboard the ship was a 'young Moor' whom the local king wished to accompany the Portuguese home so that the king there 'might know how much he desired his friendship'.

During this peaceful respite the crew tended their sick and recovered their strength as best they could after a passage in which they had all 'been face to face with death'.[273] Yet, just five days after their arrival, and despite the auspicious nature of relations, Vasco gave the order to set sail.

Departure so soon from this friendly port seems reckless in retrospect, but the Portuguese had no way of knowing how long it would take for the crew fully to recover, if in fact they ever would, so they could not judge what was to be gained by remaining. Moreover, the friendly reception extended to them here on the coast of east Africa in Malindi was the exception. They were otherwise surrounded by opposing Moors. The sultan in nearby Mombasa had already demonstrated his hostility towards them, and it was perfectly reasonable to fear that he might mount a final attack, one that could succeed with the crew in such a debilitated state.

The number of the crew still remaining had now probably dipped to under 100, approximately half the number that had left Lisbon. The condition of many was extremely weakened and the *Roteiro* suggests that deaths continued. Of those remaining, very few were fit enough to man the ships under sail.

Although the local ruler and regent appeared friendly, Vasco could not know to what degree, if any, that friendship extended to the Muslim population in general. The situation at Malindi could change in a heartbeat, especially if a war party arrived from Mombasa and called on the faithful to join in an assault. They had already been attacked more than once, and that prospect now could not have been far from Vasco's thoughts.

The surviving Portuguese ships had also seriously deteriorated and were in danger of quite literally dissolving beyond reclamation. But perhaps most importantly, with more than half the voyage behind them, home loomed closer than ever and pulled at the weary, increasingly heartsick men like a siren's call.

The ships passed Mombasa without incident and then, two days after weighing anchor, they stopped, offloaded the remaining supplies from the *São Rafael*, then transferred the crew, including Paulo da Gama, the captain, before setting fire to the ship. '[I]t was', according to one account, 'impossible for us to navigate three vessels with the few hands that remained to us.' Also taken from the *São Rafael* was the figurehead that had been mounted for good fortune and God's blessing on the prow of the ship.★

It may be that the crew had been reduced to fewer than 100 men even while the Portuguese were still off the coast of India. This would account for the decision there not to careen and service the *São Rafael* when the other ships were seen to. And it

---

★ The carved wooden figurehead remained with the Gama family as an heirloom and token of good luck. It was carried by family members on many of their subsequent expeditions. It can be seen today at the church in Belém, where the author viewed it.

may also be that the 'difficulties' with the *São Rafael* alluded to but never explained in the *Roteiro* had nothing to do with the number and condition of the crew, but referred instead to some problem with the ship itself, although when the vessel was abandoned, the reason given was lack of adequate crew. This left just Vasco's ship, the *São Gabriel*, and Nicolau Coelho's small shift caravel, the *São Miguel*.

To effect the changes Vasco anchored the ships off a small town and the Portuguese now remained for fifteen days as they continued to recover and prepared the remaining vessels for the long passage that still lay ahead. This suggests that the Captain-Major had not been confident of his position in Malindi. At this village the Portuguese bartered for fowls which they acquired in abundance in exchange for bracelets and shirts. On 27 January, a Sunday, a favourable wind carried the two ships southward.

Any threat from Moors was now safely behind them. What remained was sailing and seamanship – surely refreshing, and reassuring, challenges after the protracted drama in India and off the coast of east Africa. The next day the two ships passed close to the island of Zanzibar and on 1 February they anchored at the small island off Mozambique where they had held a Mass on the voyage north, and there they erected another *padrõe*.

The previous March it had been at nearby Mozambique Island that relations with the sultan had become so violent. This time their presence was disregarded, probably out of fear, given the trouncing they had received earlier. With only minor setbacks the vessels made steady progress south, assisted by the same winds and the powerful Mozambique Channel current that had been such obstacles when they sailed north exactly one year earlier.

On 3 March the ships anchored at Mossel Bay, where the Portuguese 'caught many anchovies, seals and penguins, which we salted for our voyage'. It had been at this bay that Bartholomeu Dias had first realized he had successfully doubled Africa and where he had slain a threatening Hottentot with a crossbow. And here on his outward voyage Vasco had remained for thirteen days reprovisioning the ship and bartering for both cattle and sheep from the locals. Although relations had in general been good, there had been incidents. The Portuguese had erected their first *padrõe* on this shore and been enraged at their departure to see the Hottentots pull it down and break up the cross.

There is no record of any further contact with the Hottentots and it is unlikely there was any, given the nature of the previous encounters. If the locals were in the area, it is likely they avoided them. The Portuguese remained for nine days replenishing their supplies, and failing in their first attempt to leave by adverse winds.

'Those who had come so far were in good health and quite robust, although at times nearly dead from the cold winds which we experienced', the *Roteiro* reports. 'This feeling, however, we attributed less to the cold than to the heat of the countries from which we had come.' The *Roteiro* adds, 'We pursued our route with a great desire of reaching home.'

The second attempt to pass the tip was successful and on 20 March the ships joyously rounded the Cape of Good Hope.

> They took down many bearings and marks of this coast, and soundings, which they took lying-to . . . They ran under full sail, and seeing the Cape remain behind, and that they had passed by it towards Portugal, the pleasure of all was so great that they embraced each other with great joy; they then all knelt down, with their hands raised up to heaven, uttering great praise and prayers for the great benefits which had been granted them.[274]

At some point in the homeward voyage Paulo da Gama, Vasco's beloved older brother, took seriously ill with tuberculosis, adding a sense of urgency. The adverse winds and ocean currents that Vasco had avoided with his epic *volta da Guiné* now worked to the Portuguese advantage, permitting them to take a more direct route. The ships were pushed forward by brisk winds astern and the Benguela current for twenty-seven days after rounding the African continent. Slowly the familiar constellations reappeared, along with the North Star. The talk of the crew aboard the two ships was of nothing but home.

The strong winds and favourable current swept them on, though with growing difficulty given the reduced numbers and wretched condition of the diminished crew. The seams of the ships were increasingly exposed as the caulking came out and sea water poured in. 'They sailed thus with much labour at the pumps, for the ships made much water with the straining of going on a bowline.' Then, on 16 April, near the Cape Verde Islands, they were becalmed. '[T]he ships could hardly keep afloat by means of the pumps, and they were so old that it was a wonder how they kept above water, and many of the crews were dead, and others sick.'[275]

At this point the *Roteiro* comes to an end but an account of subsequent events is available from other, more sketchy, sources. The two ships made modest headway against slight, unfavourable breezes before becoming separated, presumably as a result of one of the many squalls common to the region. Unable to locate the *São Gabriel* and so tantalizingly close to home, Coelho headed for Portugal. Those, in fact, may very well have been his orders in the event of such separation. He arrived without incident at the small fishing port of Cascais at the mouth of the Tagus on 10 July 1499, landing two years and two days after the enormous festivities at the expedition's departure.

The amazed Portuguese on shore heard from these exhausted men that they had just returned from India. The Portuguese had done it! God, in His mercy, had given them the prize they had for so long sought. Word raced along shore towards Lisbon like a wildfire.

For his part, Vasco searched one day for Coelho's ship before sailing on to the island of São Tiago. Paulo's health had deteriorated steadily during the long sea passage and he appeared increasingly unlikely to recover. At São Tiago, Vasco secured the use of a swift caravel and turned command of his ship over to another with orders to proceed at once to Lisbon. Left aboard the ship were the Good Moor from Gujarat who had piloted the Portuguese so faithfully and provided invaluable information, and the 'Christian' from Goa, the *provocateur* seized off the coast of India just before departure. The *São Gabriel* arrived in Lisbon shortly after young Coelho, although the exact date is not known.

With his brother near death, Vasco set out at once for home as well, but it soon became clear that Paulo would never make it. Instead, Vasco diverted course and sailed to the island of Terceira in the Azores, as he did not wish to bury his brother at sea and he hoped for a miracle once Paulo was on land. Paulo da Gama died the day after reaching the Azores and was buried at the church in Angra. His crew gravely ill and dying, even this ship in need of repairs, Vasco remained there in mourning.

During the two years the Vasco da Gama expedition had been absent not a single word of its fate had reached Portugal. It was assumed by many during the passage of the time that the ships and men were lost. Still, the expedition had been fitted for a three-year voyage, so there were those not prepared as yet to declare the attempt a failure.

Manuel availed himself of the pleasures of his new Spanish wife as he sought to produce an heir. He continued to issue corrections to his initial expulsion order against Jews and, while still imposing cruel and all but unimaginable hardships on them, had the effect of permitting many Jews to remain and contribute to the national economy since most of the essential fluid wealth was held by Jews or Jews forcibly converted, the so-called *Christãos novos*. But some of the most valuable Jews left anyway. These included Abraham ben Zacuto, who had pronounced the stars favourable to the attempt to reach India and provided invaluable assistance to the expedition. He, like others, including at least one royal physician, moved on.

During the period of the India expedition the heir to the Spanish throne died, placing Manuel's wife, Isabella, next in line. In the summer of 1498, while Vasco was engaged with the Zamorin and Arab merchants in Calicut, the couple journeyed to Spain to obtain formal recognition of her claim. While there in August, Isabella gave birth to a son, Miguel da Paz, but died during labour. The infant's claim to the Spanish throne was recognized, but only on condition that the child remained behind to be raised by his grandparents, Isabella and Ferdinand. In March 1499 the Portuguese Cortes met to debate the troubling Portuguese succession and reached the conclusion that a Portuguese heir reared as a Spaniard should not stand, at least not without substantial concessions from Spain. While negotiations were under way with the Spanish monarchy the infant died, and Spanish succession passed to the son of a daughter married to the Emperor Maximilian. In late 1500 Manuel was to marry the fourth daughter of Ferdinand and Isabella, and with her he had ten children, one of whom, born in 1502, became his heir to the Portuguese crown, John III.[276] It was in this climate and with such adverse concerns of state that word of Coelho's arrival was received. The Portuguese court was jubilant on learning of the success. An exuberant Manuel declared 'even greater joy than when he learnt that he was to be King of Portugal'.[277]

The king wasted no time in acting. Just two days after Coelho arrived in Lisbon and confirmed the success of the expedition, Manuel dispatched a letter to the parents of his deceased wife, to Ferdinand and Isabella of Spain. Six and a half years earlier Christopher Columbus had lectured the then Portuguese sovereign on his discovery of India by sailing west. Now Manuel had his opportunity to inform the Spanish monarchs of the true discovery of the sea route to India.★

Even before Vasco da Gama had reached Portugal, Manuel had modified his titles and placed a globe on his sceptre. The king was now to be henceforth known as 'Dom Manuel, by the Grace of God King of Portugal and of the Algarves on this side of and beyond the sea, in Africa, Lord of Guinea and of the Conquest, the Navigation and Commerce of Ethiopia, Arabia, Persia and India'. The enthusiastic and exaggerated letter read, in part:

★ Letters were sent to the Pope and to the Portuguese Cardinal Protector at the Vatican, to assert Manuel's claim to the newly discovered region under the terms of the previous papal bulls.

Most high and excellent Prince and Princes, most potent Lord and Lady!

Your Highnesses already know that we had ordered Vasco da Gama, a nobleman of our household, and his brother Paulo da Gama, with four vessels to make discoveries by sea, and that two years have now elapsed since their departure. . . . [I]t has pleased [God] in His mercy to speed them on their route. From a message which has now been brought to this city by one of the captains, we learn that they did reach and discover India and other kingdoms and lordships bordering upon it; that they entered and navigated its sea, finding large cities, . . . great populations among whom is carried on all the trade in spices and precious stones. . . . Of these they have brought a quantity, including cinnamon, cloves, ginger, nutmeg, and pepper, as well as other kinds, . . . also many fine stones of all sorts such as rubies and others. And they also came to a country in which there are mines of gold . . .

As we are aware that your Highnesses will hear of these things with much pleasure and satisfaction, we thought well to give this information. . . . [T]here will be an opportunity for destroying the Moors of those parts. Moreover, we hope, with the help of God, that the great trade which now enriches the Moors, . . . shall, in consequence of our regulations be diverted to the natives and ships of our own kingdom, so that henceforth all Christendom, in this part of Europe, shall be able, in a large measure, to provide itself with these spices and precious stones. . . .

Written at Lisbon, July 1499.[278]

As the Portuguese man, Vasco da Gama, had returned with residents of India, as well as a sampling of spices and gems, there could no longer be the slightest doubt but that the Spanish man, Christopher Columbus, who had twice returned with primitives, displays of exquisite feathers, exotic plants and a bit of gold dust, had not reached India. The Treaty of Tordesillas, negotiated just four years earlier, had given Spain the West, Portugal

the lands to the East. Where Spain had failed, Portugal had succeeded, or to put it on the personal terms that existed, Manuel
had triumphed where Ferdinand and Isabella had failed.

If any measures were taken by Manuel to keep the invaluable
information just received secret, they were largely ineffective.
Literally within days detailed communications were streaming
from Lisbon bearing the news of the Portuguese success and
comprehensive information from the communications to the
king and from those who had taken part in the expedition. The
letters are remarkable not for their occasional inaccuracy but for
the wealth of knowledge so quickly acquired.

Venetian merchants living in Lisbon dispatched letters home
to report this astounding and, for them, depressing event. One,
written by Guido di Messer Tomaso Detti, reviewed the implications to the Venetian spice trade, concluding that he and his
colleagues should hereafter 'become fishermen'. The letter also
said:

> [T]his is an excellent finding and this King merits great
> commendation from all Christians, and certainly all the
> Kings and great and powerful lords who are sea-powers
> should always send out to find and give news of unknown
> things because it brings honour and fame, reputation and
> riches, and in fine, because of it they are praised by all men.
> And to such men it is well that Lordship and State is given
> . . . And thus we may say: the King of Portugal should be
> praised of all men.[279]

Another wrote of these events, 'As soon as the news [of Gama's
return] reached Venice, the populace was thunderstruck, and the
wiser among them regarded the news as the worst they could
have received.'[280]

It was understood that henceforth the flow of wealth from the
spice trade would largely bypass the Italian city-states and enter
Europe through Lisbon. The centre of European economic
power had permanently shifted from the Mediterranean west-
ward to Portugal and, within a short time, to Spain as well, with

the conquest of the Aztecs and Incas and the exploitation of the Americas.

But as yet the hero, Vasco da Gama, had not reached Portugal. A resident of the island of Terceira had sailed on a caravel as soon as Vasco arrived there with his dying brother. He bore the news to the king of the Captain–Major's location and reported that the crew with him was 'sick and dying'. Weeks passed with no other word reaching the nation. During the interim Manuel basked in the glory of his success and made plans as to how he would spend the enormous wealth that would soon be his. Of Vasco at Terceira, Correa writes, '[W]hen the ships were provided with all that was necessary, they departed for Lisbon, and Vasco da Gama was so afflicted by the death of his brother, that it very much diminished his satisfaction with the great honours that he hoped for on coming to the King's presence.'

Some three to six weeks after Coelho's modest caravel had entered the small harbour at Cascais bearing the stupendous news of triumph, Vasco da Gama at last arrived in Belém, from where he had sailed two years earlier, surrounded by an armada of 'many vessels' which had accompanied him from Terceira to bask in his glory and share in the celebrations. On landing Vasco gave thanks at the same chapel where he had knelt with his brother and officers.

A partial explanation for Vasco's late arrival lies with what he did next. Rather than go immediately to his sovereign and receive the rewards awaiting him as well as the adulation of the Portuguese people, Vasco sent word that he remained in mourning at the loss of his brother and would report to Manuel when that was over. He now remained in Belém and for nine days prayed a novena for Paulo. On hearing of the great captain's arrival Manuel dispatched the Count of Porto Alegre and other nobles to receive him.

The return of Vasco da Gama and those seamen who had survived with him completed the single greatest ocean expedition in world history to that point, and one that still ranks among the two or three greatest sailing feats in human history. For what it meant to the future of mankind it stands alone. The world as it had been was no more; the consequences for Portugal, Europe and Asia to this day are nearly incalculable.

Word of Vasco's return spread throughout Lisbon, its environs and the nation with something akin to the speed of light. Pealing church bells could be heard for miles across the countryside. The excitement at what he and his crew had accomplished was all but unbearable. Celebrations, both intended and spontaneous, occurred everywhere. In part the joy was not just at the success but because people could see with their own eyes seamen 'who seemed to be as though men risen from the dead'.[281]

From the day Coelho arrived in Lisbon, the surviving members of the expedition had returned to loved ones, visited with friends, been toasted in the *tascas* and fêted as heroes throughout the city. They had sold off those modest amounts of spices they had managed to acquire at an enormous profit. Again and again they told the story of their two-year adventure, regaling small gatherings and throngs with stories of derring-do and descriptions of the fascinating, all but unbelievable, sights to which they had been witness.

The surviving seamen, officers and priests told of the incredible and utterly daring *volta da Guiné*, that magnificent feat of seamanship that had inaugurated their voyage to India, of the three-month, 3,370-mile sweep through the central and south Atlantic, out of all sight of land, only to arrive within scant miles at their destination on the south-western coast of Africa. They told of their first encounter with the Bushmen of South Africa and the eventual hostility they overcame. They told rapt audiences the difficulties they had faced in rounding the tip of Africa through violent waters and contrary winds, how time and again their ships were thrown back, how seamen had demanded that the captain break off the attempt, but how their Captain-Major had pledged he would not return to Portugal without doubling Africa and reaching his goal.

The survivors told of the fat cattle they had eaten in Mossel Bay, then of how the Hottentots there had destroyed the king's pillar once they set sail and had been afraid to confront them when they stopped in the same bay on their return. They told of the treachery of the sultan on Mozambique Island, of the attempts to seize their ships and slay them, of the failed blandishments to lure them close to shore, of the battle they had fought before the plank barrier, of finally filling casks under hostile eyes and imminent threat of attack. They related their kind reception at Malindi, how the regent and king had seen to their every need and provided them with the essential pilot to reach India.

And they told of the peaceful three-week sailing across the Indian Ocean, their sails filled with the steady flow of the monsoon, carried through the tranquil waters as if by the Hand of God. They told of first setting eyes on India as Moses had beheld the Promised Land. They told of the port of Calicut, filled with hundreds of ships from throughout the East. They related the opulence they had witnessed and the abject poverty, told of the friendly 'Christians' who welcomed them everywhere, and of the Hindu women eager to lie with men of fair skin. They recounted the constant treachery of the Moors.

They described the market-place, the cheap and readily available spices and gems. They told of their departure when it appeared some of their number would be held captive ashore but of how their Captain-Major had cleverly got them back aboard ship. They related the attacks that followed thereafter, then the three-month-long, deadly sailing back to east Africa that nearly ended the enterprise, their struggle with scurvy and burial at sea, their salvation again in Malindi and elsewhere, how their numbers were reduced to sail just two ships. Finally, they told of the rounding of Africa again and swift return home by God's grace.

Throughout their telling one theme emerged repeatedly: without Vasco da Gama it would not have happened. There could be no doubt but that the success of the expedition owed everything to the cunning, tenacity, bravery and skill of its Captain-Major. Time and again a single error on his part would have brought disaster, as again and again their captain had seen to the success of the mission. No treachery could succeed against him, no attack nor the wile of the Moors. At every turn the Captain-Major had been the better and without him they would surely have died long ago or been cast in irons.

Now finished with his devotions, as Vasco himself was seen on the streets of Lisbon, he was cheered as a conquering hero and, because he had been the instrument through which God had fulfilled the destiny of the Portuguese people, he was revered. Just thirty years old, Vasco da Gama was elevated to a position nearly that of a living God.

Contemporaneous records of the royal greeting no longer exist, probably destroyed in the devastating Lisbon earthquake of 1755. Royal festivities are known to have been declared as Vasco made his way from Belém to the palace in Lisbon. A solemn Mass was held at Sé de Silves, the national cathedral. Vasco and his captains presented themselves to Manuel in ceremonies as lavish as those at their departure and received initial honours and awards. The surviving members of the crew, it is recorded, were amply rewarded. Manuel remembered his promise to the widows and orphans of those men who had lost their lives on the voyage, issuing a proclamation that they should come forward, though he parsimoniously granted them only half their due, just as he did to Paulo's family. Manuel distributed clothing from his personal wardrobe and gave royal horses to the officers of the expedition. There was more, according to Correa, for 'with these grants and salaries all remained rich and satisfied'.

Vasco presented personal gifts to his crew to take to their wives or families as well as presenting gifts from India to the king. These included ambergris, musk, which had been highly prized by the late queen, and Chinese porcelain as well as certain gems and necklaces. At his first private meeting with Manuel, Vasco asked that Nicolas Coelho be well rewarded, to which the king agreed, later granting a pension of 3,000 *cruzados* to the young man as well as captaincy of a ship in all future expeditions to India, which he could exercise or sell on to another.

There was now time to assess the cost and inevitably the numbers vary. Some sources report as few as 44 of the original crew of nearly 180 survived; others record the figure as 54. Also, the figure of between 170 and 180 for the original crew is at best an estimation. Some historians place the figure at 148, others at little more than 100. A Venetian merchant writing from Lisbon reported that 55 men died on the return voyage alone. If accurate, this would mean 25 more deaths after the 30 that occurred on the deadly passage from India to the African east coast, a total loss of no fewer than 85 men.

Certainly, no more than one third of the original crew had survived, a figure consistent with the toll taken of Bartholomeu Dias's crew eleven years earlier. Those who did survive this first epic voyage to India were often broken in health and the sight of such surviving seamen became increasingly common in Lisbon over the coming decades of conquest and empire.

The voyage had traversed 23,000 nautical miles, a total distance greater than that around the world at the equator. On two occasions the ships had been out of sight of land for periods in excess of ninety days. Vasco da Gama had successfully completed the first voyage in the history of mankind connecting the West and the East by sea. The social and economic life of the world was to be profoundly altered by what he and his crew had accomplished.[282]

Although Vasco had returned with specimens of cinnamon, cloves, nutmeg and pepper, as well as gems, most historians indicate the amount of actual spices as being no more than a 'handful'. It is commonly held in Portugal today that all the spices would have fitted within a bread bin. A well-informed Italian living in Lisbon wrote that the expedition returned with 'little and nothing of value'. Whatever the actual quantity, given the value of spices, it was sufficient to do more than repay the cost of the expedition.

Of far greater importance was the knowledge returned from the East. The *Roteiro* and other documents meticulously prepared during the voyage were now in the hands of Manuel's most trusted advisers and the junta. Scribes had prepared voluminous and detailed reports that accurately described exactly how the spice trade was conducted, its course from the far-off Spice Islands to India, and from there through Cairo into Europe.

Included were market prices for spices, their origins and myriad trade routes, the war-making capability of every kingdom that played a role in the production or trade of spices and precious stones, even a basic primer for Malayalam, the language spoken in Calicut. Now it was all laid out, both as a commercial enterprise and as a potential military objective, if it came to that. An example of what Manuel and his junta read relates:

> Ceylam [Ceylon] is a very large island inhabited by Christians under a Christian king. It is 8 days from Calecut, with a favourable wind. The king can muster 4,000 men, and has moreover many elephants of war as well as for sale. All the fine cinnamon of India is found here, as well as many sapphires, superior to those of other countries, besides rubies, few but of good quality.[283]

The veil of secrecy that had for so many centuries masked the trade was at last lifted. Although some of the conclusions reached were utterly inaccurate – such as that the Hindus were Christians and that large numbers of sympathetic Christians existed in the East – the information overall was remarkably accurate and made possible the blueprint for the future Portuguese dominance of the spice trade, with all that that meant for the tiny, impoverished nation. Preparations for another expedition were already under way and Manuel issued orders for it to proceed with haste.

In addition, the Good Moor and the Gôa *provocateur* were also debriefed at length, fêted, dined and displayed to the city. The man from Gôa had become quite friendly with Vasco on the long voyage home and Manuel was utterly seduced by him. He elected to be baptized and was given the name Gaspar da Gama, although he is sometimes referred to as Gasper da India. Manuel made him a cavalier of his household and he returned to India with Pedro Cabral and on several subsequent expeditions, serving as interpreter and adviser, primarily on trading matters. As a reward for his service, he was eventually given an annual pension by the crown. In time the truth of his origin was clear. His Jewish parents had fled persecution in Poland and immigrated first to Palestine and then to Alexandria, where Gaspar was born.[284]

Manuel was well known to be sparing in his grants of rewards for service rendered the crown, but when it came to the new national icon, the Captain-Major of the expedition that opened the way East, no such claim can be made, for the honours and grants were substantial, even lavish. While the initial rewards sprang from the success of the undertaking and Manuel's delight with it, others came from Vasco's persistent popularity with the people and for subsequent service rendered.

Vasco himself understood the significance of what he had brought to the king, and undertook to raise himself and his family to the ranks of the Portuguese nobility. His father had once been the *alcaide-mór* of Vasco's home town of Sines, so his first request was to be named the seigneur of the town, which the king granted. Sines, however, belonged to the Duke of Coimbra, the bastard son of John II, who had received it in part as compensation for not becoming king, and removing this portion of his lands to reward Vasco da Gama was a delicate matter that took some years and Vasco's persistence before it was finally accomplished.

More immediately, Vasco received an annual pension of 1,000 *cruzados* and the title of 'Dom', which he asked to be extended to include his sister and surviving brother. This request was granted and subsequently made hereditary. Having demonstrated his superiority in navigation, Vasco da Gama was appointed to the royal junta.

In January 1502, one month before his departure on his second voyage to India and at a solemn ceremony in the presence of dignitaries and ambassadors, Vasco was awarded a second annual pension, this one hereditary, in the amount of 300,000 *reis* and the title of 'Admiral of India', with valuable privileges attached, including a trading concession. The honour and privileges were probably modelled on those given by the king and queen of Spain to Christopher Columbus. The title of 'Admiral' was not simply an honour. It meant that Vasco da Gama could, on his own initiative and without order of the king, assume command of any expedition to India and take control of the Portuguese vessels already in those waters.

After returning from his first voyage to India, Vasco lived in

Évora, where he married Dona Catarina de Ataíde, the daughter of a well-established and highly regarded family, thereby reinforcing the Gama family's connection to the Almeida family. The Almeidas had opposed Manuel's succession and remained the primary force in opposition to his rule thereafter, so the marriage had strong political overtones. This was Vasco's only marriage and produced six sons and a daughter.

On his return from his second voyage and the presentation of valuable 'tribute' from the sultan of Kilwa another annual pension of 1,000 *cruzados* was awarded. With the grant of these three pensions Vasco da Gama was, from them alone, one of the wealthiest men in Portugal. Only six noblemen, seven bishops and two archbishops in the country had incomes exceeding his own, and this did not include the moneys he earned from the royal trading concessions and subsequent honours given to him.

At one point Manuel promised to confer on Vasco da Gama the title of 'Count', a singular honour indeed, but for a number of years he did nothing about it despite Vasco's repeated entreaties. The most likely explanation is that Manuel believed he had given enough. He may well have been jealous of Vasco's continued popularity and unwilling to put himself in the position of having to grant additional honours. Finally Vasco informed Manuel that he would emigrate from Portugal along with his family, a move that would be a slap in the face for the king.

In the last year of his life Manuel negotiated an accommodation with his nephew the Duke of Bragança, who had interceded on Vasco's behalf, to yield two towns to which Vasco da Gama was named count (Vidigueira and Villa de Frades). Vasco signed over one of his pensions to the duke and paid him the sum of 4,000 *cruzados* in gold from his own pocket to secure this final honour, which was granted shortly before his departure on his third, and final, voyage to India in 1524. The title was hereditary and represented the final step in elevating Vasco and his descendents to the nobility. Enormous as they were, there have been no suggestions that any honour and reward received by Vasco da Gama was excessive or undeserved based on the totality of his service to the king and country.

Manuel did not move so slowly in rewarding himself, that is, in enjoying the fruits of the enormous wealth he knew would soon flow to him across the vast ocean highway that Vasco had created for him. Even before Vasco had arrived in Portugal, Manuel ordered a commemorative gold coin to be struck. He also ordered the body of John II, who had done so much to make this moment possible, to be moved from the national cathedral to the abbey of Batalha with what was seen as extravagant ostentation and fawning pomp. An eyewitness reported that Manuel ordered the casket to be opened and the dust blown from the remains, then leaned down and 'kissed the dead man's hands and feet again and again' in gratitude.[285]

The king also ordered large numbers of Lisbon's picturesque olive trees to be cut down and tracts within the crowded city to be cleared and levelled. He then commanded a grandiose programme of public works. These included the palaces of Ribeira, the Casa da India, royal warehouses and additional elaborate storehouses. At the site of the small chapel where Vasco and his captains had knelt in vigil the night before sailing he directed the construction of Portugal's national treasure, the magnificent Mosteiro dos Jerónimos, which in time would hold the remains of Vasco da Gama and Luis Camoens. It endures as Manuel's and Portugal's monument to the first European voyage to India, and all it meant.

Epilogue

In the summer of 1498 Admiral Christopher Columbus set sail on his third voyage to the 'Indies', as he still insisted on calling islands and lands that were clearly not India at all. When he arrived at the Spanish colony of Hispaniola in August, as Vasco and his captains were reaching the decision they must leave Calicut, he found it in a state of revolt against his rule. His attempts to restore order only led to further difficulties. A royal commissioner arrived from Spain in 1500 to arrest Columbus and return him in irons. It was in these circumstances that he learned of the Portuguese success.

Although Columbus managed a fourth voyage to what was already being called the New World, it was an utter failure. Marooned on Jamaica, he faced still another revolt and returned to Spain in disgrace. When he died in 1506 – if not exactly impoverished, as is usually claimed – his obsession died with him. By insisting to the end that he had reached the Indies he denied himself the one lasting legacy that could have been his: the lands he discovered were named after someone else.

In contrast, although the Portuguese did not seek to rename India, Portugal's first voyage to India ushered in what is called the Vasco da Gama epoch of Asian history, lasting from 1498 to 1945. For those centuries the course of the region was largely determined by European powers.

Six months after Vasco da Gama's return to Lisbon a second fleet set sail for India. Between 1501 and 1505 Manuel dispatched virtually every ship his small nation could acquire or build. Eighty-one ships in six annual convoys set sail, carrying some 7,000 sailors and soldiers, of whom between a third and a half died on the outward passage alone. Of the remainder only a handful ever saw their homeland again.

The passage to India remained audacious in the extreme. Under the most favourable conditions, and taking the most direct route possible, the round trip consumed eighteen months, although many voyages lasted much longer and in some cases the ship was lost altogether. By comparison, the short voyage of the Spanish to their possessions across the North Atlantic took just six to eight weeks. The warm waters of the Indian Ocean were also especially destructive to the hulls of the Portuguese ships and after just three voyages massive vessels built at great cost were no longer seaworthy.

Although India had known conquerors, many of them far more violent and lethal than the Portuguese ever proved to be, their coming and that of the Europeans who followed in their footsteps changed the subcontinent permanently. Just as the Muslims had barred Europe from direct contact with India, so they had likewise barred the Hindus in India from direct European contact as well.

There is a sixteenth-century Portuguese anecdote in which Vasco da Gama is asked what Portugal would trade with India and what India would give in exchange. After explaining the nature of the mutual trade Vasco says, 'In this fashion, it is they who have discovered us.'[286] The coming of the Portuguese, and of the Europeans, ended isolation for both Europe and India with unforeseeable and enduring consequences.

The Portuguese gave to the Indian traders a new outlet for spices. They were no longer forced to deal only with the Muslims in the Middle East. Despite all his generosity towards the Portuguese, the ruler of Malindi was poorly served by them. His port was bypassed in the ensuing trade with Portugal and suffered accordingly. Immediately following the opening of the all-sea route from Europe to India new spices entered the market for which an equally insatiable demand quickly developed. The holds of the Portuguese vessels could carry not only a much greater volume but also a wider selection of spices and other exotic products.

The first Portuguese attempts to establish trade missions in the Genoese model, as Vasco da Gama had tried, were a failure and the Muslim pilot off the east coast of Africa had been quite correct – they would have to conquer, albeit in a way never before experienced in that part of the world. The Portuguese immediately understood that control of the sea lanes over which the spice trade moved was in the end all they required. Ports to service their ships and to revive their crews were established, as were trading posts from which goods and precious metals could be exchanged for spices and other Asian valuables. There was no need to conquer and hold nations by force of arms.

In the Battle of Diu in 1509 the Portuguese established naval supremacy in the Indian Ocean and a virtual monopoly in the spice trade. Once they seized Ormuz they took direct control of the Indian trade for horses, which were so essential to the strength of any Indian army. In fact, more than one king refused to attack the Portuguese in India for fear he would be cut off from his source of horses and be left vulnerable to his neighbouring states. The trade in spices was the lifeblood of the states in southern India and, once the Portuguese took control of the sea lanes, those kingdoms prospered or languished at the pleasure of the Portuguese.

Within a very short time Portugal held a string of forts and factories throughout Asia, stretching from Sofala and Ormuz to the Moluccas, Macao and Nagasaki. In 1510 the Portuguese seized the landlocked island of Gôa from the local sultan and 'Golden Gôa', the Rome of the East, became its principal trading port in the region, remaining in its possession until 1961.

The Portuguese did not introduce violence into the sea lanes of the Indian Ocean; that had existed throughout recorded time. What they brought instead was a magnitude of violence and the expert way they employed it, first to wrest and then to maintain control of trade. They accomplished this from a nation a hemisphere removed and at incredibly long maritime distances.

So it was that within scant years following the first voyage of Vasco da Gama the Portuguese commercial empire spread across the world. No other nation in world history spread itself so widely, so fast, so utterly. In the Atlantic the Portuguese occupied ports and forts in Morocco, Cape Verde and Luanda in west Africa, along with islands in the Gulf of Guinea. Almost immediately after its discovery on their second voyage to India the Portuguese had communities in Brazil which soon prospered with the transplanting of the plantation system they had perfected on Madeira.

Portuguese fishermen worked the Newfoundland banks, which they discovered. From Guinea, south-east Africa and Sumatra flowed gold; from Indonesia and the Malabar Coast came pepper; from Madeira, São Tomé and Brazil came sugar; from Banda came nutmeg and mace; from Ternate, Tidore and Ambonia came cloves; from Ceylon came cinnamon; from China came gold, silk and porcelain; from Japan came silver; from Persia and Arabia came horses; and from Cambay in Gujarat and Coromandel came cotton products.

The Portuguese kings profited immensely from the nearly insatiable demand for spices, especially pepper. Production rose dramatically in the East, as did imports carried in Portuguese ships, while the price in Europe actually increased threefold. Shipped annually to Portugal was an average of 1,625 tons of pepper, rising on occasion to 2,925 tons.[287] Pepper acquired in India was resold from Lisbon for forty times the price, a figure ultimately fixed at thirty times the purchase price. Both directly and indirectly the wealth from spices made its way to the Casa da India in Lisbon in quantities that are nearly unimaginable. Annual income to the crown was reliably estimated at 1 million *cruzados*, yet Manuel and his successor managed to spend the country into near bankruptcy.

Manuel lived in such luxury as had not been seen in Europe since the Roman emperors. He delighted in nothing so much as the exotic gifts his captains and viceroys sent him, the pleasure all the greater as he was the only monarch in Europe to have them. In one grand procession through the streets of Lisbon, Manuel displayed a rhinoceros, followed by five elephants. Behind them was an exquisitely fitted horse ridden by a Persian accompanied by a leopard on a leash like a trained dog. One of these elephants, together with the horse, rider and leopard, Manuel sent to Rome to celebrate the election of a new pontiff. They were well received, especially when the elephants sprayed the cardinals and guests with water. Such acts enhanced Manuel's stature enormously.

The king sought to further his position with the church and other European monarchs by restoring Jerusalem to Christian control. Alfonso de Albuquerque was ordered to seize Aden, the gateway to the Arab peninsula and the Red Sea, then to capture Mecca and Mohammed's tomb. Manuel would then exchange Mecca and the body of the Prophet for Jerusalem. The plan was thwarted when the Portuguese were unable to take Aden, although they came very close.

While Manuel is given credit for modest accomplishments by some historians, the kindest interpretation of the squandering of Portugal's new wealth is that the country had no model to follow in controlling the expansion of its empire or in its administration. It lacked a sufficiently large middle class to draw on and, primarily because of the expulsion of the Jews, lacked experienced bankers on the scale required. The bankers in Antwerp who usually advanced the funds for a ship sailing East were ultimately to profit more greatly than the Portuguese king.

No greater evidence of Manuel's fundamental mediocrity need be found than in his inability, or unwillingness, to see that the spice trade was properly organized and managed. He neglected to order the most rudimentary of measures, and his legacy in the East was larceny, mismanagement and outright fraud. His primary concern was the flow of wealth to his feet and, as long as his representatives saw to it, they were free to loot at their leisure. The captaincy of a Portuguese ship for just a single voyage to India and back left the captain a wealthy man free to retire. The personal ships of officials were reportedly so overladen with booty that they were scarcely seaworthy, and more than one foundered in moderately active seas. Long forgotten, or no longer considered necessary, were captains such as Gil Eanes, Antão Gonçalves, Nuno Tristão, Diogo Cão and Bartholomeu Dias, not to mention Vasco da Gama.

To give just one example, shortly after the Portuguese sacked Malacca the governor's flagship sank off Sumatra on its way to Portugal. Aboard ship was a treasure of gold that included the golden throne of the Malacca sultan and gems, 'the greatest wealth ever lost in a single shipwreck', according to Correa. The wreck was recovered in 1988 and the estimated value of its cargo was $3 billion. This was just one ship among thousands.

There is no doubt but that both John I and John II, not to mention Henry the Navigator, would have properly organized and supervised the spice trade and the Portuguese sea-borne empire that followed within a short decade of Vasco da Gama's return to Lisbon. Had they done so, the course of history for the Portuguese and for millions of others in India and the Far East would have been very, very different.

To maintain this far-flung empire and to fight off interlopers Portugal required a vast number of expensive ships and skilled men. Each year some 2,400 able-bodied, largely unmarried, men left Portugal 'at the scent of this cinnamon',[288] from a population of between 1,000,000 and 1,400,000. The long voyage east killed as many half of these, while the rest soon succumbed to the fever and disease epidemic to the tropics.[289] The round trip for a single vessel from Lisbon to Nagasaki often took three years. Only a handful of the seamen who left on the ship survived the voyage.

The situation was aggravated in that corrupt captains pocketed much of the money given them to feed the Portuguese men dispatched east, starving them *en route*, depositing them on the shore of India or eastward in such a debilitated state that death soon followed. Setting aside the inhumanity of such actions, it was an unconscionable waste of the most precious resource Portugal had to give – her young men. The essential Portuguese fortress of Malacca in the Moluccas, always precariously held, was never manned by more than 600 Portuguese, and usually held as few as 200 men, yet it was the linchpin that kept the spice empire together. There was no greater failure on the part of Manuel and his son, John III, than properly to manage the gift they had been given by the lives of Portuguese seamen.

Nevertheless, so many young men left Portugal to seek fortune in Asia that vast tracks of land were abandoned and towns were reported denuded of population. Agricultural production fell and a portion of the new wealth was required to buy grain to feed the swelling populace of Lisbon.

Few women emigrated, and cohabitation and marriage with the indigenous peoples was officially tolerated, even encouraged. The children of these relationships were accepted into the civil service and armed forces of the Portuguese. Still, it is estimated there were never more than 10,000 able-bodied Portuguese and Eurasians available for service in the East at any one time. The Portuguese fleet that sustained the empire never numbered more than 300. In the East the great carracks of 1,000 to 2,000 tons were manned largely by Eurasians and African slaves commanded by a handful of Portuguese officers and gunners.

From such a lofty height there was nowhere to go but down. The Portuguese were quickly overextended and vulnerable to outsiders. The Turks had great success against Portuguese shipping in the mid-sixteenth century; Molucca was frequently blockaded by fleets from Java; the Malays enjoyed frequent successes against the Portuguese, as did both Hindu and Muslim raiders along the west coast of India.

Most significantly, the Portuguese established the opening through which much of Europe raced, for in the end the royal advisers to Manuel proved correct. Portugal was too small for such an ambitious expansion of empire. Even Dom Vasco da Gama urged the king to pull back from the maximum extension of influence, to consolidate what could be maintained. But what the Japanese would term 'victory fever' in the first months of World War II had seized the Portuguese, and there was no turning back from what could be taken, until it in turn was taken from them. More powerful rivals – the Dutch, English and Spanish – successfully wrested away their monopoly of the sea trade route to the East, though the Portuguese remained dominant players for centuries.

There were many reasons for the inability of the Portuguese to retain control of the Indian Ocean besides the lack of manpower, corruption and an adequate commercial structure. The settlement and exploitation of Brazil diverted resources and attention, while Spain's occupation of Portugal in 1580 was especially devastating to the far-flung empire.[290] Perhaps most damaging of all, the Portuguese commanders sent to Asia were primarily motivated by personal greed and usually acted against their country's long-term interests. Royal governors did not keep their promises or remain loyal to allies. The Portuguese were quickly determined to be unreliable, and in a very short number of years it was also apparent that they lacked the resources to hold what they had by force. Nevertheless, Brazil, Angola, Gôa and Macao long remained part of the Portuguese empire.

The Portuguese discoveries changed the face of the world. Maps were utterly transformed and what emerged was a largely accurate depiction of the outline of the world's major land masses and of the sea routes to them. They ended the Muslim monopoly on the spice trade, with devastating consequences for the Arab rulers. Lisbon, linked to the East, to Madeira and to Brazil, was Europe's main port, its busiest market-place and its most prosperous city. Less than 100 years after Henry's ships had begun their explorations a Spanish expedition under the command of the Portuguese captain-general Ferdinand Magellan had circumnavigated the world.

If it had not been the Portuguese, then it would have been someone else. Europeans would not have remained where they were. Ever-increasing trade, and conquest, between East and West was inevitable at some point in history, for that has always been its course. It is likely that Prince Henry, John I, John II and Manuel accelerated the 'discovery' of the world – including the Americas – by at least 100 years, perhaps more. What another century would have meant to the Indian subcontinent and to the Aztec and Inca empires is best left to others. Perhaps the greatest beneficiaries would have been the Africans of Guinea and Angola, the two regions from which most slaves for America, north and south, were taken. Without Brazil and the plantations of the Caribbean and British American colonies exerting pressure, far fewer would have been seized and by the time America was colonized and exploited the institution of slavery there would have had a shorter run.

The key captain of the discoveries, Vasco da Gama, is one of those rarest of historical figures: an individual who succeeded in every mission given him, who enjoyed celebrity, honour and enormous riches within his lifetime, and had the good fortune to die while the zenith of his nation, made possible by his accomplishments, had yet to pass.

Almost from the first, Vasco and his men were cast as Homeric heroes and their expedition was portrayed as a national epic of divine providence. To whatever degree his place in history was determined by his actual behaviour, Vasco was elevated to near deity as the central figure in Portugal's great national epic, *The Lusiads*, by Luis Camoens, which to this day is studied by every Portuguese student. The masterpiece has nearly single-handedly etched this first voyage to India from Europe in the Portuguese national character as a triumph of the Portuguese people, through Vasco da Gama, at the direction, and fulfilling the promise, of God.

Vasco da Gama returned to India twice again. His third voyage came late in life in 1524, when he was fifty-four years old. There Dom Vasco da Gama, Admiral of India and Count of Vidigueira, took ill shortly after landing and died peacefully a few months later. He was buried, first in India, south of Calicut, then at the family estate in Sines and finally at the Mosteiro dos Jerónimos in Belém.*

There is inevitably much dispute as to the course of his life after his return from his first voyage to India. Like Columbus, who has had placed on his unwitting shoulders every evil

---

* Vasco da Gama's remains were moved from India by his son and interred at the family estate in Vidigueira. In 1880 his bones were putatively removed and with great fanfare installed at the Mosteiro dos Jerónimos. Later, it was determined that the skeleton of a Gama relative had been moved in error. In 1898, on the 400th anniversary of his first voyage to India, Gama's remains were quietly relocated. There is, however, a persistent story that the Gama family did not wish to have his remains moved and misdirected officials. According to this account, Gama is still interred at the family estate.

perpetrated by a European since he first set foot in the Americas, Vasco da Gama has been blamed for every sin and every act of violence against Asians by every European since he landed in Calicut. Ignored is the reality that in both cases the regions entered by Europeans were already extraordinarily violent and rife with conflict.

The expeditions and the subsequent discoveries by the Portuguese of the fifteenth century are probably the singular greatest achievements in European, if not world, history. The epic voyage of Vasco da Gama is arguably the most significant in human history, as it brought about the first meeting of men from the West with those of the East since Alexander the Great, and from it came permanent contact and interaction.

The tenacity of the small nation of Portugal, the courage of its people, the commitment of its rulers over decades are nothing less than astounding. From this time forward Europeans were no longer bound by the confines of their nations. The ocean had become a highway across which they could explore, settle and exploit. The words of Luis Vaz de Camoens are perhaps the most fitting memorial to what the Portuguese accomplished in less than a century:

> . . . *[I]f there had been more of the World*
> *They would have reached it.*

Postscript: the dissenters

So much is in dispute concerning the Portuguese discoveries that it can come as no surprise that there are respected historians who believe it simply did not happen like this. And they may have a point, though the great weight of mainstream history is against them. What follows is a representative sample of contrary views.

Gaspar Correa in his *Lendas da India* writes that the tip of Africa was discovered not by Bartholomeu Dias but by Janifante, 'a foreign merchant, who frequently came to Lisbon'. This is perhaps João Infante, who captained one of Dias's ships. Correa writes that the king outfitted him and he sailed down the west coast of Africa. Near the Cape of Good Hope he encountered waves so powerful he could not sail on. Back in Lisbon he was constructing 'tall' ships for a repeat voyage when he fell ill and died. The king then dispatched Vasco da Gama.

Samuel Morison in his book *Portuguese Voyages to America in the Fifteenth Century* largely discounts what he considers the myth of Portuguese secrecy in their explorations. While John II and others were secretive by nature, he argues, there was no formal policy to conceal Portuguese discoveries. The kings were constantly torn between keeping matters to themselves, and in so doing making it harder for others to exploit their discoveries, and crowing about their latest accomplishment. Vanity seems to have won out most of the time. Morison argues that there is no information about many voyages and discoveries because, for the most part, they were simply poorly recorded, or never happened.

Even Henry's role in the explorations is disputed. James M. Anderson in his book *The History of Portugal* asserts that the legend of the Navigator is essentially a fiction created after his death. He points out that there is no 'contemporary reference to the school [at Sagres], the first mention of it having been made in the seventeenth century by an Englishman'. He acknowledges that Henry took some interest in the explorations but suggests he did not play the dominant role generally attributed to him. This was a fiction created to give someone in the royal family credit.

Francis Herbert, curator of maps at the Royal Geographical Society, former president of the Society for the History of Discoveries and author, argues passionately against the traditional presentation of the Portuguese explorations. He writes that the house of Coimbra and the Order of Santiago were primarily responsible for the Portuguese discoveries and for the push to India, but that credit was later usurped by the house of Viseu and the Order of Christ – in other words, the monarchy. He states that the Gama voyage was commanded by Vasco's older brother Paulo, and that Paulo sailed under orders of George de Lancastre, the natural son of John II, Duke of Coimbra and master of the Order of Santiago. The entire expedition, according to Herbert, was owned by the Order of Santiago. According to this account, Vasco da Gama assumed final command of the expedition on the death of his older brother, and when he returned in triumph King Manuel took the credit for the expedition. Such were the rewards – or bribes – he received that Vasco da Gama abandoned the Order of Santiago for the Order of Christ.

It is true that Vasco da Gama switched his allegiance to what was essentially the king's Order of Christ. It is also true that, although Manuel was heir to John II, the king's choice had been his own son George. Manuel had no greater opponent in Portugal and would have been strongly motivated to take credit from him.

Although intriguing, especially the views of Herbert, the judgement of historians to date is contrary to these views, which, of course, does not make them wrong.

Acknowledgements

I vividly recall the moment I conceived this book. My mother and younger sister had come to visit me in Cascais, Portugal, where I was living. I was showing them the neighbourhood near my apartment while calling attention to the many historical buildings. At one point I spoke the name 'Vasco da Gama'. Hearing this, an attractive young Portuguese woman stopped and in accented English politely asked if we needed to know anything about Vasco da Gama, 'the greatest Portuguese who ever lived. He discovered India and gave us the empire.' I thanked her for her interest and she briefly told my family of Vasco da Gama's contribution to Portuguese history. The Portuguese are by nature quite reserved, yet here was a young woman intruding on a conversation between strangers.

During my months in Portugal I was struck again and again by the monuments to Vasco da Gama, the other explorers and the empire itself. They are everywhere and, I suspect, as much a part of the Portuguese consciousness today as they were 400 years ago. The Portuguese assume, incorrectly, that others know of their contribution to the modern world and respect it as they do. It is my hope that I have made a contribution to changing that.

No book of this type is written without the help of others. My thanks go to Thomas Chacko for providing me with invaluable information on the Vijayanagar empire and its capital. I also thank the highly competent staff of the Phoenix (Arizona) Public Library Interlibrary Loan Department, who assisted me so often in locating obscure, long out-of-print books. A special thanks to Virginia M. Adams of the American Friends of the Hakluyt Society at the John Carter Brown Library in

Providence, Rhode Island, for her assistance in providing the location of essential, and difficult to locate, works. Thanks also to Edward J. Redmond, Senior Reference Librarian, the US Library of Congress, for his kind assistance in researching and providing copies of key historical maps. My thanks also to Sandra Cardoso and Maria dos Anjos Fernandes at the Lisbon City Museum and Tania Olim of the Portuguese Institute of Museums. Thanks as well to the staff of the National Library in Lisbon.

I also thank my editor in the UK, Grant McIntyre, for having faith in the project, for his many helpful suggestions and for his editing. Thanks as well to Matthew Taylor for his outstanding work as copy editor. As always, my deepest appreciation to my agent, Mike Hamilburg, for first suggesting my switch to this genre and his dedication in placing the project in the face of so many adversities. Thanks also to his assistant, Joannie, for always, and I mean *always*, being of good cheer and so helpful. Finally, my gratitude to Dr Phil Jackson for his assistance and encouragement.

Notes

1. B. de Las Casas, *The Diario of Christopher Columbus's First Voyage to America, 1492–1493* (Norman and London, 1989), p. 391.
2. G. Granzotto, *Christopher Columbus: The Dream and the Obsession* (Garden City, New York, 1985), p. 186.
3. S. E. Morison, *Admiral of the Ocean Sea: A Life of Christopher Columbus* (Boston, 1942), p. 344.
4. Las Casas, *Diario*, p. 397.
5. Morison, *Admiral of the Ocean Sea*, p. 349.
6. M. Kaplan, *The Portuguese: The Land and Its People* (New York, 1991), p. 29.
7. C. R. Boxer, *The Portuguese Seaborne Empire, 1415–1825* (New York, 1969), p. xxiii.
8. B. W. Diffie and G. D. Winius, *Foundations of the Portuguese Empire, 1415–1580* (Minneapolis, 1977), pp. 190–1.
9. E. G. Ravenstein, trans. and ed., *A Journal of the First Voyage of Vasco da Gama, 1497–1499* (New York, 1898), p. xii.
10. L. V. de Camoens, *The Lusiads* (London), p. 40.
11. S. E. Howe, *In Quest of Spices* (London, 1946), p. 13.
12. Howe, *In Quest of Spices*, p. 19.
13. Howe, *In Quest of Spices*, p. 18.
14. Boxer, *The Portuguese Seaborne Empire*, pp. 3–4.
15. A. H. de Marques, *History of Portugal*, vol. 1, *From Lusitania to Empire* (New York and London, 1972), p. 166
16. H. Kulke and D. Rothermund, *History of India*, 3rd edn (London and New York, 1998), p. 101.
17. As quoted in Howe, *In Quest of Spices*, p. 35.
18. Persius, Sat. V, as quoted in *In Quest of Spices*, p. 26.
19. Howe, *In Quest of Spices*, p. 29.
20. Howe, *In Quest of Spices*, p. 25.
21. J. K. S. Phillips, *The Medieval Expansion of Europe* (Oxford, 1988), p. 103.
22. Marques, *History of Portugal*, p. 139.
23. Howe, *In Quest of Spices*, p. 38
24. As quoted in Howe, *In Quest of Spices*, p. 44.

25. J. M. Anderson, *The History of Portugal* (Connecticut and London, 2000), p. 28.

26. Diffie and Winius, *Foundations of the Portuguese Empire,* vol. 1, p. 38.

27. Howe, *In Quest of Spices*, p. 55

28. Kaplan, *The Portuguese*, p. 9.

29. Diffie and Winius, *Foundations of the Portuguese Empire*, pp. 38–9.

30. S. Subrahmanyam, *The Career and Legend of Vasco da Gama* (Cambridge, 1997), pp. 25–8.

31. Anderson, *The History of Portugal*, p. 40.

32. Diffie and Winius, *Foundations of the Portuguese Empire*, p. 53.

33. Diffie and Winius, *Foundations of the Portuguese Empire*, p. 44–5.

34. Diffie and Winius, *Foundations of the Portuguese Empire*, pp. 48–9.

35. Howe, *In Quest of Spices*, p. 62.

36. G. E. da Azurara, *The Chronicle of the Discovery and Conquest of Guinea* (London, 1896), p. 21.

37. J. K. S. Phillips, *The Medieval Expansion of Europe* (Oxford, 1988), p. 193.

38. Phillips, *The Medieval Expansion of Europe*, p. 214.

39. S. E. Morison, *Portuguese Voyages to America in the Fifteenth Century* (New York, 1965), p. 19.

40. Howe, *In Quest of Spices*, pp. 59–60.

41. Anderson, *History of Portugal*, p. 54.

42. A. Toussaint, *History of the Indian Ocean* (Chicago, 1961), pp. 98–9.

43. Marques, *History of Portugal*, p. 134.

44. H. H. Hart, *Sea Road to the Indies: An Account of the Voyages and Exploits of the Portuguese Navigators* (New York, 1950), p. 14.

45. Azurara, *Chronicle*, p. 54.

46. Azurara, *Chronicle*, pp. 81–3.

47. Hart, *Sea Road to the Indies*, p. 19.

48. Hart, *Sea Road to the Indies*, p. 22.

49. E. Bradford, *A Wind from the North: The Life of Henry the Navigator* (New York, 1960), p. 256.

50. From the journal of Alvise da Cadamosto, a Venetian merchant who joined the Portuguese in 1454 and made two voyages to Guinea.

51. E. Prestage, 'The Portuguese Voyages of Discovery', p. 3.

52. Morison, *Portuguese Voyages*, p. 3.

53. E. G. Ravenstein, trans. and ed., *The Voyages of Diogo Cão and Bartholomeu Dias, 1482–1488* (Pretoria, 1986) [reprinted from *The Geographical Journal*, vol. 16, no.6 (December, 1900), p. 1.]

54. Hart, *Sea Road to the Indies*, p. 91.

55. Hart, *Sea Road to the Indies*, pp. 44–5.

56. Boxer, *The Portuguese Seaborne Empire*, p. 6.

57. Ravenstein, *Voyages of Cão and Dias*, pp. 2–3.

58. Marques, *History of Portugal*, p. 219.

59. Ravenstein, *Voyages of Cão and Dias*, p. 4.
60. Ravenstein, *Voyages of Cão and Dias*, p. 4.
61. Ravenstein, *Voyages of Cão and Dias*, p. 6.
62. Morison, *Admiral of the Ocean Sea*, p. 70.
63. Granzotto, *Christopher Columbus*, p. 58.
64. Taken in large part from J. Carey, ed., *Eyewitness to History* (New York, 1987), pp. 222–3.
65. Ravenstein, *Voyages of Cão and Dias*, p. 11.
66. A Captain Becker of the *Falke* carried this one off to Kiel, Germany, in 1893.
67. H. V. Livermore, *A New History of Portugal* (Cambridge, 1969), p. 129.
68. Morison, *Portuguese Voyages to America*, pp. 44–7.
69. Morison, *Admiral of the Ocean Sea*, pp. 74–5.
70. Ravenstein, *Voyages of Cão and Dias*, p. 15.
71. Ravenstein, *Voyages of Cão and Dias*, p. 14.
72. Hart, *Sea Road to the Indies*, pp. 34–5.
73. Howe, *In Quest of Spices*, p. 90.
74. Howe, *In Quest of Spices*, p. 90.
75. Ravenstein, *Voyages of Cão and Dias*, p. 19.
76. Hart, *Sea Road to the Indies*, p. 35.
77. Ravenstein, *Voyages of Cão and Dias*, p. 21.
78. Hart, *Sea Road to the Indies*, p. 36.
79. Howe, *In Quest of Spices*, p. 90.
80. Ravenstein, *Voyages of Cão and Dias*, p. 23.
81. Ravenstein, *Voyages of Cão and Dias*, p. 23.
82. Ravenstein, *Voyages of Cão and Dias*, p. 42.
83. Howe, *In Quest of Spices*, p. 96.
84. Howe, *In Quest of Spices*, p. 116.
85. Howe, *In Quest of Spices*, pp. 93–4.
86. G. Correa, *The Three Voyages of Vasco da Gama and His Viceroyalty* (London, 1869), pp. 16–17.
87. Hart, *Sea Road to the Indies*, p. 46.
88. Hart, *Sea Road to the Indies*, p. 47.
89. Howe, *In Quest of Spices*, p. 95.
90. Hart, *Sea Road to the Indies*, p. 48.
91. Hart, *Sea Road to the Indies*, p. 49.
92. Howe, *In Quest of Spices*, p. 95.
93. There is no record of John II honouring this commitment.
94. Howe, *In Quest of Spices*, p. 96.
95. Howe, *In Quest of Spices*, p. 95.
96. Howe, *In Quest of Spices*, p. 97.
97. Howe, *In Quest of Spices*, p. 99.
98. Howe, *In Quest of Spices*, p. 99.

99. Hart, *Sea Road to the Indies*, p. 61.

100. Howe, *In Quest of Spices*, p. 100.

101. Hart, *Sea Road to the Indies*, pp. 61–2.

102. Hart, *Sea Road to the Indies*, p. 62.

103. Howe, *In Quest of Spices*, p. 100.

104. Howe, *In Quest of Spices*, pp. 100–01.

105. Howe, *In Quest of Spices*, p. 101.

106. Howe, *In Quest of Spices*, p. 103.

107. Howe, *In Quest of Spices*, p. 105.

108. Phillips, *The Medieval Expansion of Europe*, p. 253.

109. Hart, *Sea Road to the Indies*, pp. 72–3.

110. Hart, *Sea Road to the Indies*, p. 73.

111. Hart, *Sea Road to the Indies*, pp. 74–5.

112. H. V. Livermore, *A New History of Portugal* (Cambridge, 1969), p. 134.

113. Kaplan, *The Portuguese*, p. 9.

114. Howe, *In Quest of Spices*, p. 120.

115. Correa, *The Three Voyages*, p. 17.

116. Hart, *Sea Road to the Indies*, pp. 84–5.

117. Hart, *Sea Road to the Indies*, p. 79.

118. Howe, *In Quest of Spices*, p. 121.

119. Correa, *The Three Voyages*, pp. 29–30.

120. Hart, *Sea Road to the Indies*, pp. 94–8.

121. Ravenstein, *A Journal*, p. xii.

122. Subrahmanyam, *The Career and Legend of Vasco da Gama*, pp. 59–60.

123. Subrahmanyam, *The Career and Legend of Vasco da Gama*, pp. 63–4.

124. Ravenstein, *A Journal*, p. xv.

125. Subrahmanyam, *The Career and Legend of Vasco da Gama*, p. 62.

126. Hart, *Sea Road to the Indies*, p. 104.

127. Correa, *The Three Voyages*, p. 31.

128. Subrahmanyam, *The Career and Legend of Vasco da Gama*, p. 67.

129. Howe, *In Quest of Spices*, p. 120

130. Ravenstein, *A Journal*, p. 165.

131. Hart, *Sea Road to the Indies*, p. 86.

132. Hart, *Sea Road to the Indies*, p. 88.

133. Howe, *In Quest of Spices*, p. 124.

134. Hart, *Sea Road to the Indies*, p. 89.

135. Howe, *In Quest of Spices*, p. 124.

136. Howe, *In Quest of Spices*, p. 125.

137. Hart, *Sea Road to the Indies*, pp. 111–2.

138. Howe, *In Quest of Spices*, pp. 123–4.

139. Hart, *Sea Road to the Indies*, p. 90.

140. Correa, *The Three Voyages*, p. 34.

141. Correa, *The Three Voyages*, p. 80.

Notes

142. Hart, *Sea Road to the Indies*, pp. 117–9.
143. Hart, *Sea Road to the Indies*, p. 119.
144. Luis Camoens, *The Lusiads*, as quoted in Howe, *In Quest of Spices*, p. 127.
145. Hart, *Sea Road to the Indies*, p. 122.
146. Hart, *Sea Road to the Indies*, p. 123.
147. Hart, *Sea Road to the Indies*, p. 127.
148. Subrahmanyam, *The Career and Legend of Vasco da Gama*, p. 95.
149. Subrahmanyam, *The Career and Legend of Vasco da Gama*, p. 96.
150. Subrahmanyam, *The Career and Legend of Vasco da Gama*, p. 96.
151. G. A. Danzer, *An Atlas of World History* (Ann Arbor, 2000), p. 53.
152. A. Toussaint, *History of the Indian Ocean* (Chicago, 1961), pp. 51–2.
153. Toussaint, *History of the Indian Ocean*, p. 56.
154. Toussaint, *History of the Indian Ocean*, p. 51.
155. Toussaint, *History of the Indian Ocean*, pp. 57–8.
156. J. A. Garraty and P. Gay, eds., *The Columbia History of the World* (New York, 1972), p. 350.
157. Garraty and Gay, *Columbia History*, p. 350.
158. Kulke, *History of India*, p. 155.
159. Kulke, *A History of India*, p. 7.
160. Garraty and Gay, *Columbia History*, p. 341.
161. Kulke, *A History of India*, p. 5.
162. Garraty and Gay, *Columbia History*, p. 343.
163. Kulke, *A History of India*, p. 11.
164. Toussaint, *History of the Indian Ocean*, p. 68.
165. Kulke, *A History of India*, p. 7.
166. Garraty and Gay, *Columbia History*, pp. 350–1.
167. Garraty and Gay, *Columbia History*, pp. 351–2.
168. Garraty and Gay, *Columbia History*, p. 354.
169. Garraty and Gay, *Columbia History*, p. 353.
170. Kulke, *History of India*, pp. 176–7.
171. K. N. Chaudhuri, *Asia before Europe: Economy and Civilisation of the Indian Ocean from the Rise of Islam to 1750*, pp. 362–4.
172. Subrahmanyam, *The Career and Legend of Vasco da Gama*, p. 100.
173. J. Keay, *India: A History* (New York, 2000), p. 284.
174. Keay, *India: A History*, p. 284.
175. Subrahmanyam, *The Career and Legend of Vasco da Gama*, p. 104.
176. Subrahmanyam, *The Career and Legend of Vasco da Gama*, pp. 104–5.
177. Boxer, *The Portuguese Seaborne Empire*, p. 50.
178. *Roteiro*, p. 6.
179. Hart, *Sea Road to the Indies*, pp. 131–2.
180. Hart, *Sea Road to the Indies*, p. 132.
181. *Roteiro*, p. 8.

182. Howe, *In Quest of Spices*, p. 130.
183. Subrahmanyam, *The Career and Legend of Vasco da Gama*, p. 88.
184. *Roteiro*, p. 16.
185. Howe, *In Quest of Spices*, pp. 131–3.
186. *Roteiro*, pp. 19–20.
187. *Roteiro*, p. 21.
188. Howe, *In Quest of Spices*, p. 134.
189. Hart, *Sea Road to the Indies*, p. 141.
190. Boxer, *The Portuguese Seaborne Empire*, p. 40.
191. Hart, *Sea Road to the Indies*, p. 143.
192. Hart, *Sea Road to the Indies*, p. 143.
193. Howe, *In Quest of Spices*, p. 137.
194. *Roteiro*, p. 24.
195. Hart, *Sea Road to the Indies*, p. 146.
196. Subrahmanyam, *The Career and Legend of Vasco da Gama*, p. 113.
197. *Roteiro*, p. 25.
198. Hart, *Sea Road to the Indies*, p. 146.
199. *Roteiro*, p. 29.
200. *Roteiro*, p. 30.
201. Hart, *Sea Road to the Indies*, pp. 148–9.
202. *Roteiro*, p. 28.
203. *Roteiro*, p. 33.
204. Hart, *Sea Road to the Indies*, p. 149.
205. *Roteiro*, p. 36.
206. *Roteiro*, p. 36.
207. Subrahmanyam, *The Career and Legend of Vasco da Gama*, p. 118.
208. *Roteiro*, p. 37.
209. *Roteiro*, pp. 37–8.
210. Howe, *In Quest of Spices*, pp. 135–6.
211. *Roteiro*, p. 39.
212. Hart, *Sea Road to the Indies*, p. 152.
213. Subrahmanyam, *The Career and Legend of Vasco da Gama*, p. 119.
214. Hart, *Sea Road to the Indies*, pp. 153–4.
215. *Roteiro*, pp. 41–2.
216. *Roteiro*, p. 44.
217. *Roteiro*, pp. 44–5.
218. *Roteiro*, p. 45.
219. *Roteiro*, p. 45.
220. Subrahmanyam, *The Career and Legend of Vasco da Gama*, pp. 122–8.
221. *Roteiro*, p. 46.
222. Hart, *Sea Road to the Indies*, p. 155.
223. Hart, *Sea Road to the Indies*, p. 156.
224. *Roteiro*, p. 48.

225. Hart, *Sea Road to the Indies*, pp. 173–4.
226. Howe, *In Quest of Spices*, p. 141.
227. Hart, *Sea Road to the Indies*, p. 160.
228. N. Sastri, *A History of South India from Prehistoric Times to the Fall of Vijayanagar* (London, 1966), p. 327.
229. Keay, *India: A History*, p. 277.
230. *Roteiro*, p. 48.
231. *Roteiro*, p. 49.
232. *Roteiro*, p. 50.
233. Howe, *In Quest of Spices*, pp. 139–40.
234. *Roteiro*, p. 50.
235. *Roteiro*, p. 50.
236. Howe, *In Quest of Spices*, p. 141.
237. *Roteiro*, pp. 49–50.
238. *Roteiro*, p. 51.
239. *Roteiro*, p. 52.
240. *Roteiro*, pp. 53–4.
241. Hart, *Sea Road to the Indies*, p. 177.
242. *Roteiro*, p. 54.
243. *Roteiro*, p. 55.
244. *Roteiro*, p. 56.
245. *Roteiro*, p. 56.
246. Howe, *In Quest of Spices*, p. 140.
247. *Roteiro*, p. 58.
248. Hart, *Sea Road to the Indies*, p. 178.
249. *Roteiro*, p. 59.
250. Hart, *Sea Road to the Indies*, p. 179.
251. *Roteiro*, p. 60.
252. Hart, *Sea Road to the Indies*, pp. 179–80.
253. Hart, *Sea Road to the Indies*, pp. 180–2.
254. *Roteiro*, p. 62.
255. *Roteiro*, p. 64.
256. *Roteiro*, pp. 64–5.
257. Subrahmanyam, *The Career and Legend of Vasco da Gama*, p. 141.
258. Hart, *Sea Road to the Indies*, p. 184.
259. Hart, *Sea Road to the Indies*, p. 183.
260. *Roteiro*, p. 66.
261. Hart, *Sea Road to the Indies*, p. 184.
262. *Roteiro*, p. 68.
263. Hart, *Sea Road to the Indies*, p. 186.
264. *Roteiro*, p. 68.
265. *Roteiro*, p. 69.
266. *Roteiro*, pp. 70–1.

267. Subrahmanyam, *The Career and Legend of Vasco da Gama*, pp. 142–3.
268. *Roteiro*, pp. 73–4.
269. *Roteiro*, p. 77.
270. *Roteiro*, p. 80.
271. *Roteiro*, pp. 83–4.
272. *Roteiro*, pp. 84–7.
273. *Roteiro*, pp. 89–91.
274. Correa, *The Three Voyages*, pp. 262–3.
275. Correa, *The Three Voyages*, pp. 264–5.
276. Livermore, *A New History of Portugal*, pp. 134–5.
277. Howe, *In Quest of Spices*, p. 143.
278. Ravenstein, *A Journal*, Appendix A, pp. 113–4.
279. Subrahmanyam, *The Career and Legend of Vasco da Gama*, pp. 150–1.
280. Hart, *Sea Road to the Indies*, p. 201.
281. Howe, *In Quest of Spices*, p. 143.
282. Diffie and Williams, *Foundations of the Portuguese Empire*, pp. 176–7.
283. *Roteiro*, p. 98.
284. Hart, *Sea Road to the Indies*, p. 191.
285. Hart, *Sea Road to the Indies*, p. 203.
286. Subrahmanyam, *The Career and Legend of Vasco da Gama*, p. 164.
287. Boxer, *The Portuguese Seabourne Empire*, p. 59.
288. Boxer, *The Portuguese Seabourne Empire*, p. 63.
289. Boxer, *The Portuguese Seaborne Empire*, pp. 51–2.
290. Toussaint, *History of the Indian Ocean*, p. 112.

Bibliography

A Journal of the First Voyage of Vasco da Gama, 1497–1499, trans. and ed. E. G.
    Ravenstein, Hakluyt Society (1898); repr. (New York) [*Roteiro*]

Anderson, James M., *The History of Portugal* (Connecticut and London, 2000)

Azurara, Gomes Eannes da, *The Chronicle of the Discovery and Conquest of
    Guinea* (London, 1896)

Boxer, C. R., *The Portuguese Seaborne Empire, 1415–1825* (New York, 1969)

Bradford, Ernle, *A Wind from the North: The Life of Henry the Navigator* (New
    York, 1960)

Carey, John, ed., *Eyewitness to History* (New York, 1987)

Chaudhuri, K. N., *Asia before Europe: Economy and Civilisation of the Indian
    Ocean from the Rise of Islam to 1750* (Cambridge, 1990)

Correa, Gaspar, *The Three Voyages of Vasco da Gama, and His Viceroyalty*, from
    the *Lendas da India* (London, 1869)

Danzer, Gerald A., *An Atlas of World History* (Ann Arbor, 2000)

Diffie, Bailey W., and Winius, George D., *Foundations of the Portuguese Empire,
    1415–1580* (Minneapolis, 1977)

Garraty, John A., and Gay, Peter, eds., *The Columbia History of the World* (New
    York, 1972)

Granzotto, Gianni, *Christopher Columbus: The Dream and the Obsession*, trans.
    Stephen Sartarelli (Garden City, New York, 1985)

Hart, Henry H., *Sea Road to the Indies: An Account of the Voyages and Exploits
    of the Portuguese Navigators, together with the Life and Times of Dom Vasco
    da Gama, Capitão-Mór, Viceroy of India and Count of Vidigueira* (New York,
    1950)

Howe, Sonia E., *In Quest of Spices* (London, 1946)

Kaplan, Marion, *The Portuguese: The Land and its People* (New York, 1991)

Keay, John, *India: A History* (New York, 2000)

Kulke, Hermann, and Rothermund, Dietmar, *A History of India*, 3rd edn
    (London and New York, 1998)

Las Casas, Bartolomé de, *The Diario of Christopher Columbus's First Voyage to
    America, 1492–1493*, trans. O. Dunn and J. E. Kelley, Jr. (Norman and
    London, 1989)

Livermore, H. V., *A New History of Portugal* (Cambridge, 1969)

Marques, A. H. de Oliveira, *History of Portugal*, vol. 1, *From Lusitania to Empire* (New York and London, 1972)

McNeill, William H., *Plagues and Peoples* (New York, 1977)

Morison, Samuel Eliot, *Admiral of the Ocean Sea: A Life of Christopher Columbus* (Boston, 1942)

——, *Portuguese Voyages to America in the Fifteenth Century* (New York, 1965)

Newby, Eric, *World Atlas of Explorations* (New York, 1975)

Nowell, Charles E., *A History of Portugal* (New York, London and Toronto, 1952)

Phillips, J. K. S., *The Medieval Expansion of Europe* (Oxford, 1988)

Prestage, Edgar, 'The Portuguese Voyages of Discovery' [lecture given at King's College, London, 26 January 1939]

Roberts, Gail, *Atlas of Discovery* (New York, 1973)

Sastri, Nilakanta, *A History of South India from Prehistoric Times to the Fall of Vijayanagar* (London, 1966)

Subrahmanyam, Sanjoy, *The Career and Legend of Vasco da Gama* (Cambridge, 1997)

Toussaint, Auguste, *History of the Indian Ocean* (Chicago. 1961)

Veseth, Michael, *Mountains of Debt: Crises and Change in Renaissance Florence, Victorian Britain, and Postwar America* (New York and Oxford, 1990)

Wink, Andre, *Al-Hind: The Making of the Indo-Islamic World*, vol. 2, *The Slave Kings and the Islamic Conquest* (Leiden, New York and Cologne, 1997)

INDEX

Index